ANDREI, FIRA AND PITCH
Scenes from a Musician's Life

ANDREI, FIRA AND PITCH
Scenes from a Musician's Life

by

ANDREI GAVRILOV

Andrei, Fira and Pitch
Scenes from a Musician's Life
Copyright © 2017 by Andrei Gavrilov
All rights reserved.

Asteroid Publishing, Inc.

ISBN: 978-1-926720-44-9

No part of this book may be reproduced or transmitted in any form without the written permission of the publisher/author.

Photograph contributors: Andrei Gavrilov, E.S. Bulgakova
Cover design by Katie Alberts

*To Alice Jondorf and Igor Shestkov
without whom this book
would have not become a reality*

Contents

To the Reader 1
Instead of a Preface 2
Fa-Re-Do-Si 5
Chopin 9
Standing to attention 13
Polya 17
Yura Egorov 23
Lyova 29
The Competition 35
Gudauta – Salzburg 43
I am your slender ear of wheat 53
Seppo Karlsson 63
Seppo the Creep 71
Seppo the Escapist 75
Ugly Mugs 77
Quetzalcoatl and Tezcatlipoca 79
Mark Malkovich 81
Romania 85
Anton 89
Deadmen in the Georgievsky Hall 93
The Ball 99
Handel Passions 111
Four and twenty tailors went to catch a snail 125
Cut off 135
Raisa's secrets 141
The Hunt 149
Divorce 153
I'll f*cking shoot you 157
Poisoned 159
Scriabin Sonata No. 8 165
The Angel from the Philharmonia 169
To Dyutkovo 171
The Gonzaga Theatre 179
Depression 185
Flat on his face on the tarmac 195
The new carpet 201

Titan	207
A right one	213
Astronaut	217
Cadaver	221
Hiding in the loo	227
Richter's protégé	231
The Enigma	233
The third year of the travel ban	243
The coffin with ropes	253
On the staircase at Lubyanka	257
Piano Concerto for the Left Hand	267
Tigran	271
Only with you	277
Crashed and burned	283
A story with bowler hats	289
Stalactites under the belly of the piano	303
Gidon	307
Caviar, Forshmak and Foie Gras	315
Uncle Zhenya	321
Vishnya and Buratinka	327
Gorby	335
Tour in Russia 2010	349
Piano Concerto No. 1	357
Conclusion	363
Index	369

 *QR link to the Chopin Nocturnes performed by Andrei Gavrilov*

To the Reader

I asked myself at an early age, why does everybody live as though they were on an enormous skating rink? Why does an invisible force make everyone race around in a circle without looking back until the day they die? People who have no wish to run with everyone else are viewed as losers. Those moving in the opposite direction are considered crazy, dangerously arrogant or dissidents. I ran with everyone in the "only right" direction. I triumphed in various competitions, won gold medals, plates, discs, gramophones, silver spheres... I had the courage necessary to put an end to the hideous race. I stopped. Then I set off along my own path. My sense of reason, poisoned by fear, tried to push me back. I resisted and fought as hard as I could. I smothered the eternal terror of the modern individual of being surplus to requirement.

For a long time I had no success. After a decade of intensely difficult work and prayers at my instrument, musical revelations started to appear. Not illusory ones, but genuine. More and more people started to discern in my music every intention of the composer I was performing. My music stopped humming, jangling, crackling and giving off sparks. It started to talk unobtrusively about what was really important. I ceased to be aware of time; it lost all meaning for me. The so-called "meaning of life" opened up before me. It turned out to be infinitely simple – give love and seek no reward. Reciprocal love is your reward and the meaning of life in its entirety.

Instead of a Preface

Andrei, Fira and Pitch deals with my life in the Soviet Union. It tells of the period between my graduating from the Central Music School in Moscow and my move to the West (1973-1985). It is the story of a young pianist who was sent by the Party and the government to lose the International Tchaikovsky Competition, but who won it. It recounts how the career of a musician who had entered the world's performing élite was cut short at the whim of musical smugglers. It describes what happened at the Kremlin's Georgievsky Hall during the celebrations for Brezhnev's 70th birthday, and during celebratory concerts in the Kremlin Palace of Congresses. It is the tale of private, apolitical resistance by one musician to the Soviet totalitarian machine. I have tried to put into words what most affected me in my native land – the good and the evil, and to recall my peers, and to tell of the triumphs and tribulations of a performer

My recollections of Svyatoslav Richter, or Fira as I called him, occupy a particular place in the book. There is a well-known Latin phrase that states "Of the dead speak well or not at all." I have always been against this rather suspect edict, and see it as the product of a patrician morality of dubious character. I am convinced that the opposite is true. It is impossible to analyse or seriously consider someone who is still alive, who has not yet completed their path through life, not spoken their final word and shuffled off this mortal coil. Any in-depth study into historical figures can and should begin only after their demise. If we go along with the Roman deception then we will never understand the actions and motives of dictators and tyrants and will be unable to benefit from the lessons that history has to teach us. On the other hand, we will also never be able to penetrate the characters and the mysteries of the works of great pioneers and thinkers. They will remain forever gilded, lifeless, idols. Fira for me is not a dead musician, but a critical voice that lives within me; one of the most crucial voices, a tuning fork. Everything that I play he hears, appraises and passes comment. Ultimately, I have decided that to speak "well" in the saying means to speak "the truth" and that to speak "not at all" is cowardly, cynical, deceitful suppression! Therefore I intend to write about Fira in exactly the way I remember everything. With no preconceptions. He was an extraordinary man who needs no counsel for the defence.

Andrei, Fira and Pitch is not an academic book, not a tome of musicological musings, nor is it analytical or political. It is a collection of semi-ironic texts which are somehow connected to music. There are dramatic and comic episodes from my life, opinions, portraits of people alive and dead, dialogues, concerts, thoughts about music, extracts from letters; in short, everything that I have LIVED THROUGH is reproduced here in the form that it has remained in my MEMORY.

Fa-Re-Do-Si

In 1985 I left the USSR.

My entire being was permeated with pain and incomprehension. I didn't understand why. How was it possible?

My Soviet life seemed to me to be a bad dream in a poisoned Looking-Glass World.

It was impossible to live or work with such a burden on my heart. I wanted just one thing, to forget my past as quickly as possible and start my life afresh with a clean slate.

I buried myself in my work. New impressions; endless commercial and charity concerts; recordings; rehearsals; travelling the world from London to New Zealand; ceremonial meetings with members of various royal families and leading politicians from different countries; interviews on the BBC and Voice of America; cigarette breaks with Freddy Mercury and steaks with Mick Jagger. The maelstrom of this new life pulled me in and made me forget about the past for a while. Years went by.

Unfortunately, it proved not so simple to forget the best years of my life which had been mangled by a remorseless system. Just as a drowned body will float to the surface, so surrealist nightmares of what I had lived through in the anti-world of the first half of my life came floating up from the depths of my soul.

The problem was that terrible memories were tearing me apart, and the monsters of my past lived inside me and continued to distort my consciousness, my inner world and my perception of my surroundings. In the early 1990s I realized that I couldn't play another note with real feeling. The fluttering butterflies of Chopin became stinging wasps under my fingers; the sounds and scents of sweet violets vanished, and the air turned to brittle glass. I realized that I would need to fight to liberate my muse until my dying day.

Ten years of touring, recording and concerts had not freed me from my neurotic, uneasy heaviness. My heart closed up, my emotions disappeared and I was like a frozen lump of wood. I performed all over the planet. My fingers raced across the keys with immeasurable speed, and I played like a man possessed... but it was not me, and it was not my music. It was the music of a man who had proved unable to break free from the torture chamber, a musician whose perception had become clouded from shock and had lost himself in the struggle for survival. My strident success back then was unhealthy in post-modern Europe, and it sprang from the sickly state of my overwhelmed spirit, rather than from my artistic achievements and innovations. I writhed on my piano stool in concerts like a man on the electric chair, and my convulsions were transferred to the audience. They shook and gyrated as though they were at a rock concert. None of it bore any relation to serious music. My unconditional success in the eyes of the public and the critics of the time stemmed from the perverted satiety of a decaying Western society, unable to survive the shock of WWII and the catastrophic failure of the whole Christian project.

The realization that I was living someone else's life, that some bilious, neurotic and cruel stranger was playing instead of me eventually forced me to leave the stage. On 4th December 1993 I was supposed to perform in Brussels at a concert attended by the Queen of Belgium. It is just two hours by car at most from my house in Wiesbaden to Brussels. I intended to leave the house at 3 o'clock in the afternoon. I woke up at half past nine, as usual, drank a glass of freshly squeezed orange juice, did my morning exercises, nipped into the sauna for a quick steam, and announced to my wife, surprising myself as much as her, "I am not going to play today!"

Natasha turned pale and asked, "Aren't you feeling well?"

"No, I just can't play."

"Oh my God!"

I phoned my agent in Brussels.

"There's not going to be a concert today."

"Have you got flu? Please, get a grip! Take some antibiotics and set out right away."

"I'm sorry, I can't. I'm healthy. But I can't play and I won't."

"Have you gone mad or are you pissed?"

I hadn't gone mad and I wasn't pissed, I really just couldn't play any more. I couldn't bring myself to look at the instrument, I felt like a cabbage, and my success revolted me. Over the next two weeks I cancelled all my concerts for the next three years.

I was fully cognizant of the consequences of this step. I bade farewell to my international musical career with a clear, cool head.

It was ten years before light glimmered at the end of the tunnel after desperate wanderings, and endless, fruitless attempts to find salvation. I returned to my house in Wiesbaden and locked myself away like a hermit.

My old friend John Willan called me.

"Andrei, I've got a really fun project for you. Bach for the masses! You have to do video recordings of Bach's preludes and fugues, but nothing too po-faced. We'll dress you up in various outfits – from a tramp to Liberace."

I flew to London. They told me there that the recordings were for the 250th anniversary of Bach's death, and they were due to be made in the trendiest building in the UK, the Walsall Gallery just outside Birmingham. A wonderful team from across England had been gathered for the shoot. The recording took place in a cheerfully intoxicated atmosphere of creativity. We improvised, and our fantasies knew no bounds. I wore a white dinner jacket to perform the E Flat Minor Prelude and Fugue from Book 1. I had a pendant round my neck, an enormous ring on my right hand and cufflinks on my shirt. All the jewellery was adorned with large yellow topazes. The stage was lit with a dense blue light… It was as though I was playing at the bottom of the sea.

I had started a new life. Neither Soviet nor Western – it was my life.

Chopin

It is possible that in the whole history of humankind there has never been another genius who could create a world as wonderful and original as Chopin. A world where we would all wish to live.

In his art the life of the human soul is presented as the continuity of the melodic harmonies of divine beauty. Chopin transforms into music the many colours in the palette of emotions, situations, movements and conditions of his lyrical hero. But Chopin's music contains more than the psychological life of a rarefied, delicate, schizophrenic, sensual intellectual in search of love; there are pictures from the natural world, battle scenes and historical reminiscences. It is a grave error to confine Chopin's music to the salon, to put it in a romantic cage of chamber music.

Alongside the lyricism, his music often also contains a struggle and a clash that is far from intimate and rages on a grand scale that is both political and social. Tragic conflicts within the individual are interlaced in his music with social conflicts; the physical and metaphysical worlds weave together in strange, bewitching harmonies.

Chopin replicates in his music the most intimate anxieties and predicaments of humanity, and yet never oversteps the boundary of impeccable taste. He tells us of passions and disappointments, of loneliness and yearning, and yet he never slips into soppy sentimentality. He carries his listener along the front line and through the battlefield after the war is over. He manages never to lurch into gloomy mysticism or morose fatalism, but always to remain a man. He remains the epitome of a man of honour.

Starting in approximately the 1830s, (Chopin died in October 1849 at the age of 39 from a chronic lung condition), people within European culture started to feel and think in the categories of Chopin's musical language. Chopin not only imparted perfect musical forms to the dilettante, sensual outlook of the salon; he not only SHOWED the sensual life of a lonely, intelligent, subtle man; he actually CREATED this man to a certain extent. Without him, not only would a whole inestimable layer of the subtlest and finest human emotions and thoughts be lacking, but there would be no repository of this emotional stratum – no honourable, profound, animated man of European culture.

Playing Chopin is incredibly difficult. In part this is because Chopin has been played to death, and trapped in "delicate sentimentality". For most people, Chopin is a well-rounded little romantic melodist, a tear-jerker, and a courteous, temperamental, consumptive salon genius. The REAL Chopin is not only difficult to perform and understand, but is an unwelcome guest in any concert hall.

The nocturne genre was developed by the Irish composer and virtuoso pianist John Field, who lived most of his life in Russia (one of his pupils was Mikhail Glinka). Critics often held up nocturnes by this composer as an example to Chopin. Why? Because Chopin's nocturnes had overtaken Field's nocturnes. They had outgrown the genre. The classical nocturne is a night-time song. A small lyrical, dreamy piece that represents the nocturnal state of nature and mankind, designed to be performed in a chamber context at night-time. The composer used sound to depict this state.

Chopin's nocturnes are more akin to diaries by the composer where he notes down and reproduces his intimate and heartfelt experiences of varying sorts. Chopin chronicled his entire life in his nocturnes. Not only the life of his own body and soul, but also the life of his people, and the tragedy of his homeland...

I am not aiming to provide a detailed analysis of Chopin's nocturnes, or decipher them biographically. The text below represents many years' experience of performing the nocturnes of Chopin in concert, of empathizing with the composer, of becoming him, and the experience of long contemplations on these brilliant pieces. I have tried to whittle my thoughts down as far as possible, and to leave only a few pointers that I believe will facilitate a better understanding of the music.

***

I shall play three concerts in Barcelona and then fly to Majorca. I shall perform at the Chopin festival in Valldemossa in a former Carthusian monastery where the composer lived with George Sand, and where he wrote the second Ballade, his Preludes, the Polonaise in C minor, and where he thought up the mystical second Sonata to which he had already written the funeral march. Orange trees grow in the monastery and there is an altar in the courtyard that is smothered in violets.

Valldemossa is situated in a valley. Even when it is 30 degrees down by the sea, in Valldemossa you need to put on a thick jumper towards evening to stay warm. Sand and Chopin lived in cold, damp cells that used to be inhabited by monks. I would suggest that Madame Sand had not fully realised the implications of this. Chopin himself was blatantly incapable of thinking in practical, medical terms. The disintegration of his lungs, which had been abated, renewed its progress. It was here that the prolific baroness wrote A Winter in Majorca.

Standing to attention

I went abroad for the first time in my life in May 1971. The headmaster of the Central Music School, Mikhail Anastasiev, took his best pupils to the anniversary celebrations of the famous Stankovic Music School in Belgrade. Four kids from Moscow were due to give two concerts with two musicians from Yugoslavia – the pianist Ivo Pogorelić (13 years old) and the cellist Xenia Jankovic (12).

As Soviet ninth-graders we were dizzy at the prospect of going abroad. We were delighted with everything. The international sleeper carriage on the train, the wonderful toilets, the washbasin in the compartment, and the foreigners! On the train we all sat together on one seat, like kittens in a row, goggle eyed and sharing our impressions with each other.

The first stop abroad was Budapest. The Danube. There were grand palaces with strange bulbous green roofs. We smoked American cigarettes and staggered arm in arm across the beautiful bridge that joins Buda and Pest. Then we travelled on to Slovenia, Novy Sad and Belgrade. What amazed us particularly? The food! You could buy salami sandwiches in the street. You could drink ice-cold orange juice. Naturally, that first day we stuffed ourselves and drank more than our fill. Our tongues were coated with a horrible white fur and we went completely hoarse. It was a good job that none of us was expected to sing.

We encountered young emancipated Europeans at the Stankovic School. The girls were dressed in mini-skirts or shorts and t-shirts with no bra. The lads wore suede shoes, jeans, string vests or lace-up t-shirts. A fair-skinned, curly-haired beauty, slender as a ballerina, came up to me. Her name was Mina, and she was a pianist. She gave me a big kiss on the cheek with her coral-red lips, which turned me red as a beetroot, and she hauled me off for a walk. She bought a sexy magazine, sat on a bench, pulled me to sit down beside her and then started flicking expertly through it, pointing at the pictures and asking, "Do you like it like that? Have you tried doing that one with anyone?"

I never did make it as far as the piano that day. That night my friends (violinist Levon Ambartsumian and cellist Victor

Kozodov) and I collapsed in exhaustion on our beds in the hostel and slept like logs.

Many of my "first" trips amazed me. There was Salzburg, and America, and Italy, and other places, too. But the trip to the freest barrack in the communist camp remained the most powerful and unforgettable experience. It might have been because I was a teenager. The Yugoslavian kids were such free people. Tito had not crushed in his people what Stalin had destroyed in his, and what is so disastrously lacking in many citizens of contemporary Russia – that sense of personal dignity, respect for others and, most importantly, an unconstrained individuality that permits a critical look at society and at oneself.

At the joint concert we Soviet kids thrashed the Yugoslavs with our perfect technique and artistic mastery. But for some reason the victory brought us no joy. Yes we had developed our programme with excellence, but we felt overwhelmed by our fanatical lessons and daily brainwashing as musical sportsmen. We were strong, free and elevated only in our music, while in our ordinary, private lives, we were clumsy and inhibited.

We outplayed the Yugoslavs in Zagreb as well, but there was no jubilant sense of triumph then either. You might beat them, but they were Europeans and they were a hundred times happier than us! They lived and enjoyed life naturally and with ease, while we didn't even know what that meant! We lived with our arms by our sides, standing to attention.

Once we had bought presents for everyone, we went home without enthusiasm. We were all tormented by the unexpected insight into the hopeless misery of our lives in Moscow.

B flat minor, Op 9 No 1

Chopin wrote his nocturne in B flat minor at the age of 17 at home in Poland. This piece could be labelled a classic nocturne. The composer is contemplating and reproducing the nature of his native land. His heart is aching with a strange longing.

The piece contains an error in terms of tempo. I am convinced that Chopin himself did not make the mistake when he played the nocturne. The fault is in the middle movement in D flat major. Almost all nocturnes are written using the A-B-A form. Usually, performers are wary of shifting the middle to an allegretto tempo, and the nocturne thence loses some of its originality and beauty.

If you do use the tempo then the music instantly wafts with the fragrant breeze of summer. Nocturnal rustlings and reverberations scamper through a dark mysterious garden. An echo rings out. The piece takes on its own aromatic breath. The transition to the concluding movement of the piece is then natural, with its mood of melancholy and heartache... Later, Chopin was more accurate in his authorial directions.

QR link to the Chopin Nocturnes performed by Andrei Gavrilov

Polya

Vishnya and Buratinka had a daughter, Polya. I was so infatuated with her! She was cute, flirtatious, almost flat-chested but feminine, slender and she had skin like satin that positively glowed. Her cheeks were a peach. She even smelt like a peach! The entire Central Music School was in love with her. But Polya was inaccessible. She might flirt with you, she might even go on a date, but anything more than that was a no-no.

The very next day she would be flirting with someone else. The boys all pined and some even slept under her window to be able to glimpse their loved one leaving the imposing entrance of the House of Composers of a morning.

One day, Polya announced to me, with her slight lisp, "If you get first prize at the Tchaikovsky Competition I'll be yours! You can forget it for now, though." I carried her words in my heart like a good luck charm.

The next two agonising years of study flew by. It was the then minister of culture, Ekaterina Furtseva, who included me in the eleven Soviet contestants for the Tchaikovsky Competition. I won. I then gave a whole slew of celebratory concerts, was constantly appearing on television, and was invited to a state reception at the Kremlin. I picked Furtseva up in my arms at the reception. She was rather tipsy, laughed like a drain and put up no resistance.

Hardly waiting till the end of the reception I raced from the Kremlin up Herzen (Nikitskaya) Street holding an enormous bunch of flowers like a spear. I went up in the lift, rang the bell of the coveted door of Vishnya and Buratinka's enormous apartment.

Polya had kept her word, and I noticed that she was naked under her almost see-through negligée. I handed her the bouquet, kissed her, stroked her wonderful body and… left.

On the way home I was sad and mocked myself. My ideal beloved that I had dreamed of for so long, had proved not a romantic girl in love with me, but a hard-nosed matron who was cold-bloodedly trying out an eligible bachelor for suitability.

The next time I saw Polya was in Los Angeles in 1985, in my dressing room after a solo concert. We had a chat, flirted mildly, and went our separate ways.

D flat major, Op 27 No 2

Chopin wrote his Nocturne in D flat major at the age of 26. It is a piece that tells of the composer's amorous adventures. Ecstasy and despair alternate. The personal life of the composer was complex – his liaison with George Sand appears to have been far from an idyllic romance.

The characteristic Polish rhythms and intonations in this nocturne are the voice of Chopin himself. In addition to this, we can hear female voices. At the end of the piece the music seems to contain a representation of a dialogue between two women who are soothing Chopin's restless soul. At the very end of the work there is an element of calm, and peace of mind that can be sensed in the music. The piece could be called the musical quintessence of feelings of love, or a profound portrait of love. The Nocturne in D flat major was included in the soundtrack of one of the best James Bond films, The Spy Who Loved Me.

QR link to the Chopin Nocturnes performed by Andrei Gavrilov

School-leavers' skit

The so-called Soviet piano school is a very conservative education. It gave me the foundation without which I could not independently have moved forward in the direction that I have now taken.

The Central Music School in the 60s was like a conveyor belt. We were taught by the very best that the Russian piano school of the late 19th century had to offer. I am lucky to have learned in this tradition before it disappeared. It was around the time that I *was finishing the Central Music School (in the early 70s) that the agony of the Soviet Union was beginning. The wonderful old music teachers, the last bearers of the pre-revolutionary music school started, as if on command, to die out. Young and old alike were passing away – Zak, Flier, Oborin, Stasik Neuhaus and Boris Zemlyansky... The time had come to settle accounts. Soviet culture was supposed to stand on its own two feet, to walk without its pre-revolutionary crutches. Soviet culture did not have its own legs, it only had the ministry of culture.*

***

I graduated from the Central Music School in the summer of 1973. We had a tradition that at the very end of school the school-leavers put on a show of skits. My friend Levon Ambartsumian and I wrote the show at his dacha. It was easy to write, and we howled with laughter, completely forgetting about self-censorship. An enormous amount of resentment had built up over 12 years of hard labour at the school. We wanted to find some way of getting our own back. We wrote music, we painted sets and prepared the stage in the main hall. We set the acoustics up. We had the violinist Alexei (Lyosha) Bruni down as our clown, but he bottled out at the last minute, just before the show.

"No-o-o, I can't. She's sitting in the hall already, come on guys, show some mercy!"

The show started. Overcoming his terror with great effort, Lyosha leapt onto the stage in a white doctor's coat and cap, with a huge red cross on his backside, holding a clyster. Lyosha was impersonating our school doctor, who was sitting in the front row. I accompanied his entry on stage with some idiotic, stirring music à la Prokofiev. Lyosha gradually entered into the spirit of his role, jumping around like a gorilla, giving enemas to all and sundry and banging on with the Soviet health slogans that everyone was thoroughly sick of hearing. Anyone that Lyosha touched would "die" theatrically, or start to limp or clutch at their hearts and writhe. I quietly played the funeral march from Chopin's famous sonata. All the spectators were laughing, except for the doctor. She looked round her helplessly, trying to catch the eye of the headmaster or other senior manager.

The Ride of the Valkyries boomed out of the speakers. I flew onto the stage as a witch on a broomstick. I was being our biology teacher, a Stalinist and sadistic old maid whom we all called "the Swotty Botanist". She was a ferocious woman who humiliated children, shouted, stamped her foot and could even strike a child. She would not leave off until she had reduced her victim to hysterics. I was armed with a machine gun, a hand grenade and a ruler. Swotty gave a particularly hard time to boys with long hair and girls who wore short skirts. She would kick up a fuss and summon parents into school. I went around measuring boys' hair and girls' skirts with my ruler, and then "killed" them with my toy gun. We had embellished Wagner's score with a diabolic falsetto cackle, explosions, machine gun fire and bloodcurdling shrieks. Swotty, sitting in the audience not far from the doctor, rose to her feet, tugged her blouse straight and with eyes narrow and hands clenched in a fist, left the hall. The funeral march rang out as I buried her victims at the back of the stage.

We then set up our school canteen on stage. Behind the counter stood our graduating students, representing our kind canteen ladies who were all brazen thieves. They were feeding the "children" with rissoles made from chopped cardboard. The "children" were gobbling them down hungrily and then clutching their stomachs, falling to the floor and thrashing in agonies, stretching out their hands to the dinner ladies and asking, "Why? Why have you done it, Auntie Katya?" Cruel Auntie Katya the dinner lady imperturbably shot the dying kids with her ladle and filled up a shopping bag with stolen food. She left the stage to much laughter and applause from the audience.

I cranked up the funeral march and Ira Timofeyeva, a wonderful artist and straight-A student all through school, carried round portraits of the child heroes who had perished in the school canteen.

Not all of our jokes were quite this gloomy. In the first year of the musical theory course at the conservatoire students had to listen to a string of eight chords and identify each chord, its key, name and function. At the Central Music School, we were played strings of 16 to 24 chords. They were played just twice, and they all had to be remembered. When we listened to the eight chords at the entrance exam for the conservatoire we fell about laughing. While kids from other schools spitted and hissed: "Those kids from the Central Music School have been trained like monkeys; how can you compete against them?" We made the task more "challenging" in our skit. We put an enormous fake forehead painted with multitudinous wrinkles on a student who was representing our theory master. This "walking cranium" did not play us chords; instead he "thought" them, changing the expression on his face depending on the chord and the key. The marvellous teacher that we were parodying, Lev Kaluzhsky, chuckled and delighted in our inventiveness.

At the very end we held a parade of freaks, where all our parody characters linked arms and formed a front line as they started at the back of the stage and advanced slowly but surely on the audience, like the white army troops in the famous Soviet film about Chapayev. Over the speakers came the theme of the Fascist invasion from Shostakovich's Symphony No. 7, starting with the quietest pianissimo, and increasing to a crash and grind that seem to burst the eardrums.

Fifteen minutes later the school's headmaster rushed into the hall. He was shouting, threatening and spitting mad. Half an hour earlier we had ridiculed him on stage. He was represented as a donkey with a sign saying "Acting Eeyore". He was only acting head at the time. Our real, much-loved headmaster, Anastasiev, was no longer at the school because he had been promoted. We had been sent an ordinary Soviet headmaster.

Anastasiev had undergone many rises and falls, all because of his passionate love of women. He had been director at the Bolshoy Theatre and had slid from there to the Central Music School after his latest scandal. Everywhere that this amazing man worked, there reigned a superb atmosphere of creativity. He was only in charge at the Central Music School for three years, but in that time he organized exchange tours with Yugoslavia, Czechoslovakia and Hungary and he established links with Central Television – I was in a live music show called *Orlyonok* [Eaglet] at the age of 14.

Anastasiev was kind with his subordinates, and firm but fair with his students. He valued and had a nose for talent! He dug out gifted children from the backwoods and gave them the opportunity of studying at the Central Music School.

Later Anastasiev met an unfortunate accident. His wife walked in on him when he was at home with another woman. He jumped out of the 10th floor window and was killed instantly.

Acting Eeyore called us a group of Fascist louts and promised that he wouldn't touch the actors, but would "award" the authors what they deserved. My co-author got away with just one unpleasant phrase in his reference. My award was somewhat harsher. The headmaster re-wrote my previous reference and backdated it. The new text stated that "Gavrilov is not a member of the *Komsomol* by conviction and has demonstrated that he is an inveterate anti-Soviet; he drew a parallel between the German Fascists and his Soviet pedagogues, engaged in tactless acts and had a negative influence on his comrades." I was going to have to present this to the admissions office at the conservatoire!

Having a reference of this description meant being totally blacklisted. The only place to go with something like that in the Soviet state was straight to the army or behind bars. I was a quivering wreck for three days. Then something happened. There was a quiet, modest boy in our class, Andrei Krylov, who was the son of a minister. He showed what he was made of and got his father to phone Furtseva, the culture minister. The all-powerful Furtseva interfered in the matter and I was given back my previous reference. Our Acting Head was sacked shortly thereafter.

The entrance exams for the conservatoire started. At the initial interview Kulikov, the rector, asked me, "So, Andrei, are you going to be arranging any skits at the conservatoire?"

"One was enough for me," I answered, and I kept my word.

"Then we'll have you," replied the rector. He was joking of course.

Yura Egorov

The conservatoire skivers sat in the canteen drinking beer and flicking matchboxes, all singing to the same hymn sheet, "Just stay where you are and don't make a move, mate! It's all been stitched up in any case. Anyway, it's only snitches or people with connections who have a hope. You'll never get anywhere, you're an outsider and that Naumov of yours won't drag you up to any great heights. He's not even a proper professor, just an intellectual do-gooder. You're doomed."

I didn't go for such fatalism. Thoughts of that kind stopped you working, which was of course the aim of the pessimist skivers, who were trying to justify their own laziness and impede the development of anyone who had strength and talent.

I was often lazy in my first term. After the inhuman drilling at the Central Music School you could happily spend two years without needing to prepare for any classes. I hung around Moscow with my mates. We went to see friends, danced, talked and drank. Sometimes we spent the night on the floor in strange flats belonging to people we didn't know. On one such adventure I met Yura Egorov who was by then a prize-winner from the Marguerite Long competition in Paris. I remember that a panic had broken out at the Central Music School in 1972. Some 16-year old kid from Kazan had got the bronze at a competition in Paris! From Kazan! What about us?

I saw him for the first time at the conservatoire. Yura was one year ahead of me. He was tall, elegant, very thin but strong and broad-shouldered. He had large, handsome hands. He was extremely modest, even shy, and his noble, pale face was framed with shoulder-length black hair. Unlike many others Yura was never jealous and never malicious. He was never crude, and he had real style. He laughed in a charming and highly infectious manner. He would throw back his head, fall to his knees, fold in half and silently laugh like crazy.

We made friends quite by chance after Yura, a few other people and I had been thrown out of a flat by the parents of a student girl who had invited us all for a party. I managed to persuade an old lady I knew, who adored the artistic lifestyle, to let all of us stay in her one-room apartment near Sokol metro station. Yura was grateful to me, as he had nowhere else to go.

Our group on that occasion consisted of me, Yura Egorov, Pasha Egorov (a pianist from Leningrad) and Vadim Sakharov. Much later I found out that all of my friends that evening were varying shades of gay.

When they shared the only bed they laughed, drew lots, were embarrassed, angry and argued, while I had no idea what was going on!

I slept in the old lady's flat for only two hours, then flew off to the conservatoire and played something for Naumov. Lyova, as he was known, looked at the black circles under my eyes, but said nothing. When I got back to Sokol, I found both the Egorovs and Sakharov having breakfast. They were having a dignified discussion about art. They were not laughing or teasing each other. They were three scholarly young musicians.

When I walked in they looked at me in amazement, as if wondering where on earth I had sprung from.

Yura Egorov and I both had Armenian mothers who were very similar to each other in appearance and in character. This brought us particularly close. We both loved our Armenian mums very much.

We studied at the conservatoire in two departments that were closely allied – with Yakov Zak and Yakov Flier.

We were therefore often playing at the same interim review concerts in the conservatoire Small Hall. We often played one after the other. Yura first and then I, or the other way round. I always listened with interest to how Egorov played. After the performances we would discuss our successes and failures over a cup of coffee in the canteen. Gradually, Yura became my only musical friend. I trusted him implicitly and believed in his assessments, despite the formal competition between us. There was no hint of jealousy in his elevated soul, or any other petty feelings that so often poison relationships between colleagues.

Just like countless other Soviet boys I had never received any kind of sex education. My only university was the street and my own experiences. I therefore had no idea about homosexuality. There was an un-written taboo on talking about it at the conservatoire.

I often gave Yura a hard time, asking him to show me his girlfriend one of these days.

"All the girls in the conservatoire are running after you, and you're hiding your sweetheart! Spill the beans, who's your bit of fluff?"

Yura brushed me aside with jokes…

One day we were walking along Herzen Street towards the Nikitsky Gate and Yura promised to show me his sweetheart. I was delighted.

"Where is she, where is she?"

"There, by the traffic light, at the crossing."

I scanned the crowd, looking for a pretty girl…

Yura was bursting with laughter, and pointed to a large, stout woman.

"There's my lovely bit of fluff," the vulgar word sounded alien coming from Yura

It was his mother.

Yura was in the lead when he got through to the final round of the 1974 Tchaikovsky Competition. He made a dreadful mistake in the third round, in the first movement of Tchaikovsky's Concerto No. 1, just before the second theme. In the exposition, the main theme is presented in broken octaves in B flat minor, and in the reprise it is one tone higher, in C minor. Yura "forgot" about this, and played his octaves in the reprise in B flat minor, while the orchestra was accompanying him in C minor, a whole tone higher! It would be impossible to make a more ridiculous or funny mistake. He would have been better just stopping altogether! But even here, in this awful situation, while he was playing, up on stage, he was laughing at himself, although it was too late to do anything about it. A petty egoist would have had a heart attack, but my high-minded friend just laughed.

It was because he understood that he was playing the piano, not performing open heart surgery. Later he told me, howling with laughter, "Lovey (which is what he called me), can you imagine –

THEY were playing in C minor, and I'm warbling out my octaves in B flat minor and cracking up so much!"

The day after the results had been announced Yura and I went to the conservatoire pay desk to get our prize money.

The students who were waiting in line at the window for their grants were alarmed and scared that because of the thousands being paid out to us, they wouldn't have enough money. Galya, our jolly cashier, reassured them, "Don't worry, my loves, there'll be enough for everyone, the money van brought the cash specially for these two from the competition." We got our thousands and ran off to the electrical goods store.

I wanted to make my longstanding dream come true and buy a washing machine for my mum. My mother did all the washing by hand on a ridged washboard that made her hands ache... They had just started to make a semi-automatic washing machine in the Soviet Union, called the Eureka. I had had my eye on it for the past six months...

Yura and I went marching into the shop like kings, processed our purchase and then lifted the machine in our strong, pianist arms and dragged it onto Nikitsky Boulevard. Mum opened the door, saw two winners of the Tchaikovsky Competition rolling about with joyful laughter, she gasped and gave us a big hug...

The Eureka held court in the bathroom. Mum laid the table...

In 1976, Yura Egorov was on tour in Czechoslovakia. Then he went to Italy and disappeared in Rome after his concert. He went missing. He turned up in Amsterdam. He never went back to the USSR. In the first interview he gave, he spoke of the reasons for his defection. "It is impossible to live in Russia. It's ridiculous, there are books that you aren't allowed to read, or even certain music that you can't play – such as Schoenberg and Stockhausen, as it is seen as decadent, capitalist art. In addition to that, I'm gay. In Russia homosexuality is considered a form of madness. I lived with the hang-up that I must be mentally ill. And if your homosexuality is discovered, then you are put in prison for five to seven years. I had to hide, and I hate that."

I missed Yura by just a couple of days in Prague. He left me his wallet with Czech korunas and message to have fun with them. An unknown Czech came and gave them to me portentously during rehearsal. I didn't understand anything. I decided that Yura had forgotten his wallet and that I needed to take it back to Moscow. This happened three days before the official announcement of his defection from the USSR. I still have his fifth-year student card from the conservatoire. Yura was supposed to pay 20 rubles to have it renewed.

Yura said to me in London in 1985, "Andrei, Lovey, you know I felt I was going crazy there. I'd started to drink, I had almost become an alcoholic…"

Yura Egorov died in early spring 1988, in Amsterdam. By that time he had already been ill with AIDS for three years. Yura died in dreadful agonies and, so his colleagues tell me, he could not bear the pain and killed himself. He was only 33, but had already made a brilliant international career for himself.

C sharp minor, Op KK IVa No 16 Posth

This nocturne was first published after the composer's death, but was written when he was 19. Chopin remained dissatisfied with the piece, and kept re-working it until he died. This nocturne could be viewed as the final result of Chopin's life. Or as a sort of musical epitaph to himself. Emotional pain, sorrow and bright impressionistic reminiscences were the principal elements in the music and in the life of the composer.

The short introduction sounds like an interrupted prayer. The melody that follows is full of lovelorn longing. The composer's soul is wounded. The central movement of the nocturne is a happy memory. We can hear delicate Polish dance and singing motifs, fingerpicking on a guitar and cheerful shouts. This all sounds exceptionally quietly. The memories are lost in a light mist of forgetfulness. At the end of the piece the heart-rending longing is replaced with sudden enlightenment. This may well be the last light before eternal night.

 *QR link to the Chopin Nocturnes performed by Andrei Gavrilov*

My parents, Vladimir Gavrilov and Assanetta Eguiserian

Lyova

You see, the words that you use to describe art have, for a long time now, lost any meaning for me.

My approach to art is elementary in its simplicity. There is one important aspect for me – is it alive, or not.

A living, talented spirit can feel that art is alive, and has no need for explanations, or for analysis. A lifeless and talentless spirit starts to theorise, to plunge into pseudoscience and to play at philosophy... But it still remains lifeless.

The dialogue between living and dead souls can lead to nothing. They are two universes locked in never-ending enmity.

Arturo Michelangeli is a great master, a man with impeccable taste and style. But, unfortunately, he is lifeless. His mastery and taste enable him to create something coldly beautiful, but he is not capable of transforming the notes into living music. He is unable to breathe a living soul into his music in the way God breathed a soul into Adam. His music is beautiful, stylish and played masterfully. It is not music, however, it is frozen shapes of sound.

Master class. Many people forget that there is a need to learn to think all the time. You need to learn about history, morals, everyday life... art. You need to know the personal file of every composer inside and out. You need to learn skills in transformation, to be at ease with religious philosophy.

You need to try to enter into the composer's soul by using your technical skills, and to touch the composer's secret and to become him while you are performing, to feel what he was feeling when he wrote the work. Yet not forget for one second that in the music of a genius there are no connectives and no bridges, and that a perfect piece of music is a living organism with the dimensions that we know, and those that we don't, of any living thing. You need to risk your life and sacrifice yourself on the journey. The chief task of a great performer is to stop being human... To become a single organism with the instrument and the composer's individuality. And that is just the beginning... Many people in Russia still retain the hope that intuition alone will take you where you need to go in creative work; that home-grown concepts of culture and art will suffice. But that won't work! You need to study experience from around the world. You need to break the mould, even though that can be physically painful. It has to be done, because it impedes you, just as kidney stones or a brain tumour will.

My musical pause lasted for almost seven years. During this time I hardly touched the instrument. The pause was painful and it was a long operation to remove the shell that had grown over the delicate, living flesh of the music. The shell was of falsely classical interpretations (the contemporaries of creative geniuses ALWAYS lag behind in understanding their ideas), stagnant concepts and habits summoned by inertia and prejudice... Don't believe a single "tradition" until you have tested everything for yourself, like a child who constantly touches objects to make sure that they are real and work out what they are for.

***

In 1970 Lev Naumov was not even invited to the traditional ceremony of presenting the best eighth-graders from the Central Music School to the professors of the Moscow conservatoire. Zak was there, as were Flier, Oborin, Nikolaeva, Milstein and Dorensky.

Studying with Flier or Zak meant receiving a gold medal at a prestigious international contest in the near future, and becoming a member of the performing élite.

Oborin was considered a representative of the Old Russian school, and studying with him meant becoming a performer of the lyricism of Tchaikovsky, Chopin, Rachmaninoff and Scriabin in the best traditions of 19th-century aristocratic salon culture.

Nikolaeva represented the "conservative" school of the pedantic Goldenweiser. She was an "omnivorous" pianist, a celebrated authority on musical literature and a wonderful contrapuntist. She had many things to teach and share with her students. She had immense authority in the world of music.

For a long time Naumov was not recognized as an authority in the conservatoire. Many people did not accept his unrestrained musical flights of fancy.

After the audition, Flier, Oborin and Nikolaeva wanted to have me in their classes. My mother, however, wanted my future musical development to continue "under the sign of Heinrich Neuhaus". She phoned Irina, one of her friends from the conservatoire, who was the wife of Lev Naumov, and agreed with her on a private audition at their home.

My mum and I went to the communal flat on Studencheskaya Street where the Naumov family lived in two small rooms. We rang the doorbell. A plump Irina answered the door. She invited us through to see Lyova, as he was known affectionately. He was sitting on the sofa watching television. It was a children's adventure film.

Naumov wore baggy black flannel trousers and a plaid shirt. Heavy rectangular glasses sat on his nose. The room was piled high with books and musical scores. There were two paths through the clutter, one to the sofa, and one to the piano.

Naumov looked like a professor from a Soviet comedy of the Stalin era. A thorough eccentric, a sort of musical Paganel... He looked rather remote, somewhere along the autism spectrum. It seemed that he was not aware of the reality that surrounded him.

Later I came to realize that Lyova was by no means an "otherwordly professor", and that he had a sharp mind and was observant, accurate and witty... He had a gigantic temperament with which his fragile body simply couldn't cope. He therefore had to take tranquilisers.

He sometimes behaved in rather strange ways. For example, he would often hail a taxi without raising his arm. He would simply stand at the edge of the kerb with his arms by his side. I knew that he was doing everything right in his mind, but the signals from his overloaded mind did not always get to his arms or legs.

I had prepared quite a large programme for this meeting of ours. The first number in the programme was the Haydn Grand Sonata in E flat major. After that I intended to play a few technically complex works with which I hoped to bowl Naumov right over.

I had been crammed to the eyeballs, and I was pretty sure that I was ready for any musical stadium or capable of giving professional concerts. I was therefore totally unprepared for what happened next. I laid into the Sonata, taking the bull by the horns straight away. But Naumov did not give me the chance to get into my stride. He broke me off immediately. After just the first four chords. And then he interrupted me at almost every phrase! He didn't let me finish a single period! I immediately stopped wanting to study with him... We never even got beyond the exposition.

I didn't yet know that music is not smooth phrases and completed periods, it is not perfect technique and a diamond sound "like Gilels", but something much deeper and more wonderful. Naumov was not impressed by what I could do. He did not need the Gilels sound, was not inspired by the smooth phrases that he had already heard a thousand times, or the finished periods. Good technique for him was something that went without saying... The sparkling, superficial music-making that wowed so many of my teachers and the famous professors was nothing but an empty husk to Naumov!

Lyova did not approve of the aesthetics of the Central Music School.

I was distraught all night after seeing Naumov. Everything that I had spent ten years learning was rubbish! What was I to do? I couldn't play a single phrase right, not one note! I was the best student at the Central Music School, and I had beaten stars like Ekaterina Novitskaya, Lyubov Timofeyeva, Mikhail Faerman! Incidentally, there are still a few old men and women in Moscow's musical circuit who mutter, "Naumov ruined Gavrilov, before going to him Gavrilov was a real treasure! Andrei's mother made a terrible mistake!"

Later Irina told my mum that as soon as we had left Lyova collapsed on the sofa, pedalled his legs in the air and wailed, "Give me Gavrilov!"

The fact that Lyova interrupted me and scoffed at me in that first meeting was a sign of respect and hope on his part. If he had seen nothing of note in my playing, then he would have listened to the whole programme, made a few comments, praised me and never seen me again. It was a shame that nobody explained this to me at the time. It would have saved me from three or four years of a painful lack of self confidence...

Lev Naumov was a master in the medieval sense of the word; the bearer of an elevated artistic culture which was already an anachronism in the Soviet Union in the early 70s, and has completely vanished from the modern world. The "normal" conservatoire professors did not touch him; they endeavoured to belittle his significance and not let him get too near the feeding trough. They called Naumov a blessed holy fool, a musical fantasist... while Naumov steadfastly went his own way. He only "danced" to music. He did not recognize traditions. He could change his conception of a piece several times in a single day. There were only a few students who could bear the strain. The strongest ones.

Lots of the professors at the conservatoire would bend over backwards to "bring medals to the Soviet team". The conservatoire was essentially split in two. On one side lived and worked Lev Naumov, Stanislav Neuhaus and Boris Zemlyansky with their students and followers, while on the other were all the rest, the medal-collectors.

Naumov played superbly. But he lacked the nerves, the physical strength and the desire constantly to be practising to play concerts. He was not tempted by the triumphs of the pianist; he was enthralled by music itself. By the exciting, iridescent depth of music. At Fira's ball Lyova played one of his own pieces, a prelude and a fugue. Richter whispered to me after the first few bars, "I'm going to take lessons from your teacher next week!"

Naumov wrote music. He could have become a celebrated Soviet composer, but he did not want to be second-best.

Lyova never built a wall between student and teacher, and he talked to his pupils as if they were colleagues. He searched for the truth with them. The atmosphere in class was friendly and comfortable. His house was always open, and each of us could casually pop in to see Lyova, drink some brandy and have a chat about student matters with him. Students went to Naumov as if to the confessional, and he listened patiently, and helped as best he could. Lyova was a teacher from heaven; he loved every detail of this difficult work, and his students were members of his family. His flat saw birthday celebrations, weddings, the start of relationships.

Somehow it just happened that many of Lyova's pupils became prize-winners at major competitions. Without any protection, without any calls to important people, without a single move being made away from art!

Naumov changed from being a lecturer to a professor, and his students didn't even notice. Then he was awarded the state honour of Distinguished Artist. All these awards were of little interest to him... His was an example that others could learn from!

By the late 70s, I began to tire from the musical dependence I felt towards my beloved professor. It worried, exhausted and frightened me. I watched his other pupils – they were all incapable of interpreting and performing a single piece without their teacher's help. I acutely felt that the time had come to break away from my tutor and start to work independently. I stopped taking lessons with Lev Naumov in 1979. My decision upset him deeply, and he did not conceal his conviction that I would be unable to manage without his guiding hand. I equally firmly decided that nothing would induce me to follow his promptings any more.

Having lived in Europe, and having become acquainted in a practical way with European culture I realized that my understanding of Western musical culture was radically different from Lyova's. Naumov was a genius, but a national and very Russian musician. That was insufficient for a genuine understanding and rendition of European music. For some time we did not talk

It was only in the mid 80s that we re-established our relationship, and by the late 90s we were good friends and colleagues.

The Competition

The Russian musical tradition? There is no such thing. Our performing tradition is a collection of styles and methods borrowed from other European cultures.

It could even be said that the main feature of the Russian musical tradition, just as the main feature of our national character, is a certain amorphous quality, a pliability and formlessness, even insubstantiality. Something eternally feminine. While people from the West, and Western classical music, are clear-cut, orderly, almost tangible… the Russian consciousness lacks a precise form, so can easily be used to fill someone else's bronze mould, like a gas or liquid. This lightness is deceptive, but for an artist and performer it is a trap. Pouring yourself into someone else's contour does not fill you with new content!

***

In the autumn of 1973 I started thinking about the Tchaikovsky Competition for 1978. I hoped by then to have matured and to intensify my playing significantly. In my first year as a student I sometimes still played in the yard outside. Mum used to call from the eighth-floor window, "Andrei, ho-ome!"

One day in December I was knocking a puck around on the fresh ice in our courtyard. Mum called me home, but she did it in such a strange voice that I realized straight away something important had happened. I raced up to the eighth floor. My mum had gone white as a sheet and held the telephone receiver in her hand. She whispered "It's the ministry of culture, the ministry of culture!" I took the receiver. A polite voice informed me that the minister for culture of the USSR would now talk to me, Ekaterina Furtseva. Oh my goodness! The conversation was short.

"Andrei, there is a view that you need to take part in the Tchaikovsky Competition next year on the Soviet team. What is your opinion?"

A thought flashed through my mind – that was it, the end of my student life, and I hadn't even had time to have fun yet.

"I agree!"

"Marvellous," concluded the minister, and hung up.

In January 1974 I had to fill out the contestant application form and write my CV. I could only boast of eleven years at the Central Music School, and competing in the final of the national competition for musical performers in Minsk. I did not understand why those in charge had decided to send me to certain death. It was cruel to send a novice to a competition where six of the ten Soviet candidates had won major international competitions. I simply didn't stand a chance in a musical contest against such experienced fighters, some of whom were eight years older than me. They also all had influential professors standing behind them, almost all of them members of the competition jury, and such celebrated names as Zak, Flier, Malinin and Bashkirov. I felt like an ant in the path of a slow-moving steam roller. The competition promised me nothing but disaster. I was preparing myself to gain the status over the summer of the loser of the Tchaikovsky Competition.

In February they let me stop coming to lectures at the conservatoire. There were three months till the competition. Despite everything I started to prepare seriously for the contest. If I was going to die, at least I could do it to music! They gave us the score for the compulsory contemporary piece (for the second round), which had been written specially for the competition by the talented composer Alexander Pirumov. It was a highly challenging toccata piece written with a modern composing technique. Contestants were allowed to play it with the sheet music, but we "Soviet eagles" we supposed to play it off by heart. I later had the honour of playing the work in the presence of the composer. Pirumov was happy with my interpretation, and, as far as I recall, he didn't make a single criticism. This made me believe in my own powers.

The ministry of culture had made a sumptuous gift to all competition participants – we were all sent off to the composers' retreat in Ruza. We were each given a separate cottage with a decent instrument. I got a Steinway! It was such a joy to work in my "own" house just outside Moscow! Round the clock. We didn't have to worry about food as we were fed for free in the restaurant at the House of Composers. Many contestants came with their parents. I worked and relaxed with my mother.

The relations between contestants were friendly and good, as though we were not going to be competing against each other. The family of the composer Magidenko often came to see me and my mum. His daughter had been in my class at the Central Music School. She was the first person who said to me, "You're going to win this competition!"

I spent all my free time with Yura Egorov (he was also a contestant). We played our pieces to each other, showed how well the pieces in the compulsory section were moving along. All these musical competitions always make me think of figure-skating championships. Our études were no less difficult than jumps on the ice. The first round was the compulsory programme, the second round was like the free skating, and then the final round with the orchestra was very like the final show. And there were also demonstration performances at the Luzhniki stadium! The better I got to know my friend, the more I wanted Yura to win the competition. I didn't see myself as the winner in my wildest dreams!

Our whole "Olympic village" worked tirelessly, and we matured not day by day, but hour by hour, and became real musicians without even noticing. We thought, lived and breathed music, forgetting that another world even existed! Happy times!

Eventually it was time for the ceremonial opening of the 1974 Tchaikovsky Competition in Moscow, at 13 Herzen Street. I felt reverential but calm. The day came for drawing lots. It seemed then that not only our musical careers, but our very lives were hanging from a thread. We drew the slips of paper with our numbers on. As a competitor, your strategy and tactics depended on what number you drew. Everyone dreaded getting the first number because there were no pointers at the beginning, no standard and no benchmark. Even if you played like a god, there would be about two hundred pianists coming after you who would drum out any memory of you in the minds of the jury and the public over the next three weeks. Whoever drew this terrible number would be a celebrity for an hour. Everyone would discuss and encourage him, then sympathise and joke with him. And at the end of the round they would forget how what-was-his-name had played.

The Small Hall at the conservatoire... Contestants were called up in alphabetical order. Everyone's hands were shaking, temples were pounding and ears were ringing. Thank God my surname didn't begin with an A! Someone had already drawn number one. The rest of us sighed with relief. It was my turn – I pulled out a paper, opened it. Number 9! I didn't know whether to be pleased or not. I had wanted a later number.

I was ready for the first round of the contest. Once I was through with the first round there would be plenty of time to prepare for the second round! Eight people would already have played before me, including the main claimant to victory, Dmitry Alexeyev, who was the oldest and most experienced. The drawback with the later numbers was that the audience and the jury were already tired, and time would be a bit short before the second round. So, all in all, let's hear it for number 9!

The first round... I was playing effortlessly, flying as though on wings. There was nothing to lose! I romped through the technical exam in the Grand Hall of the conservatoire. I was not even thinking about the competition, or about the jury! Flier noticed this, and commented irritably, "Gavrilov is playing over the heads of the jury!" He meant to be mean, but ended up making a compliment! My Professor Naumov, meanwhile, was happy; he smiled and praised me. Straight after my performance he and I went into the famous Neuhaus class to start preparing for the second round.

The public received me well. *Izvestiya* printed a little piece about the successful performance of a lad fresh out of school. With a photograph! Those in the know told me that I shouldn't see the snippet as a good omen; it was more likely to be typical misleading disinformation.

Naumov and I slogged away from morning till night. Lev seemed younger and more cheerful, and drove me unremittingly through the entire programme. If something wasn't going right, he would say, "Go and take half an hour outside, do anything you like. I shall be waiting for you here." I was dropping dead with exhaustion, but Naumov didn't give any appearance of being tired. The first round flew past, with all the Soviet contestants playing as expected, meaning that they all did what their professors had told them to do. Word got out of who had got through to the second round, and in what order. First was Stanislav Igolinsky. He was a marvellous musician from Leningrad, but rather too introverted for public competitions. Second was Gavrilov. When Naumov and I heard about this we went straight to his house on Chekhov Street and drank a bottle of brandy. Yura Egorov was third. Curiously enough, Alexeyev, who had unanimously been seen as the most likely candidate before the competition, had not even made it into the top five!

The second round started. Each competitor had to play three major works of utmost complexity, not counting one of the preludes and fugues by Shostakovich and a piece by a 20th century composer from the country you were representing (I had Prokofiev). In addition to that there was the compulsory competition piece for which there was a special prize.

I was performing fifth in the second round, while Dmitry Alexeyev was fourth. His blood pressure rose because of this, and he was put at the end of the second round at the request of his professor and under doctor's orders. I played the programme for the second round with even greater élan. It all seemed like an exciting and dangerous game to me. Everyone was nervous and anxious, while I was calm and still having fun as I romped through it all. While I was performing, the house three times went against the rules of the competition and applauded. The bursts of applause inspired me, and I threw myself into the second and then the third piece like a courageous soldier hurling himself at the enemy with exhilaration and foolhardy audacity. My head was spinning, and with each chord I played I seemed to derive some sort of inexplicable strength from the piano, the music and the public.

Things started to go wrong with the other contestants. They were tortured by a sense of responsibility. They were afraid of not meeting expectations. My Lyova Naumov never made me feel that he was expecting anything of me; he was modesty and tact personified. But when I was sitting at the piano I felt that he was inside me, also taking part in the battle. After I had played in the second round, Lyova and I drank brandy again. We had to wait almost two weeks before we knew how everyone had done in the second round.

The second round finally finished. In the meantime Pirumov the composer had praised my playing in the press, and had written that Gavrilov had played his composition best of all. The prize was given to the American David Lively, however, who was presented by the press originally as the leader of the US team and a possible contender for victory in the contest. In the end he barely made it through to the third round, and was not awarded a prize (8 out of 12 finalists got awards), and he received a consolation prize from the jury. He really was a marvellous pianist and was only left without a prize certificate because of the unusually high level in that year's competition, which included many of today's concert stage superstars. For example, András Schiff is a world-renowned pianist now, and he only came fourth.

Rumours started to circulate. As I had expected, Yura Egorov went through to the third round as the leader, while I was second on the list, sharing the position with Myung-whun Chung, a wonderful pianist and representative of a great clan of musicians in the US.

We were both in second place with an identical number of votes and points. Today, Myung-whun Chung is one of the world's greatest conductors. Stanislav Igolinsky was in third place as we went through to the third round. Alexeyev had blatantly lost his chance of victory.

My nerves started to give way in the third round. Lyova became more serious, and I started smoking two packs of cigarettes a day. He and I would sit and play. To the point of exhaustion. We'd be almost falling over. Lyova would lose his temper and shout at me. Rightly so. I mean, I hadn't prepared for the third round! I hadn't thought that I would get through. I had almost completely forgotten the text of Rachmaninoff's Concerto No. 3.

Obstinate Naumov sat with me in the Neuhaus class and bashed away at the text with me, page by page. It took us about four days to get it back together again, to work through all the possible pitfalls in this very difficult concerto. The performances in the first two rounds had left their mark on me, and I felt battered and dog-tired.

Alexeyev was due to play first, and I was second. Again his blood pressure rose, and an appeal was submitted to move his performance to the end. But this time the chairman of the jury demonstrated some principle, for the first time, and said, "If he's ill then he can go home and get some treatment!" Alexeyev had to play before me. The jury listened to two finalists a day. Alexeyev played quite well, but he had already been written off! As for me, Tchaikovsky flew out from under my hands! After the first movement there was applause! After the end of the concerto they gave me a standing ovation! It was unheard of! I ran offstage for five minutes. My course-mates all embraced me. Levon Ambartsumian poured a can of orange juice straight down my throat.

I came back on stage like a bull into the ring to play Rachmaninoff's Concerto No. 3. I'd played the first movement, and the second. I notice that some people had tears in their eyes. The finale... The last page of the giant concerto... The beloved chord culmination that carries on endlessly in unison with the orchestra... Only many years later I learned to control the orchestra in this culmination as it floats forwards and back, and then transforms to a roar. Because of aberrations in the sound the orchestra can sound like a furious organ, or like a cosmic explosion that just goes on and on. I was playing the concerto for the third time in my life then. I threw back my head rapturously in triumphant ecstasy... and left the orchestra about four bars behind. When I realized what I had done it was too late. There was nothing else for it but to sit and wait until the great machine of the orchestra crawled up, like a division of tanks, to me in my bunker. I took my hands off the keys.

A mistake! The musicians in the orchestra saw my gesture and started to fall apart. The French-horn player heroically saved us from disaster by playing his solo so loudly that we came out of our confused state and played the coda to the end. I had fallen just a few metres from the finish and barely managed to crawl to the end of the concert.

Lyova came onto the stage, he embraced me and whispered, "You were holding the gold medal in your hands until the very last minute, and you let it go." We went to drink brandy. A little man rushed up to me on the staircase at the stage door of the Grand Hall and tried to smother me in an embrace. It was Vardanyan, the deputy head of the culture department of the Party Central Committee. I had seen him a couple of times at various meetings. Had I been more experienced, I would have realized that people from the Central Committee don't just pick musicians up and waltz them around for no reason. Lyova and I drank for the remaining five days of the competition. We didn't witness Yura Egorov's terrible failure, and we only turned up on the final day for the start of the jury deliberations in the Small Hall of the conservatoire. Thousands of people had filled what was then Herzen Street, from the Manege to the Nikitsky Gate. Contestants and journalists were allowed into the foyer where a Russian tea had been set out with cakes and caviar nibbles.

It was nearly two o'clock in the morning, and the jury was still deliberating. I was smoking my hundredth cigarette. Then someone touched me on the shoulder. I recognized a journalist from the *Moskovsky Komsomolets* newspaper.

"Write down what you're feeling right now!"

He shoved a piece of paper into my hand. I wrote, "I'm happy to have gone through to the third round among such wonderful performers."

Then another reporter, a special correspondent from *Izvestiya*, thumped me on the shoulder.

"What are you writing? You've won the gold medal! You've won! Unanimously!"

My heart plummeted down somewhere and then leapt back into my chest. A blinding halogen light struck my face and the NBC TV camera turned on me. I heard voices as though they were coming from a different planet.

"We are taking an interview from the winner of the fifth Tchaikovsky Competition, Andrei Gavrilov. Andrei, what can you say at this thrilling moment? What are you feeling?"

I was as silent as the crowd in *Boris Godunov*.

The First round of the Tchaikovsky Competition (1974)

Receiving the First Prize of the Tchaikovsky International Competition (1974)

Gudauta – Salzburg

It is very difficult to establish a rapport with an instrument. There is no such thing as a perfect instrument... In my collection at home I prefer my Steinway C-grand, from Hamburg, which I bought in 1987, and which is the same size as an early 20th century New York grand piano.

I played on a Bluthner in Vladimir that was pale and blunt and had a maximum sounding of mezzo forte. My muscles couldn't take the strain, and on the third day of work they became inflamed from the constant forcing of the sound. I cancelled the concert as a result, which is something I do extremely rarely.

An instrument can change from one encounter to the next. It all depends on who has played on it, and how, and how well it has been taken care of. One and the same instrument can sound wonderful today, and an absolute disaster tomorrow. And vice versa. More than anything else, an instrument requires love, since it possesses a living soul. As for the keys and the mechanism, they just require an appropriate reaction when touched.

***

After my triumph at the Tchaikovsky Competition I was "basking in rays of glory". I was intoxicated and stupefied by success! I feverishly played the "display" concert at the Luzhniki stadium. I went to receptions at the Kremlin, I received congratulations from ministers, gave countless interviews, let myself be photographed, and beat off admirers. Everything was mixed and caught up in a celebratory whirlwind. I felt that I had to get out of Moscow as fast as possible. I went to Gudauta to relax. I went with Naumov, Levon Ambartsumian, my mother and older brother.

It was always crowded and noisy in the summer at our house in Gudauta. By contrast, in the winter there was only Kolya in the house, a lonely artist from western Ukraine who was in love with the sea. Kolya had served three years in the navy and had stayed on in the Caucasus, not going back to Ukraine. He had met my father, who had suggested that he live in our house and keep an eye on it. He was handsome and well-built with raven-black hair, very even features and eyes like black olives. That was Kolya, a Ukrainian with a hopelessly romantic soul.

Kolya was no stranger to the bottle. In fact he was a loving friend. In Abkhazia there are reasons to love the bottle. The wines from thereabouts brought us all so much pleasure – there was the light, sharp Lykhny made from the Isabella grape, then the pomegranate-red Apsny that turned your head, and the Bouquet of Abkhazia that whacked you round the legs. We all loved Kolya, in spite of his weaknesses. He was a wonderful painter – I can't count the times my father offered him the opportunity of going to one of the Moscow art colleges, guaranteeing him a place. Kolya would pack his stuff up unwillingly, say goodbye to us, go out onto the breakwater to bid farewell to the sea, sadly gaze at the waves and then stay at home.

Kolya called himself a "master of the sad portrait". The locals in Gudauta used to order full-length graveyard portraits from him, which are placed by the gravestone in the Caucasus tradition. Kolya painted the portraits from photographs. Sometimes even from tiny passport photos. Occasionally the snapshot would show the deceased in such an enormous hat that the face wouldn't even be visible. But the clients were always satisfied with Kolya's work. One time, Kolya had been drinking and had forgotten that he was supposed to hand over the latest "sad portrait" the following day. The clients woke him up in the morning and poked him in the ribs meaningfully with their sharp knives. Then they said, "Go on, do the picture!" and Kolya, sweating with fear and from the drink, painted a virtuoso portrait and gave it to the clients with 20 minutes to spare before the funeral…

Kolya drowned in the Black Sea. His body was thrown ashore by a storm. He was buried in Gudauta cemetery.

Gudauta is a small seaside town in Abkhazia, and is similar to the small towns on the southern coast of Italy, or Corsica. Blood feuds were no rarity, and the whole town knew which clans were at war with each other. Exotic funeral processions with professional mourning women would pass along our street. The hired mourners would put ash on their heads, tear their clothing and wail. It was often young men being buried in Gudauta, with bloody clashes taking many a youth to the grave, along with inter-ethnic confrontations, motorbike accidents and the sea.

Our local gravedigger in Gudauta, Volodya, was half Abkhazian and half Mingrel, and he was very like his witty, legendary colleague from Hamlet. He was small, bald, completely toothless, and always wore a hat and grey suit. He was a brilliant orator and philosopher. It was not only the relatives and friends of the deceased who would come to hear the funeral orations that he spoke over the open graves, but complete strangers as well. He would make them laugh and move them to tears.

Gudauta had its own "Grand Hotel" and dance floors by the sea, just like in Fellini's *Amarcord*. Pre-war life in Rimini was very similar to our Soviet life in Gudauta. The only difference was that we had it brighter, juicer and less civilized.

Gudauta... Dark mountains crowned with sparkling snowy peaks, a dark blue sea, and cold mountain streams as clear and clean as crystal, sweet scented magnolia and oleander, blood-red pomegranates cut in half with a sharp knife, the singing of cicadas in the heat of noon, and choirs of frogs in the humid Caucasian evenings.

It transpired in Gudauta that I had forgotten how to relax. Having swum as much as we wanted in the sea, Levon and I went home and lay on our beds. There was a big pile of money on the floor between our beds, which was the prize for winning the Tchaikovsky Competition, 2,500 rubles. I had spent relatively little so far, having only bought the washing machine for my mum. The rest of the money lay on the floor. Sometimes we made paper aeroplanes out of the red ten-ruble notes, and threw them at each other. We also played with my enormous medal. Levon gave it the bite test, and the imprint of his teeth has stayed on the soft metal ever since – it was high-carat gold.

This was not the first time that Levon and I had been on holiday together in Gudauta. Before I had got rich, money had always been a bit tight. We used to take back the bottles that Kolya had been drinking all winter for the deposit. For an empty litre-bottle of white Psou wine, the recycling point gave us 18 kopecks. We would use the money to buy wine, bread, cheese and fruit.

We went to Sochi out of boredom and a hope of finding adventure. We didn't have long to wait for an adventure as I was arrested by the Sochi police for walking barefoot down the road. I was put in the police van, where there was already a convict suffering from toothache, with an enormous swollen face. He was being taken to have his tooth extracted. The adventure ended happily, as I was recognized and let free. The keepers of the peace begged us not to tell anyone that I had been arrested. It could have ended badly, however, as the Soviet police, especially in the Caucasus, usually didn't go easy on their detainees. Broken arms, beaten kidneys, electric-shock torture and other such delights were not uncommon.

Then we decided to head into the mountains. We yomped up to the Malaya Ritsa lake. We climbed around on the rocks, then made our way through the boxwood forest, messed around, shouted and listened to the echo and had a snowball fight – there were still some blackened piles of snow lying in hidden shady hollows that hadn't melted all summer. We ate in picturesque village dives, in some of which I was recognized by the restaurant musicians who sang songs for me.

"We are singing this song for our friend, Andrei Gavrilov."

Other customers would ask each other, "Who are they singing it for? Who's Andrei Gavrilov?"

"Gavrilov? Probably a gangster..."

When we got back from the mountains, we went out into the open sea. Fishermen that we knew invited us to ride in their boat with them and catch fish. We took two crates of Lykhny with us that had been given to me by some Abkhazian bigwigs. We lowered the crates on ropes down to the bottom of the sea to cool them, and forgot about them. The bottles are still there on the sea floor to this day.

On the fifth or sixth day of our holiday, Levon and I were lounging on the pebbly shore of the Black Sea, enjoying the blissful sea air and the morning sun. My mum came up to us in agitation and handed me an urgent telegram.

"To Comrade Gavrilov. Urgent. You must fly to festival in Salzburg with concert to replace Svyatoslav Richter who is ill."

My mother and I took the first flight back to Moscow.

There were ten days until the concert. In this time I had to go through about five "exit" commissions, try to get hold of a concert outfit, process the paperwork for an international passport, become a member of the *Komsomol* and prepare for the concert. I ran from pillar to post like a mad thing. I filled out questionnaires, I submitted photos and my internal passport. I was summoned to yet another commission in the district Party office. I was interviewed there by some elderly inspectors. They were checking me out for loyalty to the Soviet authorities, for ideological purity and for moral soundness. Their questions were stupid and predictable. My answers matched them perfectly. The *Komsomol* compromised in my favour, presumably following orders from above. I was simply issued with a membership card. An 18-year old student who was not a member of the *Komsomol* in those days could only go to the West if he was Jewish, and he could only go in one direction. I wanted to be able to come back home.

The tailcoat was the most difficult problem. It was unfeasible in communist Moscow in 1974 to have this chic costume made, especially at one week's notice; impossible to purchase and totally alien to the Soviet human as it was. I had to cobble the outfit together in pieces.

One performer I knew leant me his bowtie. Another leant me the tailcoat. I got the shirtfront and waistcoat from the Bolshoy Theatre. I already had some black patent leather shoes. All that was missing were the trousers. The only trousers in my size in the Bolshoy Theatre costume department were enormously wide, like the sort of pantaloons a Turkish sultan might wear. Once I'd had a good laugh trying them on in the wardrobe department I left without any trousers. I rushed around Moscow's sewing workshops. It took me a while, but I eventually found a compassionate lady who agreed to sew me some concert trousers in a day, for a fee.

All that I needed now was to prepare for the most important concert in my life in just two days. I ground my teeth from the stress, and practised flat out. The neighbours were driven mad by the noise and bashed heavy metal objects against the heating pipes.

I was invited to Gosconcert where I was introduced to a translator called Tatyana who was supposed to fly with me. This tall, slender young woman was unattractive in some elusive way. Her dark hair stood in an unpleasant bundle on her head. There was something sharp in her features, and in profile the interpreter looked rather like a bird of prey. Tatyana was friendly towards me. She smiled often, but there was something slightly wrong about her smile. I instantly realized that I would need to keep my mouth shut with Tatyana around, and that she was one of the tentacles (with an ear like a sucker) of the enormous squid that kept us all prisoner.

They announced our flight. The Jewish émigrés came out of a different exit. The old folk and the sick were carried out on stretchers, with oxygen pillows. Later I got used to seeing Jews leaving the USSR on all Aeroflot flights to Vienna or Rome, all meekly carrying their elderly. It was painful to watch this exodus; I felt sorry for the old people, and as I remembered the stories from the Bible I thought with horror of the plagues of Egypt awaiting us.

As I was making my way to my seat I stumbled upon another passenger who had dropped some small change in the gangway. I helped him collect up his money. He seemed to recognize me rather too quickly and was a little over the top as he melted like an ice cream on a hot day. He invited me to come and sit beside him after take off, and to drink a tot of brandy to celebrate our acquaintance. I willingly agreed. It transpired that this other passenger was also a musician; he showed me photographs of students in Yakov Flier's piano class that included him, about fifteen years younger. He was dressed elegantly. He had a good suit, a silk scarf, good leather shoes and a fine imported shirt. But under the shirt he was wearing a "telnyashka", a stripy sailor's vest! His name was Vilen, or Vladlen.

A pianist? His face was mischievous, and there was something about that telnyashka that was bothering me. He was a very confusing chap. Vladlen promised that he would definitely come to my concert, although all the tickets for the concert had sold out a year ago.

We arrived in Vienna. The Jews were led off by somebody. We went through to the transit lounge. It was late evening by the time we arrived in Salzburg. We were met by representatives of the festival and taken to our hotel, the Am Neutor, an unpretentious little building with three stars over the door. I went to look at the city. I was amazed by the tunnels and the mountains. In all the commotion before the concert I hadn't even had time to open an atlas and see where Salzburg was actually situated. It turned out to be right near the Alps. Everything in the city was unfamiliar and interesting. In particular the glamorous shop windows showing musical instruments. The prices had nothing in common with the pittance I was due for my performance. It took me a while to find Getreidegasse, the narrow little street that still boasts the Hagenauer House where Mozart was born. I stood for a short time on the little square before this rather ordinary six-storey house that is now a museum and did not seem to trigger off any association with the *Magic Flute* or the *Requiem*, and then I headed back to my modest hotel.

Breakfast in a three-star Austrian hotel was bad tea, nasty rolls, a tiny piece of butter and a little plastic tub of jam. Once we had gulped this down, Tatyana and I set off to meet the head of the Salzburg Festival at the time, a Monsieur Nicolas. He was famed for his eccentricity. Only eccentricity could explain his strange decision, to put it mildly, to invite a kid fresh out of school to replace the "great Richter". The effect was that he was acting out of spite towards the celebrated musician and the pampered public by saying, "You want to make things difficult? Then make do with this Soviet puppy!"

Nicolas, elegant, slightly overweight and with greying hair, looked at me dubiously. I appeared to him a young geek in a stupid suit. I was wearing my entire wardrobe. My suit was the product of another Eastern Bloc country. My mum had bought it in the Vesna shop on Novaya Bashilovka where you could get branded goods in those days. My shoes were from GUM on Red Square, as were my shirt and tie. Nicolas pasted on a smile, muttered a few standard phrases, looked with distaste at my tie, and sent me off to practice on the piano.

I liked the instrument and the hall. I started feverishly playing my programme for the evening. I did not have enough time to rehearse properly. To be honest, there were a great many areas that were frankly not ready. I was very nervous. By evening I was in a total panic.

However hard you try, it just isn't possible to get into shape in only three days, even if you are an experienced concert pianist. I had no experience of concerts. I was just a first-year student who had won a competition.

Tatyana jollied me along in the artists' room, which was certainly no bad thing. Out of nowhere my brandy companion, Vladlen, appeared in an expensive dinner jacket, wonderful shiny shoes, and a dazzling white shirt front with that same telnyashka just visible underneath!

I went out on stage in my piecemeal Soviet concert suit. I looked at the concert-goers and was overwhelmed.

What a public! What glitz! What toffs! What charm! What alien beings! It was a mirage! It was Hollywood! Michael York was sitting in the front row; Tybald from Zepherelli's wonderful *Romeo and Juliet*. The men wore sumptuous dinner jackets, with snow-white shirts, bowties and platinum cufflinks. The women were in breathtaking evening dresses, with jewels at their necks the size of chandelier crystals. Everything was shimmering, fluttering and fragrant as a glass of champagne! I was bowled over and lost my sense of reality. I floated to the piano as though in a dream and started to play. Good God! It was my last concert before inevitable death and eternal humiliation!

Even now, thirty years later, I can't understand why the audience was so ecstatic and excited by my performance. It might be that the secret behind my extraordinary success in Salzburg was precisely in my total desperation. I really did have to fight my way through terror and death to reach light and life. And the listeners accompanied me every step of the way. Aficionados were not used to such things, and were in raptures. This spoilt audience, dressed up to the nines, had come to hear a piano concert, and had found themselves at a bullfight. Theseus the pianist was locked in a fearsome battle with the Minotaur-piano in a fatal, passionate duel.

Everything blurred before my eyes, shimmering in a multi-coloured, thundering mirage. I made several mistakes in the Haydn sonata. Then I played Ravel's Scarbo. My Scarbo flitted and spun with dreadful speed and a terrifying dynamic, and really did frighten everyone, in the way that the demonic element is supposed to. The hall rewarded me with thunderous applause, and I suddenly started playing encores, as much a surprise to myself as to everyone else there. I dashed off Liszt's most difficult études at impossible speeds, maybe because I was dissatisfied with myself and wanted to compensate. Encores at the end of the first half of a concert go against all the rules. The public were roaring in delight. I had drawn them into a musical battle not for life, but to the death.

The interval flew by. I started the second, showcase half. I felt that I had stepped over some sort of barrier, and that things were starting to go right. I played at insane tempos. When I reached the coda of Islamey, which imitates a crazy *lezginka* and added some more speed (usually people slow down because of the impossible jumps in both hands), I felt that the piano was on fire.

Standing ovations. Encores. Circus tricks from Paganini and Liszt, dry intensity and cold fury from the young Prokofiev. I played everything that I knew. And the audience and I seemed to attain weightlessness and soared in Music, transporting ourselves to the territory of the Higher Life. I was frightened that I might not be able to come back myself and to bring my audience back into the concert hall. My performance ended with the public bursting onto the stage, they picked me up and carried me back to the green room, where there was total chaos. Clamour, uproar, male and female admirers, and the frantic faces of musical agents! It was a SENSATION!

I spent the night with Tatyana and Vilen. We escaped from all the fans and the agents and wandered around town. We went into a striptease club and drank champagne (Vilen-Vladlen was paying). In the morning we flew back to Moscow. As we parted, Tanya suddenly said, "And where was that Vilen of ours FROM?" I looked at her mistrustfully. She understood my glance and asked coquettishly, "And I bet you thought that I was FROM THERE as well, didn't you?"

"I still think that," I said. Tanya laughed and said, "You rotter!" We parted company and never went anywhere together again. I think that if I had made a run for it in Salzburg, Vladlen would have found me and shot me (or drowned me in the Salzach). I reckon Tatyana would have helped him. The telnyashka was a sort of distinguishing sign, like a dog's head or a broom on the saddle of an oprichnik guardsman.

F Major, Op 15 No 1

The F Major Nocturne reproduces two diametrically opposed states of mind of the composer. The light, calm and measured state is written almost in modern musical parlance. The strings of major seventh chords anticipate the technique of French composers from Debussy to Satie. It could be asserted that this music became the prototype for all contemporary lyrical music, in particular, film music.

The central movement of the nocturne is an emotional tempest. Serenity and romantic storm are the two guises, the two principal musical elements of the composer who, from 1831, was living as an émigré, far from his homeland. The first and last movements of the nocturne paint a picture of beautiful France, Paris. Chopin better than anyone else succeeds in transmitting through musical images the atmosphere of bliss, love and happiness of this most poetic city in the world. The music in the central movement of the nocturne is the raging resentment, pain and grief for a humiliated Motherland. The three-part form of the nocturne (A-B-A) is here not only the structure of the piece; it is the very reality of the composer, a wave that permeates his music and his fate. In the third movement the pain disappears, and in its place comes the tranquillity, lyricism and radiance of France; the ease and temptations of Parisian life.

 *QR link to the Chopin Nocturnes performed by Andrei Gavrilov*

I am your slender ear of wheat

The whole world loves Prokofiev, and is infatuated with his pagan strength and his cold fire, but there are few people who really understand him, which is why for the most part they play him badly. What is particularly sad is that he is so badly understood and performed in Russia, his native land. They either bash away at it like they're playing dominos, or they simplify his highly complex lyrical movements and turn him into Chopin with "wrong notes".

At the start of his journey, Prokofiev wrote clear, neo-classical music. His energetic and original harmonic combinations were not, however, filled with a rich and profound inner content devoid of formalism. Early Prokofiev is ornamental and spectacular, but not profound. During the Soviet period, in life-long captivity and as a hostage to Stalin, Prokofiev developed his psyche and attained an unheard-of depth and altitude. Mandelstam similarly attained an unprecedented level of verbal mastery after he bade farewell forever to a more or less "normal" life, and started to prepare for his inevitable arrest and agonizing death… The black Stalinist pit revealed for him and for Prokofiev the upper reaches of being…

This Prokofiev has been overlooked; this Prokofiev is not understood

The music of late Prokofiev has an extraordinary strength of grip. Its rhythms place the listener in a trance. Prokofiev squeezes the listener in his nickel pincers, as blue electric sparks fly in all directions. The diabolical, pulsating, metallic machine instantly transports the stupefied listener, eyes screwed shut, into the red-hot cranium of the composer… There the listener is transformed into a double of the composer and starts to perform his musical composition in tandem with him. He thinks, sees and hears like Prokofiev…

I experience a similar state when I play the end of the development of the first movement of Sonata No. 8; where

Prokofiev writes with his music, "This is my last sonnet, the grave is dug and awaits, this is my testament…"

At the finale of Sonata No. 8, where the metallic machine is "eating everything alive" I became something terrifying and inhuman myself, something "dangerous" as Richter used to say.

Nobody has dug down to the obvious "messages" in the mature Prokofiev, even Slava who understood Prokofiev better than most. Richter felt that the music was good and replete, but what it was filled with, he did not know. He didn't want to know, didn't want to burn his fingers… He spoke in rather abstracted terms about Prokofiev's Sonata No. 8, "This music is a tree full of ripe fruit." Slava was unable to discern Prokofiev's subtle sarcasm, with its light sardonic flair, unless the composer blatantly called his piece "Sarcasms". Slava thought that late Prokofiev music was full of humour and merriment. That is was something along the lines of Three Over-ripe Oranges. Even though after these oranges Prokofiev had to eat a fair number of bitter poisonous berries in Stalin's garden. He had to overcome fatal terror, the pain of loss and loneliness.

In actual fact, in Prokofiev's later music there is the grinding of hell, with evil griffons racing through the musical domain, and white Death itself coming from thence into our world to bite off our heads.

***

They were the most hilarious concerts I ever took part in. I look back on them to cheer myself up when I'm sad. I had to perform at about thirty of them during those unforgettable years of the Brezhnev era, with the dreadful diction of our illustrious leader. The concerts always stuck to one and the same tried and tested pattern, even though different directors staged them. The Politburo filed in ceremonial and stately order to their box. Everybody got to their feet, clapping their hands, and the much-reported "lengthy tumultuous applause" got underway. As soon as Brezhnev stopped flapping his hands like a sea lion slapping its flippers together, the public took their seats. In a metallic, formidable voice, the announcer adjured "all the radio and television stations in the

Soviet Union" and Intervision, over which a supposedly "live" transmission of the concert was taking place. In actual fact transmission was delayed by about fifteen minutes. This gave time for the recording to be edited in case of blunders.

The curtain opened, and on the backdrop whatever it was that day that was supposed to wave in the breeze did indeed wave in the breeze. When it was Lenin's birthday it was his heroic physiognomy, familiar to all to the point of nausea, which flapped in the breeze.

The choir dolefully droned out the "Song of Lenin". A huge plaster model of his head, about the size of the Statue of Liberty, stood in front of the banner. His humungous forehead seemed, by its very existence, to refute all theories of phrenology. I always wondered in horror what would happen if that infernal skull should topple over. Knowledgeable people reassured me that the head was empty, that it wasn't even made of plaster; it was just polystyrene painted to look like plaster. At celebratory concerts to mark the first worker and peasant nation in the world, it was a blood-red flag that waved in the breeze, and a song about the USSR was sung. Some charlatan singer or a choir of charlatans would pout forbiddingly, and sternly sing some patriotic gibberish that nobody believed and nobody listened to. At revolutionary festivals it was the revolutionary flag that waved in the breeze; the singers and the choir, with their chinless mugs fervently loyal to the Party, sang even more forbiddingly and sternly about the GOSR (the Great October Socialist Revolution).

At the very first rehearsal I went to the backdrop to see how attractively the enormous banner was waving in the breeze. I saw that there were two blokes with enormous vacuum cleaners switched to blow rather than suck, and they were directing them at the banner. It was total artifice; the banner appeared to be waving as though in a strong wind. The lighting crew were soaking it in ecstatic blood-red light. The whole of the USSR was just one big, puffed up, "vacuum-cleaner" illusion!

The flapping in the breeze and the ferocious start were usually followed with a lyrical number. For the sake of contrast. It would either be Nilovna tenderly wailing something about the fatherland, or it would be some enormous fat bloke (for example

Bulat Minzhilkiev) singing the song about the Russian Field. As this Kyrgyz Pantagruel ended the song with the words "Hail to thee, Russian field, I am your sle-e-e-ender ear of wheat" we other performers would all be backstage clutching our sides and rolling around on the floor in hysterics.

Then the numbers would rattle along, one after the other, like containers on a freight train. The underlying theme from the Kremlin in all things was the firing squad for the fainthearted; the builders of communism languishing in front of TV screens; participants in the battle for the harvest; international warriors and fighters on an invisible front.

"Normal" people hardly ever performed at these concerts. The ballet dancers were the possible exception to this rule. I greatly appreciated the art of Volodya Vasiliev and Katya Maximova, and used to chat to them in the pauses in the endless rehearsals.

It was impossible to talk to the singers, male or female. They were so highly strung and puffed up with the "importance of the task and the moment", and they were so intent on demonstrating their allegiance to the Communist Party, that they lost all trace of a brain or common humanity. At the less serious concerts the directors "sunk as low" as Khazanov, and once they even summoned Pugacheva. They gave her a dreadfully hard time at rehearsal, and then threw her out just before the concert in any case. They simply didn't dare impinge on the pharaonic traditions.

At the rehearsals it was the appointed director who was in charge of everything, but at the run-through (the dress rehearsal) there were already overseers from the Central Committee of the Party, and always some deputy or other from the ministry of culture. These people loved making critical comments to the artists. Kukharsky was particularly noteworthy in this respect, never passing by an opportunity to demonstrate his own eminence and humiliate a performer. The criticisms were usually made to the rank-and-file participants, such as accompanists, members of the dance or singing ensembles or the choir leaders. As a rule, the soloists were left alone. This was because a soloist could quite simply get up and go home in response to any criticism. These celebratory concerts brought absolutely no dividends. They were official recognition of a performer's status, and that was it. It was impossible to cadge anything for yourself.

So, here is a typical rehearsal. Nilovna is tunelessly booming away at something patriotic, accompanied by a highly proficient pianist who wouldn't hurt a fly. Kukharsky is trying to pass judgment and lay down the law.

"Stop! You played that introduction badly! What's the matter with you, didn't you look at the music at home? Go away and learn it, quick march!"

Backstage, meanwhile, it's the tower of Babel! The building was blatantly not designed to accommodate this number of performers. There are two or three nymphet ensembles alone, each with 50 people! Then there are symphony orchestras, brass bands, combined and military choirs, singing and dancing ensembles and corps de ballet. The ventilation can't cope. It's incredibly stuffy.

Volodya Vasiliev and I are standing, chatting in the wings from where he is going to have to leap on stage as Spartacus. Soon it is his exit. The orchestra is playing the introduction, and Volodya is very relaxed. I ask him, "How can you possibly catch a ballerina in one hand so easily when she's leaping at you from a height of a metre and a half? Then you haul her around on one outstretched arm, and she does the splits and waves her arms around!"

"It's just technique," replies Volodya nonchalantly, "manipulation, various tricks with your fingers for a bit of security, and then they can sit tight."

I don't even have time to laugh before he's tensed his muscles and is leaping out like some magical, spinning top heading upwards, and then growing taller, stretching, jumping and hanging in the air, flying, then gently landing and taking off again. He soars and soars like a demon. A genius. In the fraction of a second he has transformed into Khachaturian's Spartacus. There he is already, in ancient Rome, flying and lording it in the arena. We, the audience, are there with him. As soon as the number is over, Volodya comes over to me, barely out of breath from all his frenzied leaps, and we carry on making jokes.

Now some pathetic little nymphets run on stage in white tights. What they're wearing and what they're holding depends on the theme of the concert. They might be Little Octoberists wearing short school dresses, demonstrating their heart-melting happiness that they have been brought up by Grandpa Lenin. If the concert is devoted to the Union of Free Republics then the nymphets run out in national costumes, also only coming down mid-thigh, with Uzbek harem trousers underneath – obviously made from semi-translucent fabrics.

For those members of the Politburo who prefer slightly older and larger girls there is a "School Years" ensemble to dance. Here, older girls in full skirts whirl around fast enough for their knickers, and what they have under their knickers, to be perfectly visible to all. A feast for the eyes of the Soviet pharaohs and their servants! Then, for the "normal blokes", ripe lasses from some sort of red-banner ensemble of singing and dancing will cavort away to their heart's content. These girls will unashamedly lift up their military tunics to reveal their knickers and surrender themselves boisterously to the dance. Party bigwigs can have the cockles of the heart warmed eventually by their beloved folk groups, which really tip over the edge into total kitsch. Gallant "likely lads" will strut around like ostriches, stretching their legs out in boots, imitating village bravado. If they tried prancing around like that in a real Russian village the locals would all bust a gut laughing at them, and then give them a good hiding. The "likely lasses" will glide like swans in a "rural" manner, not forgetting, however, periodically to bare their thighs and their backsides. Towards the end of the concert Moiseyev's joyful character dancers will rush out onto the stage in a semi-circular formation. They are true artistes and know exactly how, what, in what proportions, and at what tempo to demonstrate! The Soviet Moulin Rouge.

The "soulful" Lyudmila Zykina and Olga Voronets will then sail out on stage with their enormous busts, both in exquisite Russian shawls made in Italy.

They will open wide their meaty arms with their swollen fingers glittering with diamond rings, and will wail with their dreadful "folk" voices that sound like fire engines, "I lo-o-o-ve my ho-o-o-ome so-o-o-oil, my na-a-a-ative la-a-a-and…"

If my memory serves me well, piano works were only approved for inclusion in this emporium of poor taste after my victory at the Tchaikovsky Competition. Because there was no Jewish or German blood in my body, the pharaohs particularly adored me. I must have played the finale of Tchaikovsky's Concerto No. 1 at least twenty times. Before the astonished public, I would rise from beneath the floor with the orchestra, slowly and significantly like Sadko… and then I would chafe away like the devil at the rumbustious, boisterous passages from the Ukrainian finale.

After the absurd assassination attempt on Brezhnev, performers had to show their passports to be allowed on stage. Goons were planted at the entrance to the orchestra pit and in the wings. Soloists had their own rooms, and we were hardly affected by these innovations. Not so the poor slaves in the crowd scenes. They had to get to the stage through an underground labyrinth of shared, unbearably stuffy areas, or from countless staircases where they were held in groups by artistic-director slave-drivers, and had to show their passports several times along the way to the KGB.

There was one time when I was making my way to the pit, getting ready to transform myself into Tchaikovsky. For the nineteenth time. I could hear the announcer grandly announcing, "And now, played by the winner of…. and the state symphony orchestra conducted by award-winning."

Suddenly: "Stop, Comrade, where is your passport!"

"I've left it in my dressing room!"

"Well, trot off and get it!"

I ran, breathless, through the airless dungeons of the Palace of Congresses. I got there, grabbed my passport. I raced back, like Borzov in the 100m sprint. The stage was already rising inexorably upwards, with just a 50cm gap left. I dived headfirst, got caught on something and ripped my trousers to the waist. I just made it through. A heroine among the first violinists (thank you so much) summed up the situation in a moment, took a hundred pins out of her hair and pinned my rags together. By the skin of my teeth I slid into the first B minor chord after the orchestral introduction. We gave a clean performance that rang out across the whole Socialist Bloc. It was only after I'd finished that I realized how narrowly I had escaped death by guillotine, and quivered like a jelly. If I hadn't been so fortunate with my jump the stage would have chopped me in half like a sausage.

Eventually I couldn't face playing the Pitch concerto (Pitch for Pyotr Ilyich Tchaikovsky) for the thousandth time. I asked if I could play the finale from Rachmaninoff's Concerto No. 2. I could! Brilliant. The peasants, deputies and workers fiercely applauded "their... simple, regular Russian lad, Andrei". Sometimes our whole orchestra would crawl out from underground, like the mythical city of Kitezh, for the encores. This bit was cut out of the TV transmissions.

One day the directors asked me to write a transcription for four pianos of the march from Prokofiev's opera, *The Love for Three Oranges*. My unfailing Professor Naumov helped me do this. The arrangement proved a mega show-piece! Four Steinways going nineteen to the dozen under the drive of strong young fingers! It seemed that the dynamic passages and the abrupt chord progressions were exuding Prokofiev's neurotic, sporadic light. That particular director was an innovator and thought big. He placed us on steps up the stage – four piano stars on four different levels. On the lowest floor, nearest to the audience, presided I; the next floor up was the brilliant Katya Novitskaya, who shortly thereafter emigrated to Belgium; further up was another boy and then another girl. We were all young, attractive winners of prestigious competitions from around the world. I was the "chief star in the constellation" and was supposed to stand out more. How could this be achieved, given the abundance and equality of the text on the page? The director found a way. The march begins with a drumming on the B flat of the first octave. I was given this note in all its countless repetitions. The other pianists waited for the prelude theme. The necessary subordination had been observed. Of course, it amused us all immensely. Our fourth participant was souring up in the clouds somewhere. All we needed was Leni Riefenstahl to include the scene in *Triumph of the Will*.

Now, finally, I began after the half hour it took to list all our titles and awards. I held my hand above my "personal" B flat. I was cracking up... And I missed the first note. Our quartet fell apart. We were all playing and laughing out loud.

It wasn't only the performers who were tormented by the countless rehearsals, but also the very specific public that these events had. The concerts started after ceremonial meetings that lasted for hours. People would fall asleep, grow numb and switch off from just one speech by the General Secretary! A whole team of sound engineers would clean up the inappropriate splutterings and gurgles emitted by Brezhnev as he gagged and mumbled, suffering as he did from cancer of the jaw.

They would cut the sounds all out, sure enough, and then they would edit all the grunts and slurps into one long tape to take the Mickey out of the old man, listening and howling with hysterics in the sound studios at Central Television or at Melodiya recording studios, which used to issue records with speeches by the pharaoh.

Seppo Karlsson

After my performance in Salzburg in 1974 the Soviet music bosses sat me on a diet. No plans, no conversations about future tours!

"We set you free for a few days, fledgling! Now get back in your old hen coop."

No plans, no tours! And that was when musical agents from around the world were literally inundating Gosconcert with invitations and projects; they promised stacks of money for the Soviet state freeloaders. The invitations were ignored; quite simply nobody replied to them.

Plans? Can you really plan what composer will interest you in two-three-four years? Planning for years ahead is for musical machines who rake up money like cut grass, and for me it's categorically impossible. If my aim in life had been to rake in the money then I'd have been a Wall Street broker, not sat for decades at the piano…

Western agents perfectly understood the motivations driving the Soviet cultural mandarins. They knew that you couldn't beat them in an open fight, and so they thought up all sorts of cunning ploys. For example, they would come to Moscow on tourist visas and seek out private meetings with musicians to discuss possible projects. That was what Seppo Nummi did, a musical agent born in Finland, a very rich man and an extremely eccentric individual. Seppo was a descendant of the Duchy of Courland, he was gay and he had villas in Rome and Tampere.

He died at home in Tampere from a heart attack, in his prime.

Seppo was in charge of the music festival in Helsinki which he managed to raise to the level of the Salzburg and Lucerne Festivals. While Seppo was at the helm, the best soloists and orchestras from the international music stage came to Helsinki. The intensity of Finland's festival life in the 70s was something that even Austria, the world's principal musical power, would have been proud of.

Seppo sought me out and invited me to meet him at the Metropol. The Metropol Hotel was the main Moscow base for "homo sovieticus" to spy on foreigners and talk to them. I was therefore wary of going to meet Seppo. However, curiosity finally got the better of me. I went down into the metro and took a train to the meeting. The restaurant was crawling with KGB, like an old Moscow kitchen alive with cockroaches, and I was taken to Seppo's table. He was wearing a maroon tartan jacket, had an enormous belly over which was stretched a frog-coloured polo neck jumper, making him look dreadfully like Karlsson-on-the-roof. When he smiled, I noticed that half his teeth were missing. His table held a dozen bottles with brightly-coloured labels. Seppo plainly loved expensive wine and plentiful food.

I introduced myself. Seppo looked at me attentively, then smiled ironically and announced that as he had no cash with him… perhaps I could pay for his modest meal. This request horrified me. I had a five-kopeck piece for the metro in my pocket, and nothing else. I was mortified. Seppo looked at me even more attentively and sadistically kept quiet for a couple of minutes. Enjoying my confusion to the full, he then stood up and left. He came back a few minutes later with a huge wad of cash in his sleek, plump hands, which he then proceeded ostentatiously to count with his manicured thumb. The pile of money made a pleasant creaking sound. Before paying and leaving the restaurant, Seppo asked me if I wanted to eat or drink anything. There was only one thing I wanted, and that was to get the hell out of there as soon as possible before this Karlsson could draw me into some sort of unpleasant story. But Seppo wouldn't let me leave, and offered me a solo concert in the summer of 1976 within the framework of the Helsinki Music Festival. My tongue was stuck to the roof of my mouth from the shock, and I had difficulty in explaining to Seppo what pieces I would like to perform. Seppo wrote the programme that I dictated to him on the back of the crumpled bill from the restaurant.

The meeting was over and a few days later Gosconcert informed me of the official invitation to the summer festival in

Helsinki. Seppo knew how to work with the Soviet top knobs, and always got what he wanted. I would imagine that he scattered expensive gifts to right and left.

My season in 1975 was pretty meagre. I gave solo concerts in Leningrad, Kiev and Moscow, and in these same cities played orchestral concertos by Tchaikovsky, Rachmaninoff, Ravel and Prokofiev...

In September I started playing with Kirill Kondrashin, a very severe gentleman, and a profound and powerful musician. After a few concerts (in Dubna, Chernogolovka and at Moscow State University) we were playing really well together, and thereafter we gained immense pleasure from working together and spending time in each other's company.

Over the years we worked together, Kirill was kind enough to teach me the subtleties of conducting. Since then I have never been afraid to take up the conductor's baton with any orchestra. In October we set out for Poland, where we engaged in an extensive tour with Rachmaninoff's third concerto.

In Poland I visited Majdanek, the former Nazi death camp near Lublin. I arrived on a day that it was not open to the public. The small, stooped museum curator let me into the camp. I wandered along through this enormous death factory, saw a canister of Zyklon B gas, whole walls of shoes belonging to people who were killed, barbed wire fences, crematoria, a huge pile of black ash and a horrific dissection table. I asked to be locked alone in the gas chamber for half an hour....

I couldn't understand how this horror had been possible. I thought then about how many of our Soviet Majdaneks were successfully functioning in the not-so-distant past. Is there a single museum in one of Stalin's former prison camps?

In 1976 I went to Prague to the Prague Spring festival, which was already famous then, with solo and orchestral concerts... I spent two weeks there and went to Italy, where I played a show-piece solo concert in 40 concert halls around the country. From there I flew to France, via Moscow, to Richter for a programme of compositions by Scarlatti, Tchaikovsky, Ravel and Balakirev. After that I went to Helsinki, where the artful Karlsson-on-the-roof – Seppo Nummi – was waiting for me.

His people met me at the airport and took me to the Vaakuna Hotel on Mannerheim Square, where the statesman's proud equestrian statue stands. Seppo was living at the same hotel, which he stubbornly and contemptuously referred to as the Vagina Hotel, and had a luxurious suite on the top floor. He found his house in Helsinki too boring. He was surrounded by countless pretty boy secretaries.

Seppo continued to laugh at me in Helsinki. At the first celebratory dinner he sat me next to some Chinese guests. In between two Chinese secret service officers, dressed in terrible black overalls, sat the wonderful pianist Li Ming-Qiang, in an identical black overall. It was he who had the fingers on both hands broken by the Red Guards (just like his brilliant colleague, Liu Shi Kun). Li's face twitched.

Karlsson was sitting opposite, staring at me and smiling ironically.

Chinese and Soviet propaganda machines had announced as an "invention of the West" the story of the broken fingers of the Chinese pianists Li Ming-Qiang and Liu Shi Kun, who had, incidentally, won third prize at the very first Tchaikovsky Competition. At the Moscow conservatoire we were indoctrinated with the fact that this had never happened.

Not so long ago I met Li and asked him about it. Instead of replying, Li silently raised his hands and showed me his twisted, disfigured fingers and palms...

Now Li Ming-Qiang is professor of piano at the conservatoires in Hong Kong and Shanghai...

In the evening I went to rehearse at the Finlandia Talo, the hall that was built for the Conference on European Security. Later it was turned into a concert complex. I entered the hall and Gilels was sitting at the piano. He was rehearsing Chopin ballads for his concert the following day. Gilels couldn't get the top notes of the repeating passages in the third ballad. He replayed it again and again. I quietly waited my turn, as it would never have occurred to me to interrupt the work of the Maestro. I knew Gilels through the conservatoire, and also through my mother, who had once had lessons from him. I was always fascinated by the acrimonious expression on his face. There were stories that he was prone to take offence. Finally, Gilels stood up and noticed me.

"A-ah, hello Andrei!"

"Hello, Emil Grigorievich, I hope I didn't disturb you?"

"No, I had already finished. How are you? How is your mother?"

"Thank you, everything is fine, I just wondered if I could try out the piano?"

"Go ahead."

"Thank you."

I sat at the instrument while Gilels was getting his things together. As he left he quietly said, "Good bye."

"Good bye, Emil Grigorievich, allow me to wish you…"

I hadn't even managed to say "wish" before Gilels blew up like a balloon, stood on tiptoe in his rage, and yelled in an unexpectedly shrieky voice, "It is I-I-I-I- I who wish yo-o-o-o-ou…"

He had been deeply insulted by my attempt to wish him a good concert the following day. "Nutter," I whispered to myself, "nutter!"

The following morning I was brushing my teeth in my room. Suddenly someone stuck their hand through my legs from behind and grabbed me by the balls. I pushed away the unknown hand and turned round… with my toothbrush in my mouth and tricolour toothpaste dribbling down my chin.

A sniggering Karlsson stood before me.

"Do you think I'm crazy?" Seppo asked me.

"Fuck off!"

Seppo didn't try out any more tests of my sexual orientation. As compensation for his crudeness he introduced me to various girls, and I even went to a save-the-whale demonstration with one of them. He also gave me a whole suitcase full of illegal Russian literature.

I stopped sleeping at night, and read and read the truth about Russia, chilled to the bone with horror. With trembling hands I turned over the dreadful pages of our history. Marchenko, Delaunay, Chukovskaya…

After this week in Helsinki I became a different person. Many of my childish insights were confirmed. I understood that the freedom of thought, of creativity and of the individual that we so lacked were more than just empty words, they were not mere seasonings to spice up well-being, they were the only foundation for human life.

I travelled back to Moscow by train. I could not bring myself to part with my hoard of outlawed literature. In the meantime, we had arrived at the border. The customs inspection started on the train, although it was more like a prison shakedown. It was only now that it dawned on me what I had done. The most lenient punishment for a suitcase full of forbidden books in the USSR at that time would be exclusion from the conservatoire and the army, or they could even lock me up…

The customs inspector was working thoroughly, staying a long time in each compartment. I was ready to wail in desperation. My compartment was the last in the carriage. Beyond me was the carriage attendant, who had been very kind to me. She had brought me great chunks of rye bread with butter… I ineptly covered my books in the suitcase with a couple of shirts and waited resignedly for disaster.

Having combed through the last compartment before mine, the customs officer, a skinny man with a yellow face, suddenly clutched the small of his back, crouched down and groaned, "It's come again, damn it! My kidneys! Who else have you got there?"

The attendant shouted back, "Just a kid in specs, a weedy student!"

The customs official waved his hand and crawled to the exit. The train moved off and I was saved!

In the autumn I went on my first big tour round West Germany. The country astonished me with its reinforced-concrete stability, its wealth and general aspiration towards prosperity. I can remember asking an official in the Soviet embassy in East Berlin, a tall thin fair-haired man with thin lips who looked like a Fascist from Soviet cinema, "When are we going to West Berlin?" I shall never forget his answer.

"There is no such thing as West Berlin; there is only one Berlin, the capital of the GDR."

I wonder how they live now, all those former workers from the embassies, consulates and representative offices of the former USSR. All the innumerable lecturers and professors in Marxist-Leninist philosophy, the political economy of socialism, and academic communism.

A whole army of teachers of Soviet history, flocks of propagandists, political information officers, district Party officials, regional Party officials, personnel in the First Departments in charge of secrecy, hordes of corrupt journalists, newspaper and television broadcasters, millions of KGB foot soldiers and officers, and so on and on and on. An army from hell. What has become of them in modern Russia? Nothing at all. Some of them have died. Other designated ones have grown rich. The rest are doing what they have always done. They simply have new masters now...

I was driven to the "Western sector" by a thin, gloomy silent man with a long nose and an elongated head. His face was morose, he wore a hat and mackintosh, and his name was Afonsky. He looked as though he was on his way back from a funeral. As soon as we had crossed the border, Afonsky suddenly said, "Free at last!"

A couple of years later I discovered that Afonsky was a spy working for the West, and that he had been arrested and shot.

I played about 20 concerts in the FRG and in West Berlin. I was very well received. The Germans stomped their feet after my performance. It would appear that only in Germany is appreciation for a musician expressed in this way. The public suddenly start stamping their feet fast and furious. If you are not expecting it, it sounds intimidating. They saw me off stage to a standing ovation. In Cologne, after I had played, the manager of the concert hall came running out into the street after me.

"Herr Gavrilov, please, come back in, just one more exit onstage. THEY are wrecking the hall!"

I went out on stage dressed for the street in my fur coat and hat. I could see that the public were breaking chairs in a frenzy! Alexander the Great was of course a great hero. Until this concert tour it had never occurred to me that Germans had such fire within them. I would have been more inclined to expect something of the sort from the Italians, Spaniards or Greeks. But no, the Mediterranean public is considerably calmer, and although they experience music intensely, they do it on the inside. I remembered all the sagas about the ancient Germans, and for some reason I thought of Majdanek. NOTHING had changed in life since the ancient, Barbarian age. All that had altered was the setting and the habits of the masses. Our whole "highly developed civilization" was merely the thinnest of veneers covering the animal essence of life. The moment that cover is breached, eternal Armageddon commences.

Seppo the Creep

After my first trip to Helsinki (1976) I made friends with another Seppo, this one was Seppo Heikinheimo, a music critic. By no means all influential representatives of the Western music scene were welcoming of Soviet musicians. This second Seppo was a typical example of a Westerner who "had it in for" us.

All his life, Seppo had worked as a wannabe Chekhov: a beard, pince-nez, a pocket watch on a silver chain. He even specially ordered suits that looked like Chekhov's. Seppo Chekhov was the chief cultural commentator in the Finnish national newspaper, *Helsingin Sanomat*. It seemed that he just couldn't live without Soviet musicians, or Chinese, Czech, Polish, Bulgarian performers; anyone who came from the communist bloc. Seppo needed us Soviets as self-affirmation. Against a background of us, he felt he was an important Western man.

Seppo spoke Russian fluently, but with an appalling accent. It wasn't easy to understand him. He always introduced himself to Soviet touring concert musicians as "My name is Seppo Heikinheimo, people's critic of Finland, and hero of capitalist labour." He was immensely proud of his invention, and thought he was incredibly witty.

Seppo loved to shock and perturb his contacts from the Soviet Union. He was the Western music critic who flew to see me in Moscow after the scandal of the cancelled concerts and recordings with Karajan, he talked to me, photographed me under a nude painting, and then published a sensational "report" from my flat, without my authorization.

Seppo was delighted, even proud, when he succeeded in embarrassing or frightening any Soviet artist, who in actual fact was intimidated enough already. He could talk endlessly about the stupidity, greed and baseness of Soviet people; he knew and recited countless jokes on Soviet topics.

At one of the first music festivals in Helsinki I was invited to the sauna after the concert. It was a luxurious sauna located right under the Finlandia concert hall, on the shore of the bay. Once you'd sat long enough in the delightful heat inside you could go out to breathe the air and cross over a special gangway to the bay, to dive into the cold, Baltic water. In the sauna changing room were cold bottles of beer, damp with condensation, awaiting the bathers, along with delicious Finnish sausages. You could cook the sausages yourself on the open fire, using the medieval rapiers that hung on the walls.

I was steaming in the sauna with Gidon Kremer after a concert we had given together. Almost melting with the heat, we went along the gangway to the bay and dived in. Stark-naked, naturally.

There we were, two serious classical musicians, leaping about, splashing and turning somersaults like kids.

Malicious Seppo brought some members of the public out of the hall and led them to the path – there are your beloved musicians – look and enjoy! The public were flabbergasted. We were discombobulated. After quite a long hiatus, someone threw us some towels, and we somehow made it back to the sauna. Seppo managed to take some photos of us. He deserved to have a couple of teeth knocked out for pulling a trick like that. However, to be fair, Seppo did understand the limits of a joke of that sort. He later showed us the photographs, and then destroyed them, together with the negatives, there and then.

Seppo loved photographing Soviet musicians. But he didn't have any desire to take nice pictures, instead he always endeavoured to snap the performer with mouth stupidly gaping, or face horrendously distorted. He liked his models to come out looking like mentally ill freaks. Seppo once showed me a whole collection of large format photo portraits. I didn't like looking at them at all, but Seppo used to solemnly present the photos to his "victim" with sardonic exultation.

When I stopped being allowed to travel, Seppo managed to bring me a whole stack of anti-Soviet propaganda across the border. But he didn't bring me books, he brought me propaganda pamphlets, posters, prospectuses and other rubbish like that. It was a sadistic diversion for him, while for me it could have led straight to the clink. My mum packed all this crap into a big black dustbin bag and carried it out to the rubbish dump under cover of darkness.

Seppo gave me a copy of the typed original manuscript of Solomon Volkov's *Testimony* in Russian, 600 pages bound like a book, with a felt-pen signature on every page, "I've read it, Shostakovich". I remember that I galloped through it in a day. Seppo told me later, "It is Volkov's only good book. The rest lack talent, but this is genius, so it must be genuine."

After I had read the book I took it to Richter.

The following day, Slava said to me, "HE is completely alive here!"

"What about the family's protestations? Maxim refused to recognize the book… The expert assessment… Everybody has said that it's a fake!"

"I don't care about any of that. Expert analysis, the family's reaction. It is HE, I knew him like that, he is alive on every page. Incidentally, I need urgently to write in my will that my desk should be burned the day after I die." I started at him in amazement. "Can you believe it, Andrei, a stage director sits at his desk now.

Dmitry Dmitrich is scarcely cold in his grave and there's already a strange man sitting at his desk. I don't want the same thing to happen to me. It's revolting. Perhaps I had better set fire to it myself."

Seppo was particularly energetic in his gloating when Gorbachev came to power in the Soviet Union.

"The new Soviet leader has something impossibly funny up his sleeve," hissed Seppo, rubbing his hands. When the USSR collapsed, Seppo became deeply depressed. He simply couldn't live without communism; his life had lost all meaning. Seppo committed suicide.

Seppo the Escapist

After Seppo Nummi left the post of Director of the Helsinki Music Festival for health reasons, the new director was a delicate young man in horn-rimmed glasses, Seppo Kimanen. This third Seppo was a dedicated escapist, an open and kind man. We immediately took to one another. Kimanen made sure I enjoyed myself in my spare time between concerts. He took me out to the northern countryside that he so loved. He invited me round to his house. His wife, a beautiful Japanese woman called Yoshiko, was in charge at home. Seppo taught me Finnish, and we had a laugh.

"I love you" in Finnish sounds like "minä rakastan sinua."

I really wanted to repay Seppo's hospitality in kind, and to show him our beautiful country...

In 1977 I invited him to spend his holiday with me. Seppo was delighted to accept my invitation and came in the summer. My girlfriend, Anechka, was a devout believer and also lots of fun. She and I met Seppo in Leningrad, and got a room for him at the Europa Hotel. We roamed around the city to our heart's content, went to museums and restaurants and saw all the sights in the city. We even went to Arkady Raikin's new show, *Leaves*, at his Estrada Theatre. Seppo didn't understand a thing, but smiled politely all through the evening...

From Leningrad we flew to Pitsunda, where the deputy minister for culture, Vladimir Popov, who was holidaying there in the Party rest home, had promised to help us find a room.

Popov helped Anechka and me get a room in a private house, but refused point blank to help us find somewhere for our Finnish visitor...

"You're on your own with that Finn of yours, Andrei. I can't, and I don't have the time to do it for you."

With immense difficulty we managed to organize a room for Seppo in the only hotel in Pitsunda. It was the sort of place with "thirty eight rooms and only one toilet..." Incidentally, there was always a tremendously long queue waiting to use that one lavatory. By night, the hotel guests drank, sang loud songs and danced national folk dances. Our poor escapist was unable to get a wink of sleep for nights on end.

It took me a couple of days to realize what a terrible mistake I had made. Seppo couldn't eat in the hotel restaurant. The naïve Finn had been buying *khachapuri* cheese bread and Abkhazia kupaty sausages with some very dodgy sauce. He had a terrible upset stomach. The poor European was having a really hard time of it. The sun made him feel unwell. The poor chap couldn't begin to think of going to the beach. Seppo lost weight, grew pale, became positively emaciated and in a few days' time started to look like the sort of skeletal waifs that Evgeny Ginzburg and Varlam Shalamov described in the labour camps.

Vladimir Popov invited Anechka and me to sumptuous meals in his privileged Rest Home with its private beach, its own pine woods, tennis courts and yachts. The poor Finn was never invited... Fortunately Anechka and I found an Estonian woman for Seppo to pour out his woes to... The woman translated his complaints for us...

I cursed my own stupidity, and it was only there, in Pitsunda that I grasped in what unhygienic and extreme conditions we Soviets lived; completely deadly for any ordinary European...

I visited Seppo several times a day in his stinking hotel in the centre of Pitsunda. Seppo told me, shaking with disgust and writhing with stomach pains, about having to stand in line for that "terrible toilet, all covered in brown slime with a hole in the middle." Sometimes Seppo wept in my arms. I cursed myself and counted the days till his departure.

Finally, we took Seppo to the airport in Adler. We literally carried him onto the plane to Petersburg. Seppo was breathing heavily and rolling his eyes.

Once his plane had taken off, Anechka and I rushed to settle up for his room. We went into a small cubicle that could have passed for a prison cell. There was a fly-spotted table in the room, a crude stool and a horrendous bed... There was a piece of notepaper on the table, on which Seppo had written just two words – Rakas Yoshiko. It was a farewell note to his wife...

Ugly Mugs

Summer, beautiful weather and I'm in an excellent mood after winning the competition and my success in Salzburg, my student life is not interfering with my professional activities. Everything is marvellous! The fame from the competition and the money I have earned meant that I have been able to buy an enormous flat in a block on Suvorovsky Boulevard (now called Nikitsky). The city centre and the conservatoire are just a stone's throw away! There's as much work as I want. I've bought a second grand piano. It's a dream come true!

Now the doorbell rings. I open the door. There are two blokes standing there. One is thin, wearing a suit and with no face. The second is older, and has a mug that seems sort of bloated with pus, and with a droopy blue-ish nose, but also somehow with no face. However much you look at them, you just can't remember what they look like. I've never seen such revolting faces in my life. Later, when I'd seen loads of them, I got used to it, and could even pick them out in a crowd.

"Can we come in?"

The older one says, "I'm Nikolai Ivanovich, and this is Seryozha; we work for state security. We need to have a little chat with you."

They showed me their ID. "Nikolai Ivanovich" tipped out a pile of tiny photographs from a large envelope of thick paper.

"Have a look and see who you can recognize here."

I look at the carpet of horrible little photographs. I start to recognize various people – Masha Speranskaya, a translator and expert in Slavonic studies from Germany; Lyuba Khormut, the well-known producer at Ariola-Eurodisc records, and girlfriend to David Oistrakh. I recognize other people on the photos that I am in touch with via work and outside of work. On the whole they are foreigners.

"All of these people are spies," says Nikolai Ivanovich, who subsequently was sometimes also Ivan Ivanovich. I notice that he is drunk, really drunk.

"This is a dangerous spy network that we need to have a serious talk about, and you need to come and see us tomorrow to do that." To Natasha Kochuevskaya Street to house number whatever...

They left. My mood was completely ruined. I did not yet understand then that my mood had been ruined for the rest of my life in the Soviet Union, that the levity, sunny disposition and delight in being would never again be experienced by me here. My happiness lasted less than three years.

Incidentally, the stumpy building on Natasha Kochuevskaya Street where I was summoned for my "chats" has been demolished. It is no longer there. I looked for it recently. Instead of the building there is now an empty space. Nearby stand posh new houses. It turns out that in Moscow, business-Lubyanka has triumphed over the never-ending cruelty-Lubyanka. I so wanted to go in... It was fascinating there... It was a tiny little townhouse. A typical building from the early 19th century... The sort of house that a moderately wealthy merchant would have owned... with only one door... The door was made of wood, like a bath-house door. You went in, and there on either side were two bulldogs with machine guns. Behind them was a cast steel door. This door had no lock. It could only be opened from the inside... The gates of hell... Beyond the door were corridors and corridors, with staircases going down and whole floors under the ground. Officers, offices, and so many that it was impossible to understand how it all fitted inside one little one-story townhouse... Some sort of special KGB space extension... In the offices, the snoopers plugged away day and night...

Quetzalcoatl and Tezcatlipoca

There came a time when my inner development came to a halt. My playing became less convincing. Each new piece filled me with dread. Its structure and form were clear to me (thanks to my teachers – they really taught me), but the "content" of the work remained a riddle to me, a mystery that I couldn't unravel. Where was it, what was it, this much talked-about content, did anybody understand it? Or was everybody playing on intuition alone? Were they reproducing the sounds more or less proficiently, but without understanding the meaning of the music? I thought about this persistently all through lectures at the conservatoire and on Kabakov's "roof" where Moscow intellectuals used to congregate. One evening I listened to a lecture there by Travkin "About God". He was much admired by the Moscow Carbanari, who shuddered with sweet pleasure at the domestic freedom of speech. I listened and thought to myself, "What should I want with Travkin and his God? What am I doing listening to this stuff? Will this lecture help me understand the content of a piece of music? No, damn it!"

Kabakov's "roof" was a huge studio with incredibly high ceilings that could have hosted a whole battalion of Carbonari if they'd wanted to. There were pot plants, indoor creepers and a warm stove.

Travkin was sitting on a chair in the middle of the room, slightly raised as though on stage, head down as he proved the existence of God for the third hour running.

He was very persuasive. People were listening in silence. Smoking. Neuhaus was playing through the speakers, Chopin's Concerto in E-minor, so the guys here had taste, that much was certain. Eventually, Travkin raised his head, gave a childish smile and stopped talking. It was time for the debate. Good God, what started now!

Almost all the intellectuals were bald, with large beards. Their big round heads looked like bowling balls. Within half an hour, these bowling balls had totally demolished Travkin and his God. They knew everything! Everything, and then some! The first bowling ball called Travkin a fool, and destroyed him with the help of Spinosa, Newton and Bacon. The second called them both idiots and disproved the arguments of both Travkin and the first bowling ball with the aid of the Vedas and Upanishads. Other bowling balls joined the fray. A parade of quivering beards began. Everything you could possibly think of was used in the battle – Moses and Krishna, Berdyaev and Florensky, Marx and Blavatskaya, Moloch and Astarte and even the totally unpronounceable Aztec gods, Quetzalcoatl and Tezcatlipoca.

I was sitting on a little chair further away from Travkin, and was getting very bored. My own stupidity was making me sick. Without waiting for the end of the debate I left. As I was making my way down from the 12th floor I noticed a pair of goons guarding the stair well. There's no point in going on, I said to myself, I'm never going to be that clever. But they aren't geniuses, they're just ordinary Moscow physicists, mathematicians and engineers. How can I understand musical geniuses if I can't even understand engineers?

But I didn't only want to understand the content of a piece of music, its secret meaning; I wanted to climb into the composers' souls, to experience and feel what they felt when they were writing their works; I wanted to manipulate them, to possess the sacred knowledge of the essence of music.

Burning with shame I decided to give up my concert activities and go to work for the ambulance service.

Mark Malkovich

In June 1976 I was surprised to find myself in America. Gosconcert had had no plans to send me to the US, but Mark Malkovich, an exceptionally charming man, pitched up there and must have melted the stony hearts of the pen pushers. It only took him a few weeks to cobble together a contract. Mark took advantage of a historical moment, when the USSR decided to play with the West at "defusing international tension".

Malkovich was granted permission to invite me to the States to prove to the Americans that the Soviets were all right too, that they weren't brutes, and that they could even play the piano.

Mark Malkovich had made money in chemical plants, and led the life of a millionaire. But, as he said, the smell of chemical plants always made him sick. Mark was crazy about classical music. He gave up everything and became lifelong director of a musical festival.

I flew to New York from Moscow. I was nervous, as it was my first transatlantic flight. JFK Airport. I was awe-struck by the impossibly huge scale of the internal spaces and the amazing architecture of Eero Heinonen. I heard an announcement repeated a few times, distorting the Slavic surnames, "Mister Gawrilow, Mr Malkovik is waiting for you somewhere or other." I ran to meet him. Mark broke into a warm grin, embraced me and led me down some corridors to another terminal, to the private planes. My eyes were popping out of my head, and I tried to remember everything I saw so that I could tell my mum and my friends later. We got into a small plane. Here we were, soaring over the Hudson, with a captivating view over the skyscrapers of Manhattan. The twin towers of the World Trade Centre stood proudly above the tremendous city, whereas the Statue of Liberty, presented by the French, stood on its island looking much smaller than I had expected, just slightly taller than the towers of the Kremlin.

Mark winked at me and pressed a button on a panel for a cupboard that opened into a bar. The bar contained dozens of bottles with brightly-coloured labels. Mark pressed a second button, and a deep tray of ice cubes slid out of the wall. We drank Russian vodka with American ice.

We arrived in Newport, Rhode Island. The ocean shoreline was fantastic, with islands, beautiful private homes. Vanderbilts, Kennedys, Morgans. Mark had a large house in an exquisite setting. He had four children, and it was impossible not to fall in love with the youngest daughter, a cheeky little six-year old called Kara. Kara rode around on my shoulders and we ran along the beaches.

I was shown the downcast mother of the Kennedy boys, sitting on her veranda barefoot, in a lightweight, white tunic, gazing out to sea through a telescope. Who or what was she hoping to see there?

I found it all terribly exotic. I was also able to surprise the Americans, however; for one thing with my good knowledge of English. It turned out that my parents were right to hire an English governess to teach me as a child! I was given an enormous guest room to sleep in, with a four-poster bed. I woke up. Mark and his household were delighted to see me wake up, and wished me a good morning. They had gathered round my bed in their nightgowns, like the dwarfs around the sleeping Snow White, in their impatience for their guest to open his eyes. I felt like a Russian chimera of some sort, and laughed. They laughed, too.

My first concert in America was in the Vanderbilt mansion, on Ochre Point Avenue. The mansion contained washbasins of silver, sinks of pink marble and mahogany door handles. Malkovich bought me some jeans, a Stetson and a cowboy shirt, and I instantly looked like an American. I played a spontaneous concert in that outfit either at the Kennedys' or the Rockefellers'. I was met with great kindness wherever I went.

At the Vanderbilt concert I played with ease, as though I was singing a little song. My spirit was flying to meet the friendly Americans. Oh, if only the people in my own country could learn at least friendliness or politeness from the Americans. Or just their white-toothed smiles that they so love to mock. The following day the papers in Newport were full or warm reviews. I remember one headline:

"Gavrilov – from Russia with love!"

My Soviet stereotypes went flying out the window, and I fell in love with America. I am still friends with the Malkovich family. On 31 May 2010 Mark Malkovich was driving his car in Minneapolis to meet one of his three sons. His car overturned on the road. Mark was killed.

Mark Malkovich

With the Malkovich family (1976)

Romania

In spring 1977 I had a tour in Romania. The day before I was due to leave I had a temperature, a cough and a cold. What would any normal musician in any normal country think in a situation like this? Better get some treatment. But what does a Soviet performer think? THEY will decide that I am deliberately avoiding going to a socialist country! They will suspect me of a malicious lack of loyalty, and will stop letting me out of the country altogether. Up until this time I had only gone to Poland with Kondrashin in 1975 and to the Prague Spring in 1976. I had managed to wriggle out of all the other socialist trips without causing any fuss. A temperature and a cold? Not to worry, I won't die! A visit once a year to the rest of the Eastern Bloc wasn't that hard. I went to Gosconcert, took my various bits of paper from the "solicitous" secretary (you're one of those faceless crowd!), said my farewells and flew to Bucharest. Romania it was. It should be picturesque. It couldn't be any worse than the Soviet Union, could it? Yes, it could, by far.

A tall bottle blonde, desperately trying to appear younger than she was, met me at the airport. She was the interpreter. She had a hat, a white raincoat and gloves. She had a hooked nose, lips like worms and the expression on her face was disdainful and sardonic.

"Hello, Andrei, my name is Nonna Furman."

I told Alik Slobodyanik about my "interpreter" later in Moscow. Alik shuddered and frowned.

"That Furman of yours is the most poisonous informer and provocateuse they have."

It would appear that I was the only musician that Nonna never informed on.

Bucharest was a beautiful city. The Athenaeum concert hall where I was due to play 24 études by Chopin was just marvellous! But the hotel! What a dump! There was running water from four till eight. Electricity from eight till eleven... My jaw dropped in astonishment, and I couldn't close my gaping mouth for the whole tour.

Nonna was thrilled with my reaction. She had no need to "provoke" me to swear at Ceausescu's dictatorship, and to "denigrate" the socialist reality in Romania. The country itself gave ample provocation. I should like, however, to emphasise the point that it was not the poverty and the squalor that shocked me most in Romania; I had my own experiences of poverty. What was most shocking and incensing, just as in the USSR, was the dissonance between the ideological picture of the world and real life. The standard of living in Romania in those days was considerably lower than in the Soviet Union. The ideological and "direct" oppression by the Ceausescu clan, however, was harsher and more extreme than under Brezhnev.

I was hungry, and Nonna took me to the station. I had only ever seen stations like that in films about the war. There were beggars everywhere. They were rolling up their eyes, showing amputated stumps. A sea of gypsies... Street kids begging... Crippl..es. Filth, stench, cacophony, clamour... What the devil was I doing in this hell, and with a cold! Nonna bought me some *gogosi*, which were something halfway between a doughnut and a Georgian *khachapuri*. I could barely choke the *gogosi* down. Nonna enquired mockingly whether I liked Romanian food. The *gogosi* were not so great. They gave me terrible heartburn. I needed to rehearse and practise.

My concert in Bucharest was attended by a well-dressed, intellectual, cultural public. Where did they all come from? When I was older, I understood that spiritual culture does not die as quickly as material prosperity. In the mid 70s there were still the older, pre-communist generations living in Bucharest, bearers of European culture.

At times dictatorship and state ideological oppression stimulate a person's spiritual development more than a free society does. People turn to Bach or Mozart and immerse themselves in their music in order not to hear the persistent racket of the present. Unfortunately, there are few opportunities for this protest culture, or the culture of people divorced from reality. People are like metals in that they suffer from fatigue. They tire of living, tire of struggling. They suffocate in their own hovels.

The concert in Bucharest was unusually successful! When I am in poor condition I play better than when I am healthy. Where does this strange anomaly come from? Of course a really serious illness doesn't help, it can only blight. But a non-fatal ailment that merely exhausts us enforces a more serious attitude towards the performance, a concentration of energies, and the use of mental reserves that contain secret energies and the precious rays, the Holy of Holies in creative work.

I was emphatically gallant with Nonna, sweetly polite. I could feel that every cell in her poisonous being, with all her hang-ups, demanded nothing less. It was not only difficult to play the part of a society lady against this setting, on this stage; it was also humiliating. Nonna was afraid that people were cruelly laughing at her. This fear gave rise to her constant readiness to rebuff and avenge. Nonna's only means of revenge was by informing.

We travelled around the country with the concerts. Timisoara, Târgu Mureş, Cluj, Baia Mare. Fabulous countryside, beautiful cities, picturesque streets… Everywhere was poverty, decay, dirt, gypsies, beggars, street kids, hunger… The people were handsome thoroughbreds. I wanted to shout out loud, there in Romania, "Hey, people, how have you let yourself end up with a life like this?!" But I didn't shout once. Not in Romania, nor in the Soviet Union. I played all the concerts on my tour. I kissed Nonna goodbye. She had plainly relaxed in my company; she didn't have it in for me, and she even introduced me to her pretty daughters. I flew back to Moscow.

Anton

Don't believe performers and professors who assure you that the music of a particular composer must only sound like this or that. It's pure snobbism. Who knows how Beethoven was meant to sound? He didn't even really know himself! He constantly changed his attitude to his own compositions and played them in different ways. Then he went almost stone deaf, and started to hear music in a distorted form, which is where, like Columbus, he came across a new musical continent and made extraordinary discoveries...

***

Anton Kireyev became my friend in the first year at the conservatoire. He was a skinny lad in thick-lensed horn-rimmed glasses. He had a large forehead, a blobby nose and sad brown eyes. He always had a slightly nasal voice.

Anton had finished school with straight A's and was accepted at the conservatoire from the Gneissen School without having to take any exams. He graduated from the conservatoire with top marks as well. Anton never needed to prepare his homework or take notes in lectures because he had an extraordinary memory and remembered the lectures in their entirety, almost word for word. Even when he gave the impression of not having listened. At the age of 20 he knew everything in the world. There are people like that; their knowledge doesn't come from books, or even from their own experience. It comes from on high. His brilliant capabilities and extensive knowledge did not turn him into a pedantic conservatoire know-it-all, because he had a marvellous sense of humour and looked on himself critically and not without irony.

Anton was a master at wordplay. He spoke quietly, as though muttering to himself.

"A female singer can be full-throated, but a male singer can only be full-bodied or full-blooded, isn't that right, Andrei?"

Anton thought up a funny word to mean the audience – the Multiface, as in many faces. It caught on, and after concerts we used to ask each other, "So? Was the Multiface any good today? Discerning?"

Anton married early and unhappily, to another student, and they had young children. They all lived crammed into a horrible flat not far from the conservatoire. The teachers and students loved Anton. He had a very individual way of playing the piano. Anton never imitated anyone else, and it seemed he never even intended to learn with anyone. His playing was persuasive. I didn't need to talk with him. We often spent several hours together in silence, while engaged in an intense exchange of information and energy, altogether at a different level of being. Later on in life the only person with whom I experienced something similar was Richter. The radiation coming from Slava was dark, destructive, Wagneresque. Anton radiated warmth and attention to those around him. His aura was similar to the warm, very Russian luminescence of Pyotr Ilyich Tchaikovsky's soul…

A used to go round to Anton's at night. He would climb out of his window on the relatively low first floor, and we would drive somewhere out of Moscow. We went out along the Yaroslavsky highway, calling in at a small, ancient town to watch the sun rise, admiring the onion domes on the churches, and listening to the dawn chorus. He and I both found Soviet festivals aggravating, and so we would leave Moscow the night before all those May Days and Great Octobers.

We would then sit on the Kremlin wall in Rostov the Great, or in Suzdal and watch the pathetic and poignant provincial parade. Girls with hula-hoops, boys with hand weights. Half-dead, tipsy veterans with medals.

One time Anton saved both our lives. After a night run out of Moscow, and a long day at one of these celebrations we were racing back to Moscow in my green Lada. I desperately wanted to sleep. I actually fell asleep at the wheel. My head slumped on my chest. Anton noticed that I was driving on the wrong side of the road and immediately gave me a great shove and yelled at me. Just in time I managed to swerve back onto the right side of the road.

Anton had some sort of chronic illness that he never spoke to me about. He used to have to be admitted to hospital often. If he was in a ward on the ground floor, I would climb in through the window to see him. When he was in a ward higher up, then Anton would lower a rope or some sheets tied together, and I would tie on a three-litre jar of red Isabella wine. Anton would pull up the jar and the ward would have a lot more fun.

When the KGB laid its heavy paw on me I started seeing less of Anton. I didn't want to place a family friend in a dangerous situation. It was a really hard time. There were lots of people dying stupid deaths around that time. Others were running away from the country like the plague.

One day, in autumn 1981, Dima Klimov, a mutual friend of Anton's and mine phoned me. He told me that Anton had died

He had caught a cold, a fever, bronchitis. His wife had called the ambulance. The doctor gave Anton an injection of an antibiotic to which he had a fatal allergic reaction. He died with the doctor's needle still in his vein.

***

Many of Mozart's tunes are easy to listen to if a person is musical, or tone deaf. What more could you want?

The scene of Don Juan sinking down to the underworld is orchestrated and executed in a way that only Mussorgsky could have thought up in an alcoholic delirium.

Mozart was tormented by self-doubt. Those in power often held him for a fool, considered him a musical prattler, and treated him like an amusing toy rattle. Mozart was not accepted in high society, either. Maria Theresia wrote to her august brother, "Do not let the Mozarts over the threshold; they are as vulgar as gypsies!"

What is often interpreted in Mozart's music as his self confidence was in fact his mask, his attempt to assert himself, a protest against humiliation, and a struggle for his own dignity and place in society…

He was stifled, and he demonstrated confidence and levity where there was none at all.

Listen to his phrases. Sometimes he "forgets" that there is a need to protest and affirm himself, and then Mozart is genuine, great and tragic.

The genius of Mozart that is apparent in his best pieces cannot be characterized in human words. No human epithets apply, and he leads us into infinity itself, to the impossible and the inconceivable...

In this respect he is very close to Pushkin.

In almost all of Mozart's works there are scatterings of diamonds, but pieces that are pure diamond, from first to last note, could be counted on the fingers of one hand. His Concerto in D minor, K.V.466 is one such pure diamond.

Pushkin pre-Eugene Onegin is also frequently garrulous and empty. After Onegin, Pushkin acquired greater evenness. Pushkin seemed to mature eleven years earlier than Mozart did. Mozart attained maturity in the period he wrote The Magic Flute and Requiem. Just before his death.

Pushkin's prose has never been surpassed in mastery; not by Tolstoy, nor Dostoevsky, nor Lermontov, nor Gogol. The Captain's Daughter and the Tales of Belkin reduce me to tears.

Pushkin is delectable. You read him... and it is like golden champagne sparkling in a glass. Mozart's music was like that. Elves.

Deadmen in the Georgievsky Hall

(Brezhnev's 70th birthday celebrations)

Emigration. For many centuries Russia was an ignorant despot, but now she is also a brigand and a thief...

Before, there used to be privileged Soviet head honchos, Party and *Komsomol* bosses, functionary boors, corrupt officials, KGB stranglers, army generals, cynics and professional layabouts, policemen, executioners and bribe-taking cheats... Almost all of them sabotaged Gorby's attempts to humanize the USSR. They were scared to death of what our "great peasant" was aiming for. Their chief nightmare was the prospect of losing their privileges, being stripped of their government sinecures... Now it was time for them to settle the score. They tossed aside their Party membership and the communist ideology they no longer needed, just like snakes shedding their skins.

Having changed their image, the vampires once again found their niche and latched onto the people's jugular and the country's natural resources. Ground down by mundanity and addicted to drink, the public no longer notice what the new masters of the land are doing to them. Did you leave the country? Absolutely right. You rescued yourself, your wife and your children.

***

I arrived in the morning in time for a recce. I needed to try out the piano and get the hang of the new setting. I had a special permit to park my Lada near the Manezh, and ran to the Kremlin through the sub-zero temperatures in a typical Soviet trot. I showed my pass at the entrance. I proudly extracted the document from the inside pocket of my Bulgarian sheepskin coat. I ran to the sumptuous Georgievsky Hall, which is covered in gilded inscriptions of names from Russia's bygone glory. I gazed at the carved ceiling and at the walls. I glanced into the room itself and... burst out laughing. Generals in trousers with red-stripes running down the seams, in exquisite military tunics with ribbons and medals, were walking around the hall. They were holding the sort of plastic misters usually used for pot plants. Their faces were unbearably serious, as though they were engaged in some crucial state business, and they were squirting the air with some sort of Kremlin aroma. Their hefty paunches were jutting forward and they looked like a corps de ballet of teddy bears. It was impossible not to laugh.

I remembered this image many years later when I watched Fellini's *Amarcord*. In the scene where the prince is being treated to the delights of the local beauty, Gradisca, the chamber of love had also been "prepared" by caricature generals. Dressed in fantastical uniforms, crowned with grotesque headgear, and wearing elegant boots, they perform clumsy dance steps, suitable for a general. They do knee bends as though warming up before making love, and hold champagne flutes... Before leaving the room, one of the generals wags a finger at the languishing prince in a highly suggestive manner... Fellini's scene was invented and performed as a sweet caricature, a parody and a lampoon. Our Georgievsky teddy bears, with their turned up noses, were serious and focused, as though they were sitting an exam, and of course they had no inkling of how ridiculous they were. The trinkets on their tunics shook from side to side like the teats on a mongrel bitch. Ding-pshsh, ding-pshsh...

Various performers were slouching around the hall – the pride of Soviet culture. I recognized the Gypsy and the singer known as Nilovna who always roared like a rocket turbine. She had been given the nick-name by envious colleagues for her warm friendship with Pyotr Nilych Demichev, who was minister of culture at the time, having been demoted to minister from Politburo candidate member.

The humorist Khazanov was wandering around among the censors – they were concerned about what he could say, and what he couldn't. Khazanov was taking his very first steps in the corridors of power; he giggled inhibitedly. The national Russian Bass was walking around the hall, an unbearably serious chap. Mr Bass took immense delight in anticipating a rapid rise up the career ladder.

Fire-eaters, snake women, hula-hoop performers, jugglers and actresses singing sweet songs with appropriately sweet figures, were not invited to the Georgievsky Hall in the Great Kremlin Palace. This contingent was widely used for picnics at out-of-town dachas and receptions for foreign visitors from fellow communist countries. There were none of the usual nymphets in the hall either, with tutus pulled up to the nose so that everything underneath could be clearly seen. I can remember having to look away from these starched knickers, skin tight on childish bean-shaped backsides. For some reason these poor girls and boys, who were herded in their hundreds backstage at the Kremlin Palace, always had legs covered in purple goose bumps, which made them particularly pathetic.

I tried the instrument, and it was a perfectly tolerable Steinway. I was scheduled to play a Scriabin étude and the Chopin Revolutionary Etude, which was inevitable at events like this, and so set the teeth on edge. I checked the acoustics. Not bad, at least it didn't "boom" as so often happens in large halls with no furniture that are not designed for concerts. I went back to my place at Dynamo to snatch a rest...

In the evening I was taken straight to my seat. The members of the Politburo and the Central Committee of the CPSU were already sitting in state at the large, T-shaped table. The big cheeses were on the bar of the T, and the lesser mortals were down the leg. Set slightly apart was an improvised stage, about one and a half metres tall, with a grand piano. The table for the performers stood in parallel to the long table, almost up against the stage. The security guards were ensconced over by the walls and kept out of the way.

Their faces immediately made me feel sick. Almost all the head honchos were pint-sized; Brezhnev, who always looked such an imposing chap on the news, was in actual fact a paunchy munchkin. The faces of all the Party leadership were a revolting colour, with bad, often pock-marked skin. Their tobacco-stained, widely spaced teeth looked like little blackened grains of sweetcorn. All the bigwigs were dressed in imported suits that had been altered to fit their misshapen figures. In the middle of the table, sticking up like a beanpole, was the "ascetic" Suslov, looking like a vampire with a pale, blueish face. Beside the fat cats sat their wives. They were almost all fat, stupid country girls. The expression of greed in their faces, distorted with blubber, stuck in my memory. Their little piggy eyes...

The people sitting before me were criminals, convicts and con-men. Previously I had judged them on the basis of the portraits that hung everywhere, and their pictures on telly. Leonid Brezhnev visited a factory, gave out crucial instructions. He presented honours and medals to leaders of fellow socialist countries. Brezhnev was seen by many as a lovely Russian bear, Uncle Leonid who understood everything. We were all sheep having the harmless, kindly image of the wolf foisted upon us day in day out by the state machine. We lived in a constant optical illusion, a mirage. In pretty much the same way that the majority lives now, and always will...

It was impossible to look at THEM in the Georgievsky Hall. Although they were almost all still pretty lively, rushing around and guffawing, I felt that they were deadmen who had left their graves to make an uproar and joke around at the birthday celebration of their deadman chief. After the banquet and the concert they would all head back to the cemetery, to their damp crypts and the worms.

So there we sat at our performers' table. All around us were piggy snouts, vampires in suits and sows in brightly coloured dresses. Toasts, grunting, oinking and the chink of crystal... From time to time, at a signal from a man in civvies, one of us would rise to our feet and climb onto the scaffold stage. The singers howled in turn. The Gypsy whinnied. The Bass rumbled. Nilovna had already wailed her bit. THEY liked it. I shot off my études. THEY listened, and even stopped guzzling. The magical power of art. For THEM the main thing was that it should be loud and "with feeling"! For the intellectual Soviet public the exact opposite was true. You needed to play quietly and coldly. Melancholic and aloof, without sentiment.

Khazanov was up on stage. The poor thing was confounded because there was nothing left of his lines, only his bleating voice. He imitated a fool who knows what he's doing. THEY even liked that. It is enjoyable to watch an actor making a fool of himself, exhausted by servility. What fun to watch the grimaces of a humiliated New Soviet Human.

Despite the high positions occupied by these geese, arching their short fat necks with self-importance, they seemed to be tormented by agonizing complexes. Did THEY understand that their whole band was made up of freaks, scumbags and gangsters? Lords of half the world's surface... The downtrodden, sick half... I think that yes, they did understand it then, and their heirs today also understand it now. That is why they are so furious when they encounter proud, independent, free individuals.

I greedily watched the exotic action playing out before my eyes at the Kremlin circus. I was surrounded by rare creatures in the natural world. Monsters... While Khazanov was struggling on stage I became an unwilling actor in a mime scene which amused and embarrassed me. Opposite me, at the foot of the "T", sat an extraordinarily huge woman in a flirtatious, colourful dress.

Although the dress was made from very expensive crêpe de Chine it looked like the sort of cheap gaudy rag you'd find at a village dance. This woman in the dress started to beckon me with her finger, and nod her huge head and tiny little eyes coquettishly at me. Oh, dear, I thought, someone's very level-headed wife is summoning me in a completely unambiguous way. What should I do? I got to me feet and looked around me. The nodding intensified. One of the security gorillas stepped away from the wall. He looked at me, pulled a grim face and shook his head emphatically from side to side, signifying "No, no, no; no way." I sat back down, and this damned woman started nodding even harder, beckoning me with her finger, and displaying evident signs of annoyance. I rose to my feet again, and the gorilla pulled a face at me again, "No, no, no." I sat back down. And the woman carried on nodding and gesticulating. Hell's bells! I made up my mind to sit as though nothing had happened. I flung back my head and feigned weariness after my performance.

I sat like that for about an hour, until Khazanov poked me in the side. I looked round. A bloke in a dark suit (with smoke-stained black sweetcorn teeth, debauched face, dry skin and dead eyes) was talking to the musicians. Mr Gypsy was waving his arms around, Nilovna appeared to be displaying like a capercaillie, and the complacent Bass was hooting away with a servile leer on his face. Khazanov enlightened me, saying that the bloke in the black suit was a bigwig, head of culture in the Central Committee, Comrade Shauro. He was capable of resolving a huge range of different problems. You could ask him for a car, a flat, a residence permit for relatives, be awarded an honorary title, even the illustrious Hero of Socialist Labour (jokingly known as Gertrude in a play on words in the Russian) – anything that the typical Soviet punter could wish for once elevated to the dizzying Kremlin heights of celebrity!

Comrade Shauro perched not far from me. I instinctively pressed my knees together and shifted away. He moved intimately closer, breathing his foul, Central Committee breath on me, and said, "Good evening, Andrei, permit me, on behalf of the Central Committee, to express our gratitude for your performance. How would you like the Council of Ministers to review the question of issuing you with a Steinway concert piano?"

Is it even worth mentioning that I dreamed of having a Steinway, and that I had at the time one elderly Bechstein that had originally been taken as a war trophy? My answer came out on autopilot, as though it was not even me speaking, "Thank you very much, I already have two excellent instruments, and I am perfectly satisfied with them."

It appeared that Comrade Shauro was happy with my reply. "Well, thank you again, and if you need anything, just ask us. Now the Politburo will thank the performers, and personally..."

We stood in a row, and the members of the Politburo rose from the table and came over to the musicians in single file. They burbled something politely, shook hands. Brezhnev ruffled my hair and planted a big smacker on my right cheek. He bantered with Khazanov on a lavatorial theme (that was the only gag he'd been allowed to keep in, about an idiot who pissed himself). Brezhnev was in good spirits, cheerful and entirely glamorous. After the handshakes and the kisses, the gang moved off, with the men in black rushing after them from out of the walls. The celebrations were over.

The Ball

In 1978 it was as though Richter and I snapped the leash we had been held on. It was a year like no other; it was the honeymoon of our friendship. It was captivatingly fascinating to spend time with each other. When we used to meet, we would both bounce around in excitement, like monkeys. Richter came to see me on Nikitsky Boulevard, but he never came into the house. He would collect tiny pebbles on the road and throw them at my window. I would wake up, come outside, and we would tear off together somewhere.

"Andrei, we're going to Povtorny!"

"What's there?"

"There's a film on, *The Composer Mussorgsky*, but we have to run, it's five to ten already!"

Ten o'clock was the time for children's séances in Moscow cinemas; we sat alone in an empty cinema. Cherkasov-Stasov, wearing an enormous beard, drank a glass of milk and pronounced in a sleek bass from the screen, hamming up his accent, "Archaeology, music, art. Curse them to blazes!" A fretful Mussorgsky mused pathetically, "If all works out well for my people .... That is all that matters!"

"Now where?"

"Let's just wander round Moscow!"

"Shall we go to Pyatnitskaya Street? The Rastrelli architecture's incredible there."

"Now to Fili, that's where my favourite church is."

That was how we spent our days when we were not on tour. One day I said to Slava, "Slava, I need to do my exams. Give me three days."

"Three days?! Let's go to the conservatoire. I'll stand in the courtyard, not making any fuss, and you point me out and complain, as though we are going to be late for a rehearsal."

It worked! That was how I passed my theory, musical history and some other nonsense. I stood in the exam as though embarrassed about something. I went over to the window and made a gesture as though saying "There's no way I can, I've got an exam." The teacher drifted over to the window, looked to see who I was gesticulating to. And there stood Slava, waving his cap imperiously like Lenin. The teacher empathised and let me go, "Off you go, I wouldn't dare delay you. That's the best school there is!"

That was how Richter passed my exams with his hat!

We were such close friends that we didn't even want to go on tour. I was expected in Japan in May. We both wept at the prospect of parting. Slava also didn't want to go anywhere. We did go our separate ways, however. I flew to Japan for the first time in my life, and Slava went off to his festival in Tours.

My time on tour in Japan was spent with Chopin études and the incessant Tchaikovsky Concerto No. 1. The trip left no lasting impression on me. Young Japanese girls screamed as though they were at a pop concert. They wouldn't leave me alone and the police had to surround me and hustle me out. I grew to understand and love Asia much later when I was no longer an "eligible bachelor prize winner". What stayed in my memory most from that first trip was not the skyscrapers and lights of Tokyo, but the flight over. I was on the plane with the national volleyball team, whom I greatly admired. They were genuine sports stars: Zaitsev the genius captain, Poleshchuk the attacker and various other guys from the CSKA team. We made friends and after that they came to my concerts, and I was able to use my connections with them to buy sports goods that were unobtainable for the average Soviet Joe Public. Without a similar exchange of favours (I help you, you help me) it was impossible to live in Brezhnev's nation.

After Japan I went to London, then Italy. In the autumn we were both back in Moscow. I rushed round to Slava's house on Bronnaya Street, and he.... He was sitting wrapped up in a blanket in a darkened bedroom. His face was like Pierrot the clown's. His eyes were awash with tears. I had never seen him like this before.

I was terrified for his life.

"What's the matter, Slava? What's happened?"

Slava waved his hand in a gesture signifying that everything was so hopeless life wasn't worth living.

"Slava, let's go for a walk!"
"No-o-o-o."
"Shall we have some wine?"
"No-o-o-o."
"Shall we have a smoke?"
"You don't know how, do you?"
I lit up a cigarette in indignation.
"You call that smoking?"
"How are you supposed to do it, then?"
"Hand over your cigarette."

I gave it to him. Slava positioned it between his palms (like people do when smoking dope) and sucked in the smoke with his enormous lungs. One pull used up half the cigarette. He held his breath, went green, and only then let out the smoke from both nostrils, like a dragon.

"If you're going to smoke, do it like that. Not like how you were, nibbling away at it with no pleasure and no high!"

If I did smoke like that I'd be dead in a week! Richter finished his cigarette and turned his face to the wall. He started crying again. It was Slava's first depression since we had become friends. What should I do? It was going to kill him. How could he be brought out of this state? I did not even suspect yet that these depressive sufferings not only tormented Slava, they were also essential to him. They were a sort of punishment for an unjust life, as a means of acquiring spiritual equilibrium, gathering and binding together his mental fibres. Richter's depressions were heavy, and lasted for months. In fact they did not kill Slava; they helped him survive.

"I missed you so much."

"Re-e-e-eally?" Slava whispered huskily, using just one percent of his vocal chords.

"Well, I'll be off. I don't want to disturb you."

"Go-o-o, co-o-o-ome ba-a-a-ack tomo-o-o-or-ro-o-o-ow."

That lasted for about ten days. Then Slava "cracked".

"Andre-e-ei, the only thing that would help me…. But I can't do it myself. You know Buratinka and I arranged a masquerade ball many years ago, in fact it was rather good, but I always wanted something else, I would love to hold a...." Slava moved his lips and looked at me quizzically.

"A ball! A ball! Here on Bronnaya Street, in the flat."

Slava said this, to my surprise, in a healthy, ringing voice.

"A ball, like at the Larins', or more modest; in the old Russian style of the landed gentry!"

"U-u-u-urm, a ball in the flat. We can do that, why ever not?"

I spoke as though I'd done nothing for many years but arrange balls. I was already feverishly going over different ideas for various aspects of the plan in my head. I was afraid that if my friend didn't get his ball he would die of pique, to spite everyone.

"So you're not refusing?" Richter asked me, recovering suspiciously rapidly.

"Me? Refuse a ball? What do you think I am? Stupid?"

Slava glowed and leapt out of bed.

"Then let's start talking it through and preparing everything? Right away?"

"Urm, of course, let's start!"

"Let's go and talk to some artists about decorations and style!"

"Let's go!"

We rushed outside like mad things, and Slava tried to get into someone else's car, as always, although to be fair this one was at least green like my Lada. Richter was totally incapable of remembering cars. He couldn't notice any difference between them. They all looked the same to him. We got in the car and drove off. Slava asked, "Drive more slowly, with more pleasure. You drive too fast, and that isn't interesting. You need each leaf to be visible, each twig!"

I wasn't worried about the decorations for the ball. I come from a family of artists from Maslovka, so Moscow's entire art world were either friends or friends of friends. Take your pick! You want a sound system? No problem. I had the best speakers of all descriptions at home, various microphones, tape from EMI suppliers; everything of professional standard.

We just had to think up the concept and develop a script for the ball. That was easy! That same day Richter and I went to see some of my friends who had lots of experience in organizing shows of the sort, and they gave us valuable advice.

We decided to concentrate on the draperies first. The next day we arrived at the fabric shop on Gorky Street, near the central telegraph office. For some reason, in Moscow shops, Slava was often mistaken for an army general or some other big cheese. Probably it was because of his imposing size, the expensive imported clothes he wore and his way of speaking in a manner that broached no discussion. Salespeople were scared of him, expecting either to be hauled over the coals or subjected to an inspection. This helped us considerably.

We took ages fussing around with the fabrics and then ordered such a vast quantity that the assistants, who had been scared enough as it was, promptly lost the power of speech. Having bought half the contents of the shop, we took the material back to Bronnaya Street and told various male and female helpers (all from among Richter's menials) what needed to be done. In a few days' time all the rooms in Slava's flat had been miraculously transformed. The walls were covered with expensive gold fabrics that sparkled as though it was the bedroom of Cleopatra or Aspasia. Engineer and electrician friends were already hanging up strings of lights made from shells.

We still needed to determine the musical and dancing aspects of the ball. Richter and I brainstormed. We wrote down on a huge piece of poster-sized paper all the dances we could think of from world literature. The list would have sufficed for a good dozen balls. We then chose the ones that we liked the best. After that we set off for the sound recording archive to record all the music we wanted. In a week's time we already had hours and hours of the very finest dance music, ranging from Viennese waltzes to foxtrots, cha-cha-chas and sambas.

"Slava, what shall we start the ball with, a polonaise?"

"Naturally!"

"Which one? If the ball is like the Larins' ball, then we need to take it from the finale of *Eugene Onegin*."

"I agree, there's a wonderful polonaise there!"

We listen to the recordings: Rakhlin – no good, Golovanov – no good, Svetlanov – perfect! Excellent!

It took us two days to choose the polonaises. We were tired out. We wanted some Chopin. We listened to various pianists. All of the performances of the polonaise were "unfinished" somehow. We finally listened to one old sibilant recording. Rubinstein! In Polish style, proud, simple and it made you want to dance. One week later our "Master tape" was ready. It had dances, classical and modern music. Six hours of carefully selected music in the most brilliant renditions!

Each day the outline of the ball grew clearer and the shape more real. I asked Slava: "When are we going to give the ball?" Slava replied, without thinking, "The 7th and 8th of November."

No comment required. So simple, like everything of genius... We decided to use the Vienna Opera Ball as a model. There they have two orchestras playing in turn – classical and jazz-pop. We also had musical numbers that alternated between old and contemporary. Slava knew nothing about modern pop music, whereas I knew everything. What's more, I had already been working for five years with the London recording studios that produced the hits that had the whole world shaking their tail feathers.

In the meantime, the artists and set-designers that I had invited were busy painting views of gardens, ancient ruins and other appurtenances of classical surroundings. These painted vistas were placed in the windows and walls, and covering doors that were not needed. The space in the flat on Bronnaya Street expanded like in a fairy tale. The idea of "flat", "house", "street" disappeared, communist Moscow evaporated and dissolved in the fabrics and sounds. I understood what it was that Richter wanted. He wanted all THAT squalor to disappear! Out of sight, out of mind! No Soviet flats, hideous streets, department stores, portraits of Lenin and no stinking, primitive cities! No more Russia, red in tooth and claw! No Soviet authorities! Only ancient ruins. A mystical theatre of dreams, dancing couples and heavenly music! Culture as cult.

It was time to address the most difficult part of the business – working with people. Who, might I ask, will open a ball with a polonaise in Soviet Moscow in 1978, who will hop like a mountain goat in a mazurka and caper in a polka? Nobody but a specialist can tell the difference between a mazurka and a krakowiak. Our programme also contained the polonaise, hopak, minuet, and czardas. We decided to invite professional dancers who would dance all the numbers and take the public with them. The waltz, tango, lezginka, Charleston and samba were to be danced by everyone. In a couple of days we had engaged eight couples from the ballet troupe at the Bolshoy Theatre. They started putting the dances together and rehearsing.

In addition to the dances, we planned tableaux vivants, pranks, forfeits, surprises, ghost stories and musical offerings. It was awe inspiring. We thought up themes for our tableaux vivants – "The Pharaoh's Tomb", "Don Giovanni", "Dream of the Argonauts" and "Death of Cleopatra".

The pranks were ordinary objects that behaved unpredictably when you touched them (a teddy bear that exploded in a shower of confetti; a little Christmas tree that ran away on its own legs; a picture on the wall that roared). A whole institute of engineer friends was working on these. They also prepared the "surprises" which comprised an indoor garden in Slava's study (with birds bursting into song at midnight), and a little chamber of horrors with chests that creaked open to reveal skeletons and mummies, skulls, chattering teeth, highwaymen hanging from gallows, a black Faustian poodle and a witch on a broomstick.

Who was going to be master of ceremonies?

"Vitya" suggested Slava, unwillingly. We made a handsome but silly loudhailer for the MC.

The entire flat was packed full of sound equipment, and a different bird could be plugged in at the bottom of each tree in the indoor garden. The living room had eight powerful speakers, three tape machines and amps from EMI.

The endless dance rehearsals were in fact approaching completion. Everything was more or less ready. We sat in the winter garden. There were two nights and one day until the ball. Suddenly Slava slapped himself on the forehead.

"Andrei, we're numbskulls!"

"What's the matter?"

"We have an indoor garden, don't we?"

"Yes, but what's the matter? Stop teasing me!"

"We don't have a FOUNTAIN in the garden!"

"Where are we going to get a fountain in two days? You should have thought of it earlier!"

"Andrei, I'm begging you!"

Slava knitted his brow. I went to see my godly girlfriend, Anechka. Her uncle worked in one of the technical institutes. I went from Anechka's to her uncle's. The kindly uncle understood everything at once, put on his coat and we went to look at the indoor garden without the fountain. It was late in the evening on 5th November. Slava was sitting in the indoor garden with a doom-laden expression on his face. The unruffled uncle asked, "Where shall we pipe the water we're circulating? Via the window or through the bathroom?"

"It would be best through the bathroom. Otherwise it might start soaking people in the street."

By morning, the fountain was in place! It was an old-fashioned style, with looped chains and lighting from underneath. Slava whispered imploringly, "Pebbles, we need to put pebbles round the fountain!"

I'll just fly to the Crimea now, collect some pebbles on the beach, and fly back... What was to be done?

I took the young Prince Obolensky with me and went to look for pebbles in nocturnal Moscow. We went all round the new districts – no pebbles. We looked in the parks – no pebbles. Then I remembered that there were some pebbles lying around somewhere at the Moskva open-air swimming pool. Should we climb into the swimming pool at night? Worth a try. There was a building site not far from the pool. The site office stank to high heaven. We got in; there was nobody about. We found some filthy overalls and struggled into them. Then we grabbed two spades to look more convincing, and climbed over the wall of the pool. We found the pebbles! We collected two sacks full and climbed back. We bunged the sacks in the Lada and raced back to Bronnaya Street. We placed the pebbles round the bottom of the fountain. Slava was thrilled!

Slava told me, "You know, Andrei, I knew Nikolai Obolensky. He could really dance! His eyes would burn like hot coals!"

"Let's invite him to the ball. The Obolenskys are alive and well, and I'm sure they'd love to demonstrate their skill to us."

I dragged the Obolenskys to see Slava the next day. After Nikolai Obolensky's very first frisky steps in the mazurka I bit my tongue in astonishment and awe. I had found the answer to the old chestnut of a question that had been bugging me for years... I had often wondered about the reason for Pushkin's death, as had many other people. I couldn't understand why Goncharova had the hots for Dantes when she had beside her the "cleverest of Russia's men". In contemporary memoirs there are several mentions of Pushkin's lack of skill in dancing; how clumsily he moved and looked like a fish out of water at balls, while Dantes danced beautifully... What rot, I thought, what loathsome superficiality! To fall in love with a pair of legs? Having seen Nikolai Obolensky dancing the mazurka I understood what a compelling power there was in these dances! I couldn't take my eyes off him! What posture! The skill! The breeding! Now I get it, I thought bitterly. Pushkin at the ball was a nonentity, a sarcastic, awkward Moor. While Dantes was a Maestro, a looker. She fell in love with him, the stupid woman.

On the sixth of November we did a proper rehearsal with the active participants. Great! On the next day we were expecting our guests. Elegantly-dressed couples started arriving by eight o'clock in the evening. Everyone you could think of was there! Vasiliev and Maximova, Slobodyanik with Chizhik, Kremer with his young wife, Tretyakov with a new girlfriend, Bashmet with his girlfriend. The academicians, Kapitsa and Ginzburg. The actors and readers, the Zhuravlyovs; Director of the Pushkin Museum, Irina Antonova; Silvia Neuhaus, wife of Heinrich; the famous and much-loved Yura Nikulin, a neighbour of Richter's; the beautiful Karina and Ruzanna Lisitsian with their scientist husbands; the entire Tchaikovsky clan; Galina Pisarenko with her academic husband; Natalia Gutman and Oleg Kagan. There were a great many people that I didn't know. It seems that the only person missing was Vysotsky. Slava would not let him into his beau monde, fearing his "wildness". The entire Moscow "aristocracy", all the "celebrities" of the late Soviet period were at our ball!

Fanfares blasted out, the polonaise struck up and the ballet pairs moved off, tapping their heels in a circle as the ball began! Half of the public lost their nerve. But the ballet dancers from the Bolshoy demonstrated that everyone can dance the polonaise. By the time they had done one circuit almost all the guests had formed a line behind them, even the diffident Gidon Kremer and the somewhat bemused Alik Slobodyanik, who had been led there by his wife. In the middle of the polonaise, in the lyrical section, the varied lines of "thread the needle" that followed would have made the Bolshoy Theatre jealous!

Dance "stars" shone out among the guests. There was the massive and seemingly un-balletic musician, Bogoraz, who demonstrated such class that everyone gasped! He became the king of the dance. Bogoraz kept glancing proudly round at everyone exultantly – just look at me! The mazurka was of course the domain of Nikolai Obolensky; not even the ballet professionals could surpass him. The queen of the ball was Chizhik, who did not miss a single dance in her glamorous pink muslin gauze dress!

Everything was a success. The guests started and gasped at the pranks, delighted in wonder at our tableaux vivants – our consummate beauties and handsome boys looked no worse than their prototypes from antiquity.

Vitya, of course, was off his face. He got as drunk as a skunk and was spouting rubbish. He messed up on the first foxtrot after the polonaise. It was being performed on the grand piano by the greatest of the greats – Erroll Garner. The Black Bottom Foxtrot.

"Black Bottom!" yelled Vitya, stumbling gratuitously.

"A flight recorder, in a sense," he added, and giggled drunkenly. Slava's face contorted, and I felt weary. Slava wrenched the loudhailer from Vita and announced all the numbers himself. Slava and I played our musical forfeit. I played almost all the tracks from Romeo and Juliet, and Slava played the famous Nocturne by Grieg, a couple of Landlers by Schubert and then we played some Schubert marches together, for four hands. Everyone messed around and limped like crazy to these hilarious marches.

Slava and Nina succumbed to the general hilarity and broke into a Charleston, then danced a beautiful foxtrot before finishing with rock and roll! Slava ploughed into the crowd of young people like an ice-breaker cutting through the frozen water, and started wiggling his hips and shoulders and twisting his legs so vigorously that Elvis himself would have been outshone. There was no end to the delight and laughter of the guests. Slava and I exchanged satisfied glances. The fountain spouted water without cease after midnight. All around it the pebbles glistened rotundly. The guests sat idyllically in the winter garden, admiring the fountain and listening to the trills of the nightingales. The ball ended towards morning with a gallop that was tripped up at the end. As was the intention, everyone tumbled down in a huge pile...

F sharp major, Op 15 No 2

In his Nocturne in F sharp major the composer is looking at himself objectively, to an extent. Not without irony and humour. Here we see a lazy, coquettish Chopin. It is possible to suppose, from some of the intonations, that he is in a horizontal position, maybe lying on the sofa. Chopin is plainly in a good mood (unusual in his music), and he takes pleasure in drawing a picture of himself with musical media. Beside him is the man or woman he is talking to.

In the central movement of the piece the fantasy (or conversation) rushes to the banks of the Guadalquivir. We can discern the rhythms of flamenco, and Spanish guitar chords give way to a flitting melody that is reminiscent of a Spanish seguidilla with rhythmic bass beats that imitate Spanish percussion.

The virtuoso passages at the start and straight after the conclusion of the middle of the nocturne produce laughter – at first restrained, but later, after the Spanish section, irrepressible and pearly iridescent. The author is plainly "encoding" a domestic scene from his own life. In the coda Chopin presents with genius a "coming back to earth", and the impression is created of the lyrical hero genuinely soaring in flight and subsequently landing on a musical "parachute".

QR link to the Chopin Nocturnes performed by Andrei Gavrilov

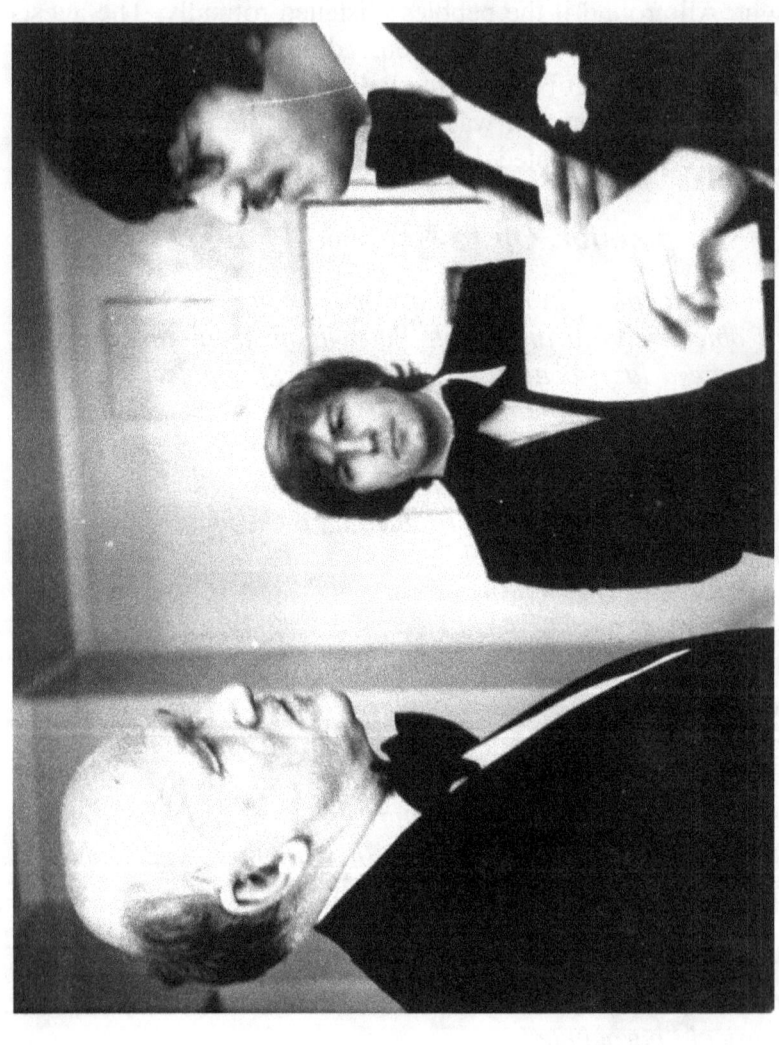

With Sviatoslav Richter and Alexander Slobodyanik at the beginning of the ball (Nov.6, 1978)

Handel Passions

I came to Paris in June 1979 to prepare for my first joint Handel concert with Richter, after a gruelling three-month tour around Europe. I also still had to play the Tchaikovsky festival in London (with Muti) and there was a major project in the Royal Festival Hall where I was scheduled to perform all of Chopin's études and a great deal of other music. In December a huge Rachmaninoff project was due to start with Karajan.

I checked in to the Ambassador Hotel and waited for Richter. I heard not a peep out of Slava. I had no idea where he was. I hung around for three days, dividing my time between studio rehearsals, lovely Montmartre and the busy, colourful night markets of Clichy back before it was cleaned up by the socialist government; and Place Pigalle where I sat stupidly in the Crazy Horse watching the girls dance. I didn't know what to do with myself. I was supposed to meet Richter as soon as I arrived, but there had been no meeting. Each time I came back to the Ambassador I asked at the front desk if there were any messages for me. There were no messages. All sorts of unpleasant thoughts crowded my head at night. I was unable to get to sleep and tossed and turned, seizing the hot air in my dry lips. It was unbearably hot in Paris. I escaped outside from my stifling room in the hotel, and rushed around the boulevards hoping to find a cooler spot, but only sliced through the hot, sticky night air with my body. After three nights of torment I managed to sink into a heavy, morbid slumber. In the morning I was awoken by the loud ringing of the telephone.

"Hi, I'm Eric, the Maestro is expecting you at his hotel. I am waiting for you downstairs."

Eric turned out to be a physically fit blond of average height with a short, almost military haircut and dark glasses. Well-developed muscles could be seen under his tight-fitting T-shirt. To all my questions of what, where to, where, he tossed back the brief "not far" and concentrated on navigating the Parisian boulevards. He stopped the car at a hotel, got out, opened my door and quietly said, "312." He then jumped back into the driver's seat and drove away.

I went into the hotel. I was astonished by the walls that were covered in black silk with a scattering of red embroidered roses and green leaves. There were a lot of roses. It was unfeasibly quiet. What a strange hotel! I got into the lift. It was so cramped! One metre square, no more. I thought – how could two people fit in the lift? I got out at the third floor, walked along a similarly flowery, gloomy gallery and knocked at the door. There was no answer. I knocked again.

"Well come in, then," groaned Richter. It was the intonation he used when he was playing up in a state of depression.

I pushed the door, which was unlocked, and went into a room that was in total darkness with the curtains tightly drawn. I could barely make out Slava lying under his blanket.

"Sit down, Andrei," he groaned quietly.

Once seated in the armchair I stared at Richter enquiringly. We were both silent, which we usually were when meeting after a long separation.

"So, shall we go and do some work?"

"No-o-o-o, I don't want to today."

"Maybe we can go for a walk?"

"Let's go, just help me get dressed. Could you hand me my briefs?"

I took Slava's pants off the back of the armchair and held them out to him between finger and thumb. He sat on his bed and started to pull them on, looking at me in a rather odd way. I turned away. It was only several years later that I realised Richter never forgave me for my squeamishness and that arm's-length pass. We left his room.

"Doesn't this hotel look like a courtesan's coffin?"

"It does, it does, what the hell are you doing staying here?"

"I have a rule never to stay twice in the same hotel in Paris; I make a note of them all and try not to repeat myself, and this hotel has a jolly reputation."

We crammed into the lift. The lift stopped on the second floor, the door opened and someone else squeezed in with us.

"This is too much," whispered Slava and let out a deep sigh.

The person who had squeezed in with us was small of stature. His hair was snowy white with age, long, thick and handsome.

His face was heavily powdered, and his lips had such a thick layer of lipstick that they seemed to be oozing blood. He was dressed in an exquisitely-cut white dinner jacket, with an enormous red carnation adorning the buttonhole. At midday! His enormous green eyes looked at us with curiosity, and the expression on the face of the man who had squashed in with us was arrogantly disdainful. He was very slender and brittle, but there was a sense that he possessed gigantic inner and physical strength. He seemed taller than us, although in actual fact he only came up mid-chest on both Slava and me. Nevertheless, he looked down on us, arrogantly and proudly. Slava stretched his eyes wide and whispered in my ear – Kinski. Then I realised. Klaus Kinski, one of the most famous and scandalous actors of the day, was staring at me contemptuously from beneath my right elbow. Our lift had an astonishingly feeble motor, and we crawled down agonisingly slowly. Thirty seconds in the lift felt like hours to me. Finally we crawled out from the tin can, like three sardines that had stuck together. Slava gave a fake, lopsided smile to Kinski, who curled his lip, tossed his hair back with his hand, while I concentrated on brushing the powder off my jacket in my embarrassment. We bowed to each other and went our separate ways.

We wandered along the boulevards, came out to the Seine and headed for a café on the bank. We sat at a table for two outside. A pretty young waitress came up to us.

"What would you like to drink?"

I ordered a Long Americano, a cocktail of Campari soda and fruit flavoured water.

"And what will your father drink?"

"I'm not his father," said Slava, going red.

"Oh, I'm sorry, are you his friend?"

Now even the waitress blushed.

"So, how do you like Paris?"

"As pretty as ever, but boring."

"I prefer London."

"I like London, too, but I always feel uneasy there. Everything is so cosy here, and it's always warm. Look, there's a chap there walking along with a guitar sweetly singing something French."

The hippy came up to us with his guitar, singing John Lennon's *Imagine*. Slava was discomfited. The first skateboarders were leaping over cars right in the flow of traffic along the embankment. There was a crackpot giving a fire-eating display.

"Well, how's Handel? I think it's marvellous."

"Slava, I'm thrilled. I've always really liked him, but never thought that he would be so good in a solo repertoire. Thank you for the idea, I'm really grateful."

"Thank YOU."

All around the café there were young male couples walking past. Slava looked at me with lively curiosity.

"Andrei, these young people seem to bewilder you?"

"No, not at all, I just prefer mixed couples; these "girls" don't whet my appetite at all."

"You're still too young."

Now Eric quietly joined us at our table. Where had he sprung from? Slava grunted and said, "Eric drives me around. He has just come back from service with the parachute regiment and is working with me."

"Paratrooper, was he?"

"Oh yes. He's nephew to Giscard D'Estaing."

"Ah, I see."

Eric bared his strong teeth, imitating a smile. He was one of those young men who think they are "hard" and demonstrate it any which way they can. Eric tried to have an effect on the people round him by staying quiet; he was a man of so few words one might think he was actually mute. He seemed to consider it old fashioned to show any expression on his face, and his sun-tanned countenance never changed its expression. He was either a robot or dead, although sometimes he clenched his jaw irritably.

The two huge gay blokes sitting at the next table had started an arm-wrestling match. They looked like long-distance lorry drivers, and huffed and puffed as they amorously pushed their heavily tattooed arms against each other. Suddenly Eric planted his small muscular arm on the table and looked at me coldly, like a Komodo Dragon.

"Let's have a go?"

"Go on, then."

We tensed and started to squeeze, smiling forcedly. The antipathy that had sprung up between us had found a point of application. We tried as hard as we possibly could to hurt each other. Where do such emotions come from? There was absolutely nothing for us to fight over. And nobody. If we had been on a field of battle we would probably have killed each other. Slava was exultant. It was impossible to work out who he wanted to win. Eric's arm was as strong as steel, he was crushing my hand and smiling more and more sweetly. The smile soon left his face with its neat little nose and cute little mole on the cheek, like Dantes. The following few minutes brought no victory to either of us. Our hands remained perpendicular to the table, in the starting position.

"How on earth am I going to play tomorrow," I thought. "My mitt's about to fall off, but I'd rather die than surrender. That creep's not even sweating."

Slava stared greedily at our hands and smiled in a predatory manner. I was starting to black out. I noticed (and was delighted) that Eric was going pale and blue circles were showing round his beautiful eyes. Was he tired? I don't know how much more time had passed, as I no longer had a clue what was going on, when Eric quietly said, "It's a draw." Slava unclasped our hands. I stood up to stretch my legs and restore my circulation. I couldn't feel my right hand. Had they set it up specially? What a stupid joke! We had to play tomorrow. When my thumping heart had calmed down I went back to the table. Slava had his right arm ready on the table and was waiting for me.

"And now with me!"

His arm was of impressive dimensions, with a long hand and a forearm the thickness of a normal person's thigh. I had not yet cooled down after my struggle with Eric, and started to press down with dreadful force. Richter was beaten within a few seconds. I looked at him and was horrified. Slava's eyes were filled with tears. Idiot, why did I do that? He sees everything in symbolic terms, I berated myself.

"Slava, let's go and work, shall we?"

"Come on, Andrei. Eric, take us to the studio, there's no need to pick me up later."

In just half an hour we were sitting in the studio, side by side at the piano. I knew that we would forget everything else in a flash, and that we would be happy like we always were when working at the instrument.

"Well then, Andrei, from A major and in order, yes?"

I started the first trill on A in the small octave. There is no text at that point, only functions and everything needs to be invented. My prelude that day sounded much longer than in the concert and, correspondingly, in the recording. I flew from modulation to modulation, not wanting to part with a single note. Slava looked at me with love as he sat at my side. The way a father looks at the first independent steps taken by his child.

"Andrei, do you improvise on themes?"

"What themes?"

"Different kinds. Play me a stone. How would that sound for you?"

I depicted a stone.

"Now ask me something."

"Do the sea."

Slava played the sea.

"And now bullrushes in a backwater," said Slava.

I gave my portrayal.

"And you do clouds."

Slava played clouds.

"Slava, your clouds sound like heffalumps!"

"And your bullrushes sounded like a bamboo thicket. Now play something completely impossible. Play me a fly."

"In a glass?"

"Go on."

I represented a fat fly by using chromaticisms in the middle register and muffled "glass tapping" in the upper register.

"Great, let's get on with the suite."

During the Sarabande, Slava tore his gaze away from the sheet music and started to gaze into my eyes. When I had finished the gigue with immense enjoyment, I also looked questioningly at

Slava. I was asking with my eyes, are we taking it in turns, or shall I play all of my portion first? Slava suggested structuring the first evening with me playing my four suites first, and then him playing his four suites; after that we could see how it went. My first set of four suites ended with the G minor and its famous Passacaglia. I always played this suite possibly with more pleasure than any other, precisely because of the Passacaglia. When I had finished, Slava said, "Do you know, Andrei, I might have made the wrong choice not wanting to play that suite, in general I don't care for things with popular themes. You know, I thought that it was impossible to play that sort of music and not make it un-... erm, unpleasant, but I was wrong." We swopped places, and Slava start his prelude majestically, with a harsh, banging sound and immediately stopped.

"What are you looking like that for?"
"Like what?"
"Well... Strangely."
"No, not at all, what do you mean."

He started more softly and looked at me significantly, holding the sound. He looked so funny, and with a deliberately stupid humour that only he had, that I burst out laughing. He shrugged his shoulders, wriggled on his seat in a very characteristic way, as though releasing his whole body, first his shoulders, then his trunk, then he shifted his backside to right and left and twitched his legs. He took a big lungful of air, held his breath, let it out, raised his chin, tilted his head slightly to the right (his fighting stance) and started to play seriously this time, and with no pauses. To my surprise, Slava was playing in a very chamber-like manner, not letting himself go in the gigues and other jolly, theatrical numbers, of which there were a great many.

The sarabandes came out restrained. The difference between our readings of the suites was striking. He finished playing his four. We were very hungry.

"Let's go and get some dinner, Andrei. Are you hungry?"
"Very."
"So am I."

Usually he would never admit the first that he was tired or hungry, and I always had to be the first to announce it. One day he confided in me, "Andrei, you know that particular state before a concert when tiredness or sleepiness are so overpowering that it is impossible to go out on stage?"

"How could I not know! Especially on a long tour."

"There is only one thing that helps. I've tested it and it always works!"

"What's that?"

"For somebody to beat you till you bleed!"

Something similar happened to me in 1989 before a concert in Salzburg. The weather in the morning had been sunny and warm, and by evening it was snowing and there was an icy wind blowing. Such abrupt changes always affect me severely. Before going out on stage I was overpowered by such deadly sleepiness that I couldn't even sit up... I remembered then Slava's sadistic advice and I asked my driver, Nikolai, to whip me with a belt. He hit me and hit me, kind-hearted Nikolai... Until he drew blood. It didn't help! I slept at the piano for the whole concert.

Slava loved reminiscing about how he was in a car accident. In Poland the car in which Richter was travelling to a concert overturned. The car was lying on its side. The driver climbed out first, and then Slava, while the driver held the door. But the door slipped out of his hand, and it landed with a thump on Slava's head.

"That is too much!" said Richter. The doctor looked at the long, deep wound and warned him, "That needs stitches. If we put the stitches in under anaesthetic then you won't be able to give the concert."

"Sew it up without anaesthetic."

Slava did not utter a sound while the wound was stitched. His concert was a great success. For a long time afterwards he played in a skull cap to hide the scar. In the Monsaingeon film there is a short episode where Richter is playing Shostakovich and wearing a skull cap – after that accident, as it happens.

Richter's courage in matters physical knew no bounds, and there was a fair amount of masochism in there. He loved to torment himself and genuinely gained pleasure from so doing. It was an interesting feature of his – when things are bad, make them worse. Then worse and worse until you "fall into nothingness" (one of his favourite expressions).

German Wagnerian characteristics, pragmatism and pedantry were combined in him with aspects of the Khlysts, the holy fool and other Russian complexes from Dostoevsky. Both of these elements attained a state of extremely high tension in him.

We walked briskly up the Boulevard de Clichy. Along the way, Richter chatted about local bars, clubs, brothels and restaurants. We paced along alleys that were lit only by signs from establishments in the red light district. There were young male prostitutes standing in the doorways, no girls. Slava looked at one lad in jeans – he stood with his arms crossed and kept an insolent eye on us.

"They're so brazen now," Slava said suddenly, becoming embarrassed and shaking his head.

I looked at him in amazement; his unexpected demonstrations of childish bashfulness always astonished me. Only just now we had been sitting in the Demagogue, and he had been "teasing" me with conversations on homosexual topics, and now he was embarrassed by looking at a cheeky boy.

The lights of Clichy were scintillating. The windows of fish restaurants lured us with their huge aquariums filled with lobsters. Gigantic flat boxes of ice contained piles of oysters.

We entered a restaurant and went on up to the first floor. Cosy little rooms with round windows were like cabins on board a ship. We sat at a table with a snow-white starched tablecloth and napkins, and we started looking at the jolly plates with blue and orange logos. Against a blue flag, a fish in a chef's hat stood on its tail and eyed a lobster that was sitting on blue letters spelling "La Champagne". I noticed that they knew Slava here. The Maître d' and some of the waiters nodded to him as to an old acquaintance. They brought some white wine. Slava started to reminisce about how we had met at his house the previous Easter. He laughed as he described his impressions from that evening and how I had fallen off my chair.

"You know, Andrei, I was struggling to stay awake all evening, and I kept dozing off on the trunk in the hall."

"Slava, I was convinced it would be the first and last day we ever met."

"Well, Klemperer's tempos are a challenge even with the most alert of heads."

"Yes, that's true, but I wasn't thinking about tempos or Klemperer at the time, my head was throbbing – shame, shame."

"What do you mean, shame! After you slid off your armchair I realised that we'd be friends."

"Thank God for that, because the memory has been gnawing away at me all year."

"I heard that you're… having a fling in Moscow."

"Who told you that?"

"We-e-ell, I heard. I have a very important favour to ask you in that connection. Never start relationships in Russia!"

"Why not?"

"They will remind you of it later and use it against you."

"A straightforward affair with a girl?"

"There's no such thing as a straightforward affair, nor a straightforward girl."

We had something to drink and got started on the oysters. Slava taught me how and in what order to eat them. He picked up a whole boiled lobster, cracked open its abdomen and said, "And this bit is the most delicious, but most fools don't realise that and throw it away." I immediately put the innards that I had laid aside back on my plate.

"Really, nobody eats it, but it's the best part."

I sensed that all this culinary chat was simply the prelude to an important conversation for Richter. Slava cracked open a thick claw with the pliers that I had been unable to cope with, and quietly said, "You know, Andrei…"

A small digression is needed here. After my triumphant performance in Salzburg in 1974 Richter, whom I had replaced at that concert, wanted a closer look at me. He did not believe in sensations in the music world. Out of ten sensations exaggerated by the marketeers of the music business to sell their product quickly, only one was genuine and all the rest were fakes and soap bubbles. A year later I received an invitation to take part in Richter's festival in Tours, on the banks of the beautiful Loire.

Each festival in Tours had its own concept. The festival in 1976 was thought up by Richter as a beauty parade of pianists. He invited many of the world's leading pianists to the festival, and performed a solo concert himself. All the invited pianists were entitled to one concert each, and put together their own concert programme.

It was fiercely hot in Paris at the time. The tarmac melted, and local residents bathed in the fountains. An elderly lady from the first wave of Russian emigration met me. I didn't like "our" French people, they were too cold, poor and constantly fretting about something. They smiled rarely. We spent half a day in Paris. It was so hot! We got on the train and travelled down to the south. We arrived by evening. I was dropping with hunger, and had swelled up in the heat. I was unable to buy anything to eat or drink as I had no money. We arrived in Tours, once the capital of France. It was beautiful. The wonderful Cathédrale Saint-Gatien with its "staring" towers. The half-timbered houses, the chateaux, the fields of van Gogh. Miles away from anywhere was a large building in a bucolic yard, an old barn.

It was romantic, beautiful and, as is so often the case with summer festivals – awkward for performing musicians. I couldn't get the hang of it. I was expecting to meet Richter. I was anxious. I saw Richter, in a blue blazer with gold buttons, coming to our barn for a concert. He was not alone, but had a sort of retinue. The Commendatore. He made a barely perceptible gesture to me with his hand and went inside. He did not welcome the novice. I desperately wanted something to eat and drink. There was nobody to ask. I also really needed to practise. My programme was crammed full of technical wizardry. I was due to play études by Liszt, the Islamey Fantasia by Balakirev, the crazy sonata by Scriabin, and various other virtuoso pieces. I was taken to a chateau to practise. Well, I thought, I'll eat at the chateau. I was left alone in a room with an instrument while they went off to a concert. The room contained just a grand piano and a table. There was a tray on the table with a large bottle of red wine and a little dish of red currants. Bastards! I practised all through the night, I can't remember where or how I fell asleep. I woke up on the floor.

I played some more. I was taken to the concert. The barn was not full, and in the first row sat Richter and Nina Dorliak.

I played like a mad thing. From rage and hunger. A dog wandered into the barn. It listened to the end of the concert with the audience and started to bark as they applauded. Success! The whole house was clapping, but Richter had disappeared. How hospitable! Nina came up to me and said something. My head was spinning. Hunger, the heat, the concert. I was taken to Paris, given a pie to munch on and sent off back to the USSR like a parcel.

Two years passed, and Richter and I already knew each other and met up. We never spoke of my concert in Tours. But I could sense that Slava had liked the concert. I started spending time at Richter's famous flat on Bronnaya Street. Slava often invited people round for shared musical entertainment. We would listen to rare pieces, Easter and Christmas music, and operas. We discussed whole musical cycles, such as Wagner's Ring Cycle.

We became real friends around mid 1978. Around that time I was helping Slava put into practise our joint ideas, and we staged all sorts of extravagant follies, the culmination of which was the huge ball mentioned above with the polonaise and the fountain. By the time we were sitting together in Clichy, we were already thick as thieves. If we had moved just one millimetre closer to each other, we would have turned into a one-bodied two-headed monster.

Slava spoke quietly, "You know, Andrei, do you remember your concert back then in Tours? From the first note you played in the Scarlatti sonata I understood that I was finished. When you played Scarbo, and La Campanella I sat and cowered as though dodging bullets fired at me.

I had never liked the Scriabin No. 4, but what you did there made me horrified at my own lack of talent. Gilels also played the Campanella well, but yours was better. I wanted to learn it once upon a time, but I never spared the time. I wanted to come up to you after the concert, but I couldn't. I cried all night, and loved you and cursed you. But I understood one thing, once and for all, that my life was over in all respects! There is not room for both of us in this world, and what is particularly terrifying for me is that if you have the exposition, then I have the coda."

Richter started to cry. I shrank into myself and was transfixed on my chair, mumbling meaningless, soundless consolations through my parched lips.

"And now, when you played Handel, I wanted to kill you. I didn't care how, just to kill you. I will re-do everything ready for the concert. You terrified me. How on earth did you manage to make that wretched Passacaglia so strong? I couldn't bear it, that's why I gave you that suite. I thought that none of your suites could be played decently; they are all flat, lopsided and primitive. And you have done them in such a way that I have to re-do everything to imitate your whole theatre and drama! You have killed me, killed me the way I wanted to kill everyone else. There is no more me, and never will be, whatever I do! I hate you!"

With Paul McCartney (London, 1979)

With Angelika von Bennigsen, Tatyana K. and "Pauli" (Moscow, 1979)

Four and twenty tailors went to catch a snail

1979 was the best and most fruitful year for my music! The Handel "duels" with Richter and my first recordings and concerts with Muti in London, after which Elisabeth Schwarzkopf herself came to see me in the green room, and I silently fell to my knees in front of her and bowed by head while she gently stroked my hair. Athletic performances with all of Chopin's études, recordings and concerts with Gidon Kremer, and a three-month tour around Europe. These were my first serious artistic steps. I was gradually transforming from an unknown student and competition winner to a musician with my own artistic style. With my own artistic destiny. I was allowed out of the country for the European tour with my mum. Apparently the KGB caught on too late. They even came out to Sheremetyevo to detain her, but were not in time. We flew out on a morning flight. I did not want to go back to my own country from the tour, but my mum refused point blank to become a defector because of my brother Igor, an artist. I did not want to live without my mother. That was why we stayed in the USSR, with "the old woman holding on to the old man, and the old man holding on to the turnip."

For modern performers, spoiled by the new Russian capitalism, it may seem strange – but when we started out, we Soviet musicians hardly got any money at all. Just Soviet wages recalculated in the currency of the country where the concert was taking place.

All the money that we earned flowed away through the Ministry of Foreign Affairs into the "national wealth of our great fatherland". Of course it was used not for the "needs of building communism", but on the whims of the ruling élite or to support communist parties and "national liberation movements". If it hadn't been for this systematic robbing of musicians by the wicked-stepmother motherland I could have provided myself with a comfortable decade of life from one happy year. But once my mother had firmly refused to defect, I, like so many performers, had no choice but constantly and reluctantly to pay tribute to the rapacious vampires.

In this same year I got married in great haste. To the seventeen-year old Kimova girl, daughter of Valery Kimov, the winner of the inaugural Tchaikovsky Competition for violinists, and the singer Raisa Bobrova. Tatyana Kimova was a student of my professor, Lev Naumov. Marriages such as this – within a tight clique – are no rarity among musicians. Unfortunately, I had no idea who was who in the celebrity musical élite of the day. I should have taken a close look at the Kimov-Bobrova alliance. I paid a heavy price for not doing so. I should have been on my guard when the parents of my sweetheart themselves shoved their child into bed with me. I woke up one day… and there was delicious Tanya sitting on my bed, with hardly any clothes on. They also befuddled my poor mother… such sweet, generous and kind people.

While I was on tour in France with my Handel and Richter, I was informed that my sweet girlfriend was pregnant, and with complications to boot. Oh my! It was like the Blitzkrieg. As an "honest man" I would now have to walk down the aisle beside her. Then my kind informer announced that my brand-new in-laws had been arrested at Sheremetyevo airport customs with a large batch of jewels which they had tried to smuggle to Europe.

"It's the end," said Pavel.

"And what an end!" I echoed stupidly.

I had never encountered things like this outside of the cinema. Everyone was convinced that "smuggling or speculation of precious metals and foreign currency" was punished in the Soviet state by execution or long prison sentences.

A little later, other well-informed individuals enlightened me that the couple had been released a few hours after their arrest, but the charges against them were not lifted. Kimov and Bobrova wanted to try asking the all-powerful minister Nilych (Demichev) for help, but Nilych would have nothing to do with them, and when asked for help he reacted with the words: "Speculators should be judged by Soviet laws!" He even held up his ministerial hand with the index finger extended, just like Lenin! A little later still, the same sources informed me that Nilych had been overridden, the customs department had apologised, and Kimov and Bobrova happily flew off on tour. I naively thought, "Well, thank God. The security forces were wrong, maybe it was their enemies who set the whole thing up."

A few days later my father-in-law turned up in Paris to run some master classes. I had to provide him with refuge in my room at the Ambassador on Boulevard Haussmann, where he disturbed my sleep with his lusty, carefree snoring. We did not discuss the topic of customs and emeralds. It's true that this was only the third time in my life that I had met him. Kimov the violinist was blithe and light-hearted. He regaled Richter with jokes about "homos". Slava laughed, while I felt totally awkward.

I got back from tour and ran down the aisle and then set off for the Caucasus in my green Mercedes to visit the graves of my ancestors. I drove back along the incredibly beautiful Georgian Military Road that I had dreamed of seeing since I was a child. Tiflis, the Terek Valley... It was marvellous! I was travelling with my young wife, and I thought of myself as splendid Griboyedov. I was forgetting, for some reason, how poor Griboyedov met his end. The only thing to disturb my happiness was my wife's parents, who were tagging along behind us in their white Mercedes. Uncharitable voices in Moscow mocked viciously, "The Mercedes has married a Mercedes!"

"They're celebrating a potential divorce!" hissed lackeys from among Richter's menials. But nobody knew, and I could not begin to guess, what a bomb had been placed underneath me by my in-laws with this wedding. A bomb that blew up my entire life.

In December I was supposed to complete this fantastic year with a tour with Karajan and a recording of Rachmaninoff concertos. The tour and the recordings were threatening to become unique, historical events in the music world. Karajan – Rachmaninoff – Gavrilov! Until meeting me, Karajan had never burned with a desire to perform the works of Rachmaninoff. The recording was supposed to be made, for the first time ever, on enormous, clumsy green machines the size of a wardrobe with the as-yet unfamiliar label – Digital.

1979 sprinkled me with diamonds from dawn till dusk. Although I was spinning like a top I started to notice strange signs that were being sent to me by fate. Seemingly insignificant events, conversations, hints. Insignificant but unpleasant and unsettling. The meetings with the KGB that had been forced on me in the stumpy building on Natasha Kochuevskaya Street became regular occurrences. Previously they had seemed to forget about me periodically, had left me alone, but now they dragged me in practically every day. Spies, conspiracies, vigilance! I couldn't not go to these abhorrent interviews, as that would have meant an end to my career as a musician in the USSR. Every time I went, Ivan Ivanovich, AKA Nikolai Ivanovich, reminded me officiously and with threat in his voice that I mustn't "recognise" Seryozha at the conservatoire. It transpired that this vile worm was constantly spying there and "supervised" the conservatoire informants. He observed and listened in places where students congregated – in the smoking room, the canteen.

One day Ivan Ivanovich was droning on as usual about nothing at all and placed a huge hammer in front of him, as though by chance. The bastard's insinuating something, I thought and offered him some American cigarettes. He forgot about the hammer and greedily grabbed a handful of Winston cigarettes from the box with his fat, clumsy fingers.

After 1976 I always went on tour escorted by "attendants".

Attendants. That was the official Soviet jargon for the "profession" of perverted, lazy scumbags who stuffed themselves on our modest incomes and interfered with our lives and work as much as they possibly could. The institution of attendants was one form of typical Soviet zoological parasitism. A "worker insect" – a musician – goes to work, and riding on his back is an attendant "insect parasite". Aphids, lice, bed bugs. Call them what you like. They fly on the plane with you, travel in the same car, stay in the same hotel, sometimes even in the same room, together, together, together. Right up until you arrive back in the country, where the parasite mounts another back and the musician has a breather until the next job. Attendants were intrusive and insolent as they spied on performers, they constantly reminded you of their presence, especially watched your contacts, and they stuck to you like a wet leaf. They ran off for "approvals" to the consulate, the "cultural attaché", and to "our comrades". Of course for them the main thing was to go shopping in the hated West, which they were doing their small part to destroy.

There were two women among the attendants who had worked in the past at Soviet concentration camps. One of them, sitting in the director's office of Gosconcert, when told by the secretary that a performer had come to see her (David Oistrakh, for example), would react with the words, "Bring him in!" They tried to unload the second one onto me for my trips to Paris and London for the Richter and Muti projects. I refused point blank.

"We are totally incompatible!" I asserted firmly when I found out precisely which vile dolly they wanted to assign me. I had travelled with her once to London, and she had driven me completely round the bend. She stuck to me like a burr. The only place I could go without her was the toilet. My announcement astonished those who "made all our decisions for us." They couldn't begin to imagine that this "reptile of a musician, this milksop who lived in a fairytale world with trips to London and Paris" could pipe up against them. Only the "chief pianist of the Soviet Union," Richter, could allow himself such a thing, and even then it was not he himself, but through his wife who knew all the ins and outs. I dug my heels in; it was a matter of days before I was due to fly out. The summonses started. I was invited to visit one deputy minister and then another.

"Surely it can't make any difference to you who is staying in the same hotel as you, and who will be going to the embassy to settle matters? Why are you making such a mountain out of a molehill?"

I was summoned to a third deputy minister! I went in and there… were all three deputies and the minister himself, Nilych, sitting in the middle. It seemed that this female-Goon bitch was of particular value to them. I had an enormous programme! I needed to be spending all night and day practising! No, you sit in this gilded ministry at the foot of the Kremlin and listen to moralising by the bosses!

Nilych muttered something ever so quietly. That was how he gave the little people a hard time. His poor subordinate would tense, strain like a violin string. Heaven forfend that you might not hear something! Large, high-ranking men fainted after visits to

Nilych precisely because of his pianissimo strategy. Nilych learnt this strategy at the same time as all the Soviet swine learnt their cruel tricks – during the Stalin era. He learnt it and used it till the end of his beneficial work for the good of the country. His first deputy was an enormous, heavy, limping man with an ugly orthopaedic boot up to his knee and with hair that was always unwashed and unkempt in a dirty dark colour with flecks of grey. His name was Vasily Kukharsky, and he did not mutter quietly. This bully boy shouted loudly and terrified musicians. On that June day I remember so well he barked at me, "For behaviour like that you'll rot in the nut house!"

I wasn't listening to Nilych, there was no point. I listened calmly to what Kukharsky said, then stood up and said, "If I'm going on tour, then I really need to prepare for it. Thank you for the meeting."

I replaced my chair where it had stood, bade farewell and defiantly walked slowly towards the exit of the enormous office. It seemed to put them in a state of suspended animation. Four cultural bosses were motionless, either with horror or rage. I walked in total silence, and could hear only my own footsteps. When I was closing the office door I heard the belated, blood-curdling yell from Kukharsky, "You'll pay for this, you stinker!"

This Kukharsky, incidentally, was considered a dear friend in the Richter family; Nina Lvovna addressed him over the telephone as "my dear". Once Alik Slobodyanik happened to hear this affectionate term of endearment. Alik's eyes opened wide and he whispered in my ear, "She's off her rocker!" Nina realised that she had slipped up, stood up from the chair where the unexpected call from the deputy minister had caught her unawares, straightened her pleated skirt, sighed and said gravely, "Needs must when the devil drives!" Then she went into the kitchen.

I went home after the meeting with Nilych and his guard dogs with a heavy feeling. Kukharsky's cry still sounded again and again in my head, like an echo. As though I was being stabbed with a knife.

To the nut house! To the nut house! I was supposed to be working on Handel and Chopin. I can imagine what they would have sung if they had had to spend time talking to Nilych, Nikolai Ivanovich and Kukharsky.

All the same, I won that tiny battle. They went back on their word and assigned me with the most cultivated and striking informer in the USSR – Pavel Dorokhov. Pavel never interfered with me in any way. It was possible to natter away with him about anything. Slava once said of him, "That one of yours is alright, he's even rather distinguished."

I had barely got my breath back after Paris, London, Richter, Handel, Muti and Chopin when Nilych summoned me again. What is it this time? I turned up. He was whispering, the bastard. I could hardly hear him. He was sending me in September-October to play thirty solo concerts in Italy "through the allied Communist Party". I already had experience of a tour like that, as I had been on one in 1977. I had given about thirty concerts. These "fraternal Eurocommis" booted me all round Italy giving concerts, from North to South, and didn't pay a thing. Apparently "for friendship's sake". They only gave miniscule per diems that weren't even enough to eat properly. What's more, the concerts were every day. And travelling every day. Around the whole of Italy's boot! The moment I got off the airplane in Milan there was a concert that same day in Cesena.

"Gavrilev! Maestro! Brother! Friend! Comr-r-rade! Rot-Front!"

With a smile all over his jeering mug a "comr-r-rade" was running towards me with his fist raised in the old-fashioned communist style, shaking it slightly. What was he, a nutter? I did not have any idea at the time what Euro-communism was. It had never occurred to me that after the bloody excesses of the Stalinist regime, and contemporaneously with the cynical, deceitful propaganda of our socialist homeland, somewhere in a normal democratic society there could still be red boys and girls who would play at all this rot-front stuff, wave their fists and belt out songs like the *Bandiera rossa*, and generally engage in all this mothball crap which only remained in the USSR in the form of jokes and textbooks! Here... not in China, not in Cuba, not in the Scientific Communism Department of the Patrice Lumumba

Institute, but here, in the centre of Europe, in beautiful Italy. What a bunch of idiots!

Later I understood that in this world there are no capitalists or communists. Just crazies. Some are crazy and happy, while others are crazy and ferocious sadists. That is the only difference.

The "mothball communists" turned out to be normal Italians – sly and jealous. It seemed that they were only interested in one thing: getting rich and having sex for free. Well, and a little more – how to foul things up for the rich and powerful, as much and as foully as possible.

We musicians were exploited so intensively that it went beyond the wildest dreams of any "capitalist sharks". My "amico" was constantly repeating all the "Avanti populo", "companiero" and "tovarishch" stuff. He came from Florence and taught Russian at school. Judging from what he said, he often taught visiting Soviet chicks the niceties of European erotica.

"You know, amico Gavrilev, your women are so beautiful, but they know absolutely nothing – they don't even know how nice it is when the man licks! They are so shy at first, almost want to fight and then, when they discover – they are so happy! I recently worked with one very beautiful woman, she was also a Russian teacher – she was so grateful when she left, she said, Mario, Mario I will never forget that, and her eyes were so happy-happy!"

I travelled the whole country with conversations like that with the sexually advanced communist by name of Mario. Like all Florentines Mario had a very high opinion of himself. Our driver, Giorgio, was a heavy-set peasant from Modena and couldn't bear the self-satisfied, smug Florentine, and exploded every half hour. He would stop the car and leap out to calm himself down with a couple of glasses of Lambrusco. He travelled at a maximum speed of 110 km per hour. There was no air conditioner in the communists' old Opel. The temperature was 40 degrees centigrade. There was steam rising from the motorway. I was swelling up. I got straight out of the car and onstage at the next theatre in the series. It was exactly the same every day of the tour.

Mario believed it to be beneath his dignity to answer Giorgio's attacks. He would start to talk in Russian, addressing me and pointing out of the window, "Gavrilev, let's learn Italian. Look, here, grande curva."

I scanned with my eyes, looking for some sort of Cabiria-curvy broad, but could see nobody. Mario was delighted.

"Gavrilev, it is not what you thought, it is a dangerous turn in the road, and amore mio is not a song about more me..."

Nilych just kept whispering. I answered Nilych firmly: "Sorry, I can't do it, after the very demanding tour with Richter, and the cycle with Muti, and the Chopin festival in London I got a stomach ulcer from exhaustion. I need to sort myself out before the December project with Karajan. I need to take my exams at the conservatoire. I still have some left-over loose ends from the fourth year."

"You needn't worry about your studies!"

"I can't go to Italy. I need to get my health in order. Urgently."

"Well then," whispered Nilych looking the other way, "perhaps WE can cure you? And you won't need to go anywhere. I think that would be right, you have worked too hard!"

The penny dropped – he was threatening me. He was putting pressure on me, like in prison, like a kingpin pressures an underling. We can cure you! THEIR treatment could end with lethal consequences. I needed to save myself and the Karajan project somehow.

"Thank you for your concern, Pyotr Nilych. The situation isn't that bad, and I saw a gastroenterologist in Paris, recommended by Comrade Richter. He prescribed me some magical medicine, Tagamet, and said that I should have at least a month without any stress."

"You decide," hissed Nilych ominously.

The audience was over. I thought that I had won a couple of months for serious preparations for the Karajan project. I hoped that Nilych would not dare wreck that project. It was already advertised all over the West, and had major money invested in it. I was wrong. Nilych and his ministerial pals, however, did not take serious measures against me.

It should be noted here that although Nilych and I were not friends, his attitude towards me was neutrally respectful, which on the scale of the Soviet nomenclature could be equated with ardent sympathy. Even I felt no particular hatred towards this big fish in his little pond. Of all the numerous Soviet monsters I had to spend time with, Nilych was by no means the worst. He cut quite a dash in his youth with his quiff, and the factory lasses were probably queuing up to give him one. By the late 1970s he was about 60. He had even features, a clear forehead, neatly styled grey hair; he even still had a perky quiff. He was always impeccably turned out in decent imported suits, and his skin was well cared for. I often gazed at this ageing village accordionist and tried to work out how much crème he smeared on his face every day. Nilych was a nice chap. If he had a soul fitted he would have been almost alive.

Some time in October 1979 I went running to Nilych off my own bat. Elton John had sent me recordings of fanfares and the anthem for the Moscow Olympics in 1980. He asked me to help promote his material. Nilych saw me without an appointment. What an honour!

"Do you have the cassettes?"

"Yes, of course," I said, and handed him two large tapes.

"I shall report this to the very top," promised Nilych, and put the cassettes in his desk drawer. Neither Elton not I ever saw the cassettes again. "The very top" didn't show its worth in any way at all. At this time Pakhmutova was being orchestrated left, right and centre; something about Misha the Olympic bear. Typical Soviet wishy-washy soppiness.

Cut off

My first concert with Karajan in the Rachmaninoff cycle at the Berlin Philharmonic was supposed to take place on 8 December 1979. I was supposed to fly out to Berlin on 4 December. Two weeks before my departure I was furiously rehearsing in Slava's sound-proofed flat on Bronnaya Street. Richter had given me the key, so that I could practice at night. The Rachmaninoff Concerto No. 2 was already flying under my fingertips. It played itself "like child's play"; it was "a doddle" as we used to say at the conservatoire. My spirit was rejoicing in anticipation of the prospective high point of my career – long term collaboration with Karajan! But suddenly...

On 2 December I was summoned to the Central Committee. Urgently! I was met by a man in a black suit. Kuzin was his surname. He was elderly, dry and dead.

"Sit down."

I sat down. Kuzin was talking in a bored tone, not looking at me, "Comrade Gavrilov, did you know that the Berlin Philharmonic Orchestra, conducted by Karajan, was recently on tour in China?"

"Yes, I had heard. I also heard that there was a little problem with the aircraft on landing. The musicians, including Karajan, were not seriously hurt."

"Well, our government does not welcome such close relations with China; we would recommend that you refrain from performances with Karajan."

"Here we go!" I blurted out in my head. My legs weakened at the knee, fury grabbed me by the throat, and blood rushed to my face. It was plain as day. China had nothing to do with it – that was for sure.

I said nothing. The *tovarishch* in the black suit also said nothing, and then suddenly suggested, "Let's send a telegram to Berlin, we'll say that you have fallen ill, shall we?"

"No," I said, "Don't do that." Molière acted out the *malade imaginaire* and died! I don't want that to happen

The suit gazed at me in even deeper boredom.

"So you are against sending a telegram?"

"Ca-te-go-ri-cally."

"Fine, off you go and we will consult."

I left the Central Committee building on Staraya Square and flew home to the telephone, to phone Berlin. At that time it had just started to be possible to phone abroad without booking the call in advance. I raced into the flat and there – was my brother in horror, and my mother in a state of shock.

What had happened? Had they heard about me? No. They told me. Someone came to see them. Who? Two men in black with ID from the KGB.

"Comrade Gavrilov? Igor Vladimirovich! Please show us your foreign passport and tickets for your flight to Rome."

I had forgotten that my brother was planning a trip to Italy for the holidays with his wife, who was half Italian-half Russian. His father-in-law had invited them. Rome, Florence, Venice. This was a compulsory programme for any artist. The wonderful old man was waiting for them in Rome, with his ranch and horses. In the past he had been a communist, now he was retired. The KGB took the passport and tickets, claiming there was some slip-up with the stamps.

"We will bring them back as soon as the inaccuracies have been corrected, don't worry."

That was the last they saw of them. I felt sympathy for my brother and rushed to the phone. I dialled. The telephone wasn't working! It was only now beginning to sink in. This was more than just a travel ban. I raced round to Bronnaya Street. There was nobody there. Slava and Nina were in Europe. I called my agent in Berlin.

"Hello, hello, Dorothea?"

Dorothea Schlosser was well known, with her monopoly of Soviet performers in West Berlin. She was an opera singer when Hitler was in power, and now she was a colourful, elderly lady with a good deal of money. The only remnant of bygone beauty that Dorothea retained was her shock of red hair.

"Dorothea, they aren't letting me out for the concert, my brother has had his passport confiscated, the telephone has been cut off and I'm phoning from Bronnaya Street, that's all, 'bye."

Dorothea told me later that after my call she sank to the floor beside the telephone. When she came to her senses she set to calling Gosconcert. That was the wrong level! Gosconcert pretty much heard the news from her. Dorothea called me that night at Bronnaya Street. "Andrei, go to Demichev tomorrow first thing and keep an eye out; the whole of Gosconcert will be there." I listened, understood and sat back at the piano.

Third of December. Ten o'clock in the morning. I went to see Nilych in the Ministry of Culture of the USSR.

"Demichev? He's busy. He has Supagin with him, the director of Gosconcert."

Aha, I think, that means they're talking about my case. Then... the opulent doors of Demichev's office, white and heavy with gold incrustations, don't exactly swing open, they burst open with a heavy kick of someone's foot. A bald, thickset, stocky Supagin comes flying out, red-faced and wild-eyed. He looks up to the ceiling, like a prophet raising his head to the heavens, and screams at the top of his lungs, "Wankers, bastards, they've to-o-o-otally fu-u-u-ucked u-u-up!"

I stood half a metre away from the contorted Supagin, but he couldn't speak to me, or even look at me; he stopped yelling and stood for a few moments with his bald head glimmering crimson with rage as he dumbly rolled his bloodshot eyes like a bull in the ring. Then he plunged down the scarlet carpeted staircase and vanished from view. The booming ministerial echo tossed back his wild shrieks for a long time, like a ball bouncing off the walls and ceilings.

Fourth of December. A black day in my calendar. This was the date in 1970 when my father died, straight after opening the solo exhibition of a friend in Tver. In mysterious circumstances. He was only 47. I don't like this day, I don't like December, I don't like late autumn and early winter. All my close relatives departed this life at the same time of year – my mother, my father and my brother.

Dorothea had still not told Karajan and the Philharmonic about my problems. There was no point. We were going to fight it to the end, and then we'd see. I came home to Nikitsky Boulevard. I went into the bedroom. There was my wife, Tanya, wailing and trembling. In a few minutes I could hear shouts, screams and stamping feet in the hall. Oh no! My in-laws were shouting something incoherent at my mother, Bobrova was having a fit of hysterics in her rage, like a crazy baboon. The howling voices of singers are unpleasant enough to listen to in the theatre… Daddy Kimov was saying something to my mother along the lines of, "You're out of your mind. How dare you. What ridiculous accusations. Tanya, get your things together!"

This is what had happened. An old friend of my mum's, a retired KGB officer, who had eaten from the hands of Dzerzhinsky, had brought with her the first news from Lubyanka. "A denunciation, a denunciation to Brezhnev! Via Galina, from the Kimovs. There is an order to arrest Andrei. Brezhnev himself ordered it!"

Mum had hauled the Kimovs over the coals and spilled out everything. They had spat and had hysterics, roaring like wild beasts, and then taken their daughter away. Bobrova was particularly impressive, and I later heard that special "timbre" from other female singers. Do they teach them how to roar like that at the conservatoire?

They had been phased by the fact that Mum had found out about their base tricks so quickly. You might ask how mum's friend got hold of the information. It's straightforward. This was the Soviet Union! Even strategic information leaked out from kitchen to kitchen. My case was by no means strategic. It had sprung a leak.

Fifth of December. Berlin. News from the first channel of West German television.

"Today, 5 December, Herbert von Karajan and the Berlin Philharmonic Orchestra waited four hours for the soloist, the Soviet pianist, Andrei Gavrilov. Andrei Gavrilov did not appear at rehearsal. In the second half of the day a telegram arrived from Moscow, from Gosconcert, with the message that you can see now on your screens."

The camera zooms in on the telegram and shows it in close-up. It is not a telegram, but a telex, glued on to a piece of paper. I saw a recording of this news bulletin six years later in Berlin. I saw the telegram as well; I was even given it as a present.

"Andrei Gavrilov unfortunately cannot fly to West Berlin because of intensive touring around the Soviet Union."

That was all. They did not even have the imagination to write anything else. The fact that the contract had been signed a year ago by the Soviet side, that dozens of companies were involved in the project, that the concerts and recordings had been discussed and endorsed at the very highest level – ministerial and political – all this was suddenly forgotten in the Soviet Union. Lapses in memory at the personal, collective and even public level are highly typical for our "generous" land that stretches from the Baltic to the Pacific Ocean.

B Major Op 32 No 1

In his Nocturne in B Major Chopin draws his listeners into a romantic intrigue that is reminiscent of a love triangle. The start of the piece is a narrative from the point of view of the author. Gradually, dissatisfaction breaks through into the musical fabric. Or perhaps it is anger. The musical narration comes to an angry and abrupt halt. Two female voices appear, a soprano and a contralto. The two female voices seduce the lyrical hero, lull him. Chopin tries to change the situation in irritation – he tears the musical fabric as though saying, "That's enough, I'm sick of it!" The female voices insistently, sweetly and languidly persuade him of something, promising him delight. They are interrupted by a Polish musical exclamation. This is the author's voice. The first cry is annoyed, the second has the bitter intonation of hopelessness. The female voices start up their magical singing once again. Once again the author rudely "rips up" the music. After all of these ruptures in the musical fabric, the female "powers" assiduously recreate the extraordinary erotic atmosphere of this nocturne. After two unsuccessful attempts by the author to break the entrancing chains, death suddenly enters the nocturne. A sepulchral cold blows through. In the coda the sounds seem to be coming from beneath the ground, and they freeze life.

We can hear the musical signature of death interrupting the progress of the piece. I see this piece as genuinely prophetic.

QR link to the Chopin Nocturnes performed by Andrei Gavrilov

Raisa's secrets

The West made a lot of noise, but didn't do anything. Richter disappeared. Even if he had been to hand, he wouldn't have helped. He was not the right person. I tried to hear something that would make sense on the radio, but the jammers were working at full blast in that wretched December of 1979. The USSR propaganda machine was preparing for a new phase in its confrontation with the whole world. The major invasion of Afghanistan by the Soviet Army was about to begin. It seemed to me that all I could hear over the radio was rumbles about my scandal. I sat at the 18th-century oval table under my dad's beautiful painting of a nude, and hugged the teddy bear I had had since I was a child. I massaged my temples. I asked myself countless questions, and was unable to answer any of them. My brain was fogged with an incomprehensible force that paralysed my willpower. Seppo Heikinheimo found me in this unenviable state when he flew out from Europe to support me. His support consisted of spending an hour chatting to me and then disappearing. Before going he took my picture with an instamatic camera with a flash. Under the painting, with my teddy bear. A week later Nina Lvovna Dorliak told me, "There was an enormous interview with you published in all of the main newspapers and magazines in the West. You are sitting in the photograph with your head tragically clasped in your hands, and a teddy bear on your lap with a nude painting above your head."

The words of my mum's friend did not leave my mind. A denunciation to Brezhnev. Via Galina. From the Kimovs. "Via Galina" meant that the denunciation was not from Kimov, but from Bobrova. Why had my own mother-in-law decided to destroy me? What had I done to her to deserve that? I started to turn over everything in my memory, day by day, taking my time, examining the events of this crazy year from the moment I met the Kimovs. Pictures swam up in my mind's eye.

Here we are in the kitchen, Bobrova is flirting like the widow Solokha in Gogol's *Christmas Eve;* she sings something, shows off her figure, shakes her marble bosom. She shoots smouldering looks at me as though with a crossbow. We are alone. Kimov could be anywhere. Tanya is at school, preparing for her final exams. Bobrova does not love her daughter, practically kicks her around, and she has also never loved her husband. She married the gold medal from the Pitch Competition. Bobrova has talent, she has ambitions that reach up to the moon, but her success has been modest.

Bobrova had just the one love at home – her parrot. He was a strapping great thing, about 40 cm long, with a greenish tinge to his grey feathers, and his name was Styopa.

Styopa spoke, sang, whistled, parodied anyone and everyone, croaked in Brezhnev's voice and imitated the radio. Kimov taught him how to whistle the latest Joe Dassin hits. The parrot whistled even better than Dassin on his own records. In addition to this, Styopa was in love with Raisa like Othello with Desdemona! Bobrova had turned this Pretty Polly into a sex maniac. She was hot stuff! Styopa usually sat in his large cage in the kitchen, where Kimov liked to practise. So now the handsome bird sits in his cage and whistles Dassin's music. Raisa purrs at me in her warm belcanto, something erotic from her repertoire. Then she opens Styopa's cage with her delicate, slender fingers with narrow nails sharpened to points like spades on a playing card. She puts her bare, opalescent shoulder at the door of the cage. Styopa slowly sidles out of the cage onto her shoulder. Raisa pouts her lips in a kiss and starts kissing him on the beak and face. She kisses him like Zemphira kissing the gypsy in Pushkin's poem. Poor Styopa! I can see that the bird is having a hard time! He is sprawled on Raisa's arm, first he yowls like a cat (Miaow-miaow-miaow, Prrrr), then gurgles something like Brezhnev (Comr-h-rades, Hm-hm-hm), then talks like the radio (and now, industrial gymnastics – one-two-one-two). Then he climaxes in his own way, like a bird.

"Raisa, stop it. You'll give the poor bird nightmares!"

But Bobrova sings in her beautiful bosomy voice, "I lo-o-ove another, I di-i-i-ie still loving." She puts Styopa back in his cage and starts sweet-talking me.

"Andrei, my sweet, let me treat you to something. Eat my precious, my golden boy!"

What was she intending to treat me with? Raisa cooked mouth-wateringly well. Meat, soup, canapés with all different types of caviar, and wine running like a river. I had gained fifteen kilograms in a month because of Bobrova's cooking. Sometimes while she was feeding me she would quietly sit down on my lap and start petting me like Styopa. Poor Tanya would go as red as a poppy, not from shame (this family knew no shame), but from jealousy. She would bite her lips, her little eyes would flash and she would leave the room. How could I put up with caresses from this moth-balled Zemphira? I was still green and stupid myself, just like the parrot. Raisa took me with endearments and her acting abilities! I don't know if anyone could have resisted. She was a dangerous woman, Bobrova. She didn't know how to put the brakes on. She was good-looking as well, incredible sexy, talented, physically strong and as cunning as Beriya! Kimov, our famous violinist and student of Oistrakh, had been married when he met Raisa. He loved his wife, and his wife loved him. But Raisa drove him crazy. His wife suddenly took ill, came out in blue blotches and died. I was told this by a very kind lady with an extremely well-known name in the musical world. She told me, and than folded her hands on her breast in prayer and asked me with tears in her eyes, "Andrei, I beg of you, never ever tell anybody what I have told you. I'm sorry for you, and I'm afraid for you; these people are capable of anything. And remember – I have a son!"

Bobrova a poisoner? Lady Macbeth of Mtsensky District? Milady? The lady who told me might have been right. The beautiful smiling face of Rosita-Raisa Bobrova transformed in my imagination into ferocious shark's leer, with three rows of teeth and the bloody shreds of her victims trapped in them. I lived for six months at Raisa's side, and basked in her caresses like a moth-eaten cur. I ate her caviar and never noticed that she was a predatory vamp. The lad was off his head – 23 years old, tremendously busy, practising from dawn to dusk, and here was a beauty, a seductress, with a parrot, all dripping with gold, rivers of wine, a mezzo-soprano, an enchanting voice, Queen Tamara, Amneris, Lyubasha.

I tried to restore more of our acquaintance in my memory. I wound back in time. I was feverishly trying to make sense of it. Suddenly it dawned on me – I had never listened to what she said to me. I had treated her as though she was an ignorant air-head. I just watched to make sure she didn't give Tanya too much of a hard time, and didn't get too brazen. How come I never understood that she was in deadly earnest? That each of her phrases revealed details of her crimes. I thought it was all jokes, irony, the bravado of an unsuccessful prima donna. What an idiot I was! Raisa was actually a great scam artist. Kimov was her flunky with a Stradivarius, and their daughter was a toy that served as a smoke screen. The only decent person in the whole family was the parrot!

All the same, why did she want to destroy me? Why did Bobrova at first draw me in, and then send me off to the block? I can remember that everything was fine up until a certain moment, when a lull set in. Then she bit my head off, the shark. Think, head, remember what Raisa "let slip" to you. She had two conversational modes – "calm" and "hysterical". She spoke calmly when making a pass at me. She had a cool head, a cool soul and only her body was red hot. But when she laughed hysterically, that was when her soul was a-tremble. From fear and ferocity. Yes, yes, yes. I'm an idiot, but Bobrova is a master of disguise. She interspersed her conversations with hysterical laughter so that nobody would think that she was saying anything important. That was where the secret lay. If you're clever you can work it out and join in. If you're a fool you'll let it flow over you. I definitely let these passages flow over me! What had she blustered about that mess at the customs? When she and Kimov had been arrested? She had laughed hysterically at the time, which meant it was important. I hadn't understood.

I remembered. She said that she had tricked the customs officers. It was while we were on our honeymoon in the Caucasus. Raisa was sexually charged to the extreme. Every day she got more and more turned on. The sun, the salty sea air, the emerald green water, freedom, wonderful wine and a whole procession of Caucasian men around our "celebrity" group. One evening, having danced with all the handsome Georgian men, and having pressed herself in her transparent muslin dress against their muscular bodies, Raisa lost her head.

We had drunk far too much in the bar that stood on stilts in Sukhumi Port, kept by the very nice barman, Seryozha. In the dead of night, in the bedroom, Bobrova shared one of her secrets with me in a hysterical whisper. It turned out that the search had been performed because of a tip-off; someone had grassed on them. They had been taking stones and THAT across the border all their lives. They were professional smugglers. Nobody got paid very much in the Soviet Union, but Raisa wanted to live like a queen. It seemed that the informant was already rotting at the bottom of the Moskva River. They both dreamed of a "family trio with Gavrilov". We would haul grand pianos full of diamonds here, there and everywhere!

Here we are, a sultry night in Sukhumi. The violinist is snoring solitarily in the Kimov bedroom. Tanya and I are enjoying ourselves in bed… Raisa can't get to sleep. She crawls into our bedroom, greedily looking over our naked bodies. She grabs me by a place that no mother-in-law should touch. I pretend that I don't notice anything. If Tanya winces at her mother's goings-on Raisa shouts at her, "Shut up you cow, watch how you should caress your husband, you halfwit!" Tanya-the-cow whimpers quietly. She is already going crazy, but she is terrified of her mother and submits to her like a soldier obeying a general. Bobrova is drunk, aroused, babbling and laughing hysterically, "Those bastards found only the small stuff, ha-ha-ha-ha, the most worthless small fry (jewels). I had the biggest ones in my gloves, ha-ha-ha, in the ends of the fingers and the gloves were two sizes too big for me, ha-ha-ha-ha, and I threw them on the floor, ha-ha-ha-ha, as though in a fit of rage and hysterics, ha-ha-ha. They never thought to pick the gloves up! Ba-a-astards! That was where the bags and the stones were."

Stop. Stop. That was it, the key to it all! Stones, bags. Heroine? Cocaine? Of course. Zemphira let it slip in that hot bedroom! But I didn't listen to her then; I just covered myself with a sheet and pushed her hand away, loving Tanya. Bobrova was telling me the most important thing of all at the time; she was drawing me into her gang, trying to win me over me with her criminal boldness.

"Oh, Andrei, you are so seductive. But I saw, I saw, ha-ha-ha."

"What did you see?"

"I saw you and Tanya."

Tanya can't bear it, "Mum, really!"

"You keep out of this, you cow!"

Kimov is in the next-door bedroom, snoring away, and never suspecting that his better half is throwing him over. Or is he used to it? Too scared to make a noise in case he's fed some toadstools or something? One day our famous caterwauler Kozlovsky was talking to me on the steps of the Grand Hall of the conservatoire. He bent his head down and pointed towards his bald pate.

"Can you see any hair?"

"No, there's nothing there."

"Right, that's all from the ladies. You steer clear of them," Kozlovsky let out a guffaw and darted off to a young woman who was impatiently waiting for him a couple of steps higher up the staircase…

Raisa continues, "It makes no difference to me, Andrei; I have a woman, a very good friend, who often helps me, and I help her. This woman is so powerful that she can do anything, and chasing off the Moscow customs is a piece of cake for her. I have her telephone, and she'll do anything I ask her to. Of course I'll also do anything for her. I phoned her then, and we were let out in a flash, and the bastards even apologised for their mistake… They wouldn't let me use the phone for a long time."

The following day Raisa was thoughtful, even sad. I thought she must not have had enough sleep as she was pale and wouldn't look at Tanya and me. We carried on partying, going for walks, swimming, and we spent the evenings in the port under the unremitting care of Seryozha the barman. But something had happened. I can remember my heart tightening, as though I was a lamb being led to the slaughter. Raisa did not try climbing into my trousers again, but she yelled at her daughter constantly, "Shut up, you cow! Shut up, stupid! You keep out of this, feather-brain!"

Tanya wailed, and I was dejected. We hardly spoke on the way back to Moscow. Kimov was unruffled. Raisa bit her lip and often sank into thought about something, saying nothing. She tried not to look at me. I could hardly recognise her. It was then, on the way home, along the Georgian Military Road where the River Terek barely trickles through the dark ravine, that she decided to turn me in. To destroy me. Via Galina Brezhneva. She withdrew into herself, thinking how best to arrange the matter. Possibly she was even sorry for me, or holding her own little requiem in my honour. Farewell, my lover that never was, the leader of the family trio of Gavriloff & Co., the nice young man who turned down the chance of happiness. The man who knew too much... We spent the night at the camp site in Pyatigorsk. Back in Moscow we went our separate ways to our apartments – Tanya and I went to Nikitsky Boulevard, and the Kimovs headed off to their tower on Vosstaniya Square.

How straightforward it all was! It was an old story. Joseph and Potiphar's wife. I lay in my bedroom, on my bed, not stirring. I was pining. Tanya had been taken back to the high-rise.

Ever since September, when we got back from the Caucasus, she had been threatened at the conservatoire, told that she would be thrown out unless she left her husband.

After her operation, Tanya was told that she would never be able to have children. Her lips were dry from the deep anaesthetic as she asked, "How is my darling? How is he feeling?"

Tanya was torn between me and her merciless parents, about whose affairs she had not the slightest suspicion. I felt terribly sorry for her. But I was thinking of the best way to get out of the trap alive. On Natasha Kochuevskaya Street hints were made to me that there was only one way out – to work for them. Then, they said, we will tell you how to behave, how to climb out of the pit. They were bluffing. I had understood everything by then, I held all the threads of this vile story in my hands. What good did it do me?

It was with thoughts of this nature that I set off for Nikolina Gora just before New Year. Slava invited me. I told Richter that I would spend a little time at his dacha, but that I wanted to spend New Year itself with Tanya. I wanted to try and save our relationship. I was drawn towards my wife. Tanya had fixed a "secret date" with me by the house on Vosstaniya Square. At ten o'clock.

Slava was very tactful with me that New Year's Eve. He tried to convince me that I need to be patient and wait. But not wait passively, rather to work as though nothing had happened, to uphold my skills and expand my repertoire. When the long-awaited day of freedom arrived, then I could "show them all". How brilliant we all are at handing out advice when it is not us in pain, when it is not us being pounded!

I was ready to live in the way that Slava advised, but I was worried at the thought of the collaboration that never happened with Herbert Karajan. I had so wanted to work with this brilliant musician, who was at the peak of his fame at the time, and whose influence on the whole musical process in the world could not be overestimated. I felt that his era would soon pass. Indeed, by the time of my "release from Soviet imprisonment", his health was severely compromised. Our plans for Rachmaninoff melted into nothing.

Slava and I were talking away, with our usual enthusiasm, when I suddenly remembered that I had arranged to meet Tanya. I said my goodbyes and stepped on the gas of my Merc, speeding through Moscow as it ground to a halt for its New Year swoon, towards Vosstaniya Square. I drove up to the high rise at about eleven. There was nobody at the agreed meeting place, a snowstorm was raging. Tanya had not waited for me. She knew where I had been today, and had decided that I had forgotten about her "there" with "that man". I ran up and down the pavements around the tenebrous building, looking for my wife. That was how I met the New Year in 1980.

The Hunt

On 24 January 1980, Stanislav Neuhaus died. He died two months before his 53rd birthday. His pupils gathered in the sombre house that used to belong to Pasternak. Stanislav's son, little Garrik, was the subject of general sympathy in his trendy little flared trousers. Neuhaus's beautiful French girlfriend, Brigitte Engerer, was very ill-at-ease. With a scarf knotted over her hair, and her tear-stained face, she immediately looked like a Russian peasant. An orthodox priest, a former musician, started the funeral service. The Jewish professors who had come to the dacha for the funeral all went out into the garden, as though obeying a signal. They stood there with their heads uncovered in the deep snow.

The following day there was a public memorial service in the Grand Hall of the conservatoire. Slava played Debussy's La Terrasse, forgetting the text at certain points. It is difficult to play beside a coffin. Slava was indifferent to other people dying. But he was awkward at the funeral, not really sure how to behave, sometimes making inappropriate jokes and laughing. He made mistakes with the text.

Drunken idiots from the conservatoire were loafing around the Grand Hall with red armbands – they were the funeral attendants. The piano lecturer and head of foreign students, Ivan Olegov, a buffoon, a snitch and a sex maniac, was hardly able to stay upright. That is why funerals are so popular among many Russians, as it is possible to cry and legitimately toss back the vodka in public.

It was said that poor Stanislav's throat had started to bleed and that "everything burst inside". I noticed some dried blood in the corners of his corpse's mouth. Good bye, Stanislav! You left us outrageously early. Generally everything was awful! A Soviet performance of hypocrisy, Richter making his mistakes, informants and inebriation...

In February, foreign visitors started coming to see me – agents from Germany, producers from England. They were checking what state I was in physically. In physical terms I was fine. The first months of not being allowed to travel were not too difficult. You kept thinking that you would wake up in the morning and the nightmare would be over. The brain's defence mechanism. Other people with experience of imprisonment told me that the "most difficult were the second, the seventh and the eleventh years." That was their way of soothing me.

Very few people guessed who was behind the repressions against me, so people still came to see me as they had done before. Sometimes I had fun, but then I would feel terrible at night. My chest was crushed by Mandelstam's "wolfhound of the age".

When despair would come creeping up on me I would climb into my beloved Mercedes, rather than get on a trolleybus up the Arbat, and drive through the empty winter streets of Moscow until I attained total exhaustion.

Tanya would stay with me for a week, and then disappear for two. Instead of coming closer, which had so recently seemed inevitable, we grew still further and further apart. An invisible wall grew up between us. The venerable parents of my wife were falling over themselves to engage Tanya in her learning and get her to establish a career for herself. She was in the first year at the conservatoire at the time, and she needed to win medals at competitions and pass her tests and exams.

Richter was also doing everything to make sure that Tanya "left my heart" as fast as possible. He was dreadfully jealous of her in relation to me. There were some disgusting scenes. I loved both of them (in a different way, of course) and tried to ease the situation as best I could. When I was with Slava I never once mentioned Tanya's name. When talking to Tanya I forgot that Richter even existed. It didn't help much. Both Richter and Tanya could turn into spiteful and jealous quarrelsome shrews at the drop of a hat.

Slava and I went to see a well-known pianist. There was a girl sitting in his apartment. She was pretty, tall, slender. Slava screamed as though he had been bitten by a tarantula, "Is that your Dolly?" That was how I sometimes teased Tanya, because her face was like a doll's.

"No, no, Slava. Dolly is completely different, this is my friend's girlfriend."

He calmed down, relaxed, and we chatted peacefully the whole night through.

Tanya would happen to see me somewhere with Richter. Then she would yell at me at home, "You're hanging out with that old poofter again, aren't you? Aren't you sick of offering him your arse?!"

One of my long-term admirers started coming to see me around that time, a young Japanese girl called Hideko, who was the daughter of a Japanese diplomat. She took private lessons with my mother. Hideko had religiously attended all my concerts in Western Europe, and had been at the Handel evenings with Richter in Tours. Hideko looked like a fragile ivory statue, she was small and delicate and had a fabulous figure.

One day she stayed the night with me, having sat up late at the piano. The next day our local policeman came to see me. I asked him to come back another time, and he did as I requested. Although the next time he brought a document with him.

"Sign here, please!"

I read the sheet of paper.

If Hideko Kobayashi, citizen of Japan, stays beyond midnight on the territory of apartment number whatever, then you, citizen Gavrilov, will be sent to live outside the 101 km exclusion zone, in accordance with resolution number whatever...

It was an outrageous document. I signed it; what else could I do? I had known the local policeman for a long time. He also knew and respected me. That was why it was with regret that he handed over the paper to sign, and took it back as well. His blue eyes expressed sympathy and loyalty. His tightly pursed lips, on the other hand, seemed a manifestation of the age-old excuse of the executioner – an order is an order!

"Andrei, just don't break the rules!" said the policeman rather uncertainly, looking at the floor. I put my hand on his shoulder and reassured him, "I won't. I'm not going to break them."

He left, coughing in a croaky bass and shaking his head mournfully. An animal instinct told me that the hunt was on, and I was the prey.

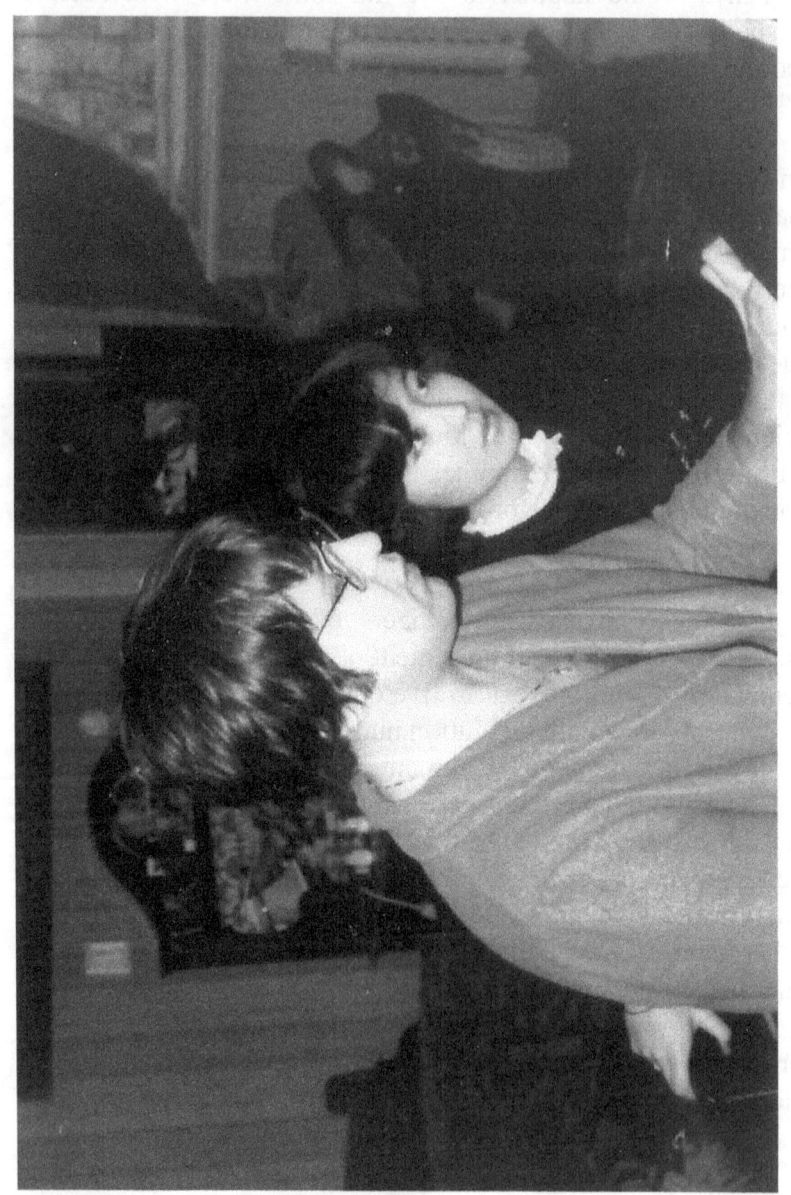

With Hideko Kobayashi (1981)

Divorce

In April 1980 I nearly killed my wife, Tanya.

I drove up to the pavement on Vosstaniya Square, where she usually waited for me. Tanya got into the car. I took one look at her trembling lips and eyes wide with rage, and I realised that there was now going to be a horrendous scene of jealousy. Some sort of spring had broken in her sweet little head. My unhappy, estranged wife was blatantly at the end of her tether. I was sorry for her. But at the same time I could feel that I had also reached the end of my tether, and I was frightened of myself. I tried to control myself.

But Tanya was already like a boat caught in the rapids of a mountain river. She was choking on her own tears and yells. She frenziedly heaped vulgar abuse on me and Slava.

I thought – there it is, the Kimov element, coming out into the open like a dragon from a cage. My little wife's perfect pitch came in useful as she remembered everything and was now squirting it all back at me like sulphuric acid. In a few minutes I stopped understanding what Tanya was shouting, and it seemed to me that her obscenities were tearing at Slava's heart like a pack of wild dogs. I recognised Bobrova's grimace in Tanya's face, distorted with enmity.

"The old woman!" I shouted in my head, in horror, just like the mad hero in Pushkin's *Queen of Spades*. My brain was getting scrambled. Unexpectedly for myself I thumped Tanya on the side of the head. She fell silent and started sliding out of the car, losing consciousness.

Aha, I thought, she's shut up, the bitch! I'll kill her!

With another blow I threw her out of the car onto the pavement, then, beside myself with rage, I reversed my Merc further away and then stepped on the gas. Thank God, the wheels skidded and the car spun on the icy road surface. Tanya managed to crawl to the steps, saving her own and my life. There were little drops of blood left on the snow where she had crawled.

My fit of passion passed as though in slow motion, just like they write in bad detective stories. Somewhere inside my head I heard Slava's thoughtful voice, "Yes, you can kill!" I did an abrupt U-turn right at the steps of the ugly Stalinist entrance. A spurt of snow fanned out from under the Merc's tyres. I raced out onto the Ring Road. By the time I had been round the Garden Ring ten times I calmed down. The image of my poor wife flat out along the entrance steps flickered in front of my eyes for a long time, along with the little drops of blood on the icy Moscow pavement. That's enough! A divorce as soon as possible! The next morning Naumov phoned, "Andrei, what on earth are you doing? Tanya's flat out with concussion!"

I asked him not to meddle in our affairs. At the same time I thought – it's a good thing she isn't in the morgue and I'm not in prison. I filed for divorce, and included a doctor's note on my wife's illness. It was accepted. I asked them to speed it up. They heeded my plea. They named the date. I had not even lived a whole year with my wife! Yet we had been through so much.

My nightmares from December, and generally all the events from the past seemed to be distant matters, long over. Time took on a crazy tempo. I was stuck, it seemed, in the dog house. But the six years of intensive touring, racing around the whole world, now seemed like a sedate Sarabande. Time... I have never understood what it is! Maybe time just goes along, minding its own business, with the Greenwich clock ticking and ticking away, while I am the pianist who has gone bonkers. My internal clock has gone crazy.

I am standing on the appointed day at the Krasnopresnensky registry office. No, I think, she won't come. She appears. But not alone; with the Queen of Spades, with Bobrova! Raisa is dressed elegantly, as ever, but somewhat unobtrusively. Tanya is wearing her long sheepskin coat with the pale fur edging and coloured embroidery, as well as woolly mittens. She never wore gloves, only mittens. I always wanted to put them on a sting and thread them through her sleeves, like a school kid. Tanya seemed poignantly vulnerable just then, caught in Bobrova's claws. Raisa tossed the last stone, "Andrei, don't do this, it won't solve anything!"

You bitch, I thought, what the hell are you doing here, anyway? All this is your fault, you viper. I took Tanya's hand and, without saying a word, I ran up the stairs with her. They told us that we were divorced. Stamp, signatures.

"That's it," whispered Tanya, through trembling lips. I swallowed the lump in my throat and, without looking back, ran to the car, as I didn't want to see her tears.

With Lev Naumov (1980)

I'll f*cking shoot you

Hideko and I decided that there was no point in tugging the tiger by the tail. Hideko stopped coming to see me, although I started going to see her more often on Vavilova Street. We hoped that the bigwigs in charge in the Soviet Union at the time wouldn't dare touch Hideko's family, as they had diplomatic immunity, and that at least there I would be left in peace.

That was how it would have been if I hadn't been hostage to a totalitarian state. You want security for a citizen of the USSR in the family of a foreign diplomat? What absurd optimism!

One icy December evening I approached Hideko's house on Vavilova Street. I drew level with the policeman's hut that stood by the entrance to the gated courtyard. All the "policemen" who worked there knew me by sight, and I knew them. I nodded to them sometimes, and they nodded in response. I knew the one who was on duty today as well, with his gingery moustache and his googly eyes like a crab's. Every time I was astonished by the combination of infinite stupidity and equally boundless aggression that never left his hideous insect face. Usually he kept quiet. But that day he had apparently received different instructions "from above".

He left his bothy and loomed up in front of me, like a living barrier, and shaking with hatred he croaked, "Not allowed!"

"What's not allowed?"

"Not allowed to visit foreigners!"

"What's the matter with you, never seen me before? I've been coming here for the last six months, and that was no problem. Have they decided to turn Moscow into a prison? Do you have any idea who I am?"

The policeman's face distorted with malice. He spoke, spitting and working himself up with his own righteous rage.

"You're Gavrilov, you whore bitch, traitor, I'll f***ing shoot you!"

For the first time in my life I saw the business end of a gun pointed straight at me. The bastard was aiming at my face. There was a glow of triumph on his base, ugly mug, and his whole lopsided form in his vile overcoat tensed and… He did not manage to pull the trigger. With my whole strength I swiped a karate chop at his hand holding the gun. A shot rang out, sounding like an iron giant coughing up phlegm. Something burned my ear.

I ran away. I called Hideko from the nearest phone box. She came out, took me by the arm and laid her head on my shoulder. Shaking with terror, she led me past the booth with the killer inside. The policeman gave no sign of any sort.

During this little skirmish I was cold as ice. In the evening, however, I was shaking with disgust and rage. THEY were prepared to kill me! I decided to wind down my visits to Hideko. It was time to have a serious think about how to live here further.

F minor, Op 55 No 1

The Nocturne in F minor could be given the title, The Lonely Wanderer. *This piece by Chopin is dedicated to a lonely man among other people. Chopin's nocturne is more laconic, abstract and convincing than the well-known Fantasia by Franz Schubert on the same theme. The lonely wanderer. The exile. The dissident. The man ahead of his time.*

The central section of the nocturne consists of musical pictures contemplating Chopin's beloved native land of Poland. The Polish cavalry can be made out in the dotted rhythms. Proud Polish officers. Rebels. Fighters for the liberation from under Russian dominance of a constantly humiliated homeland.

In the reprise, Chopin constructs a dream-like modulation that is complete genius and takes the music out into a light, triumphant mood. The sequential modulation clearly demonstrates the limitations of a tempered harmony. It is clear that this chain of broken chromatic scales should not be constrained by any harmony. Chopin has managed to weave it out of the air and space of the music. If a musician is performing this nocturne and touches the keys with his or her fingers in the right way, and if the right acceleration and mood is identified, then the listener will forget about tonality, about the piano, about themselves, and will drown in delight and admiration.

Poisoned

1979 sprinkled me with diamond rain, and 1980 sent me omens of death.

To avoid despair I set to work. I wanted to engage in something real and convincing. Something infinitely higher than this degrading life of ours. Furthermore, something that would definitely remain when the last Soviet abomination disappeared from the face of the earth. I decided to devote myself seriously to Bach. Bach's harpsichord music is more than a prayer to the Almighty on the instrument. It is more than a Gospel in sound – it is a conversation with the Creator as an equal. I said over and over to myself that Bach is stronger than Brezhnev and his bandits. I shall turn to him. He will help. The only thing that can save a musician is musical labour. That is our doctor, our medicine, our rescuer, our solace and our main reward.

I did not want to start with the most difficult. I decided to learn the concertos. Lucid, wonderful secular music. Immense possibilities, excellent training for the fingers, and a joy for the soul! I learned the Concerto No.7 in G minor within a week. I phoned my friend Sasha Dmitriev, an intelligent and cultivated conductor from St Petersburg, and he immediately included me in his next series of concerts. Sasha was then in charge of Leningrad's second orchestra, and I was ready for my speed-premiere. Two weeks later I drove up in my Mercedes to play in Leningrad, to my beloved Grand Hall of the Philharmonia. I went by car rather than on the Red Arrow sleeper train because of Hideko. As a foreigner, she needed official permission to leave Moscow. It was a shame. The Leningradsky station in those days was a great meeting place. Actors from theatre and film, directors and musicians all flashed past, like on a poster. You would come onto the platform and there would be Petersburg faces, such as Andrei Petrov, Mravinsky with his entourage, and Temirkanov. Moscow faces as well – from the actor Basov with his lovely daughter to Zhenya Svetlanov. Everybody would shake hands and immediately start coming to agreements about concerts or filming

– it was not really a station at all, more a gentlemen's club or a show business agency.

I have always been treated favourably by concert fortunes – there never were, nor are there now, empty seats at my concerts. The announcement goes out and a week later the venue is sold out. We played in Petersburg with gaiety and fire, with the audience tapping their toes in the finale on the dashing sequentias (it is said they are the work of Vivaldi). At the hotel I presented Hideko as my friend from Ulan-Bator. They swallowed the story. It would appear that Big Brother overlooked our trip. There was no provocation or emergency in Leningrad.

The Concerto No. 7 had brought me immense pleasure. It refreshed and invigorated me. I greedily set to work on the remaining six concertos by Bach. It took me two seasons to get them ready. I even collected together a string ensemble from the best musicians in Moscow for the Bach concertos. In the seasons of 1981 and 1982, I gave a set of concerts with the same team in the Grand Hall of the conservatoire and in the Tchaikovsky Hall. We added concertos by Handel to the Bach. The Moscow public was highly appreciative of these concerts. Soviet TV recorded the performances and now they are in the gold reserves of Russian television. A rarity! Almost all my recordings were demagnetised in 1985, and all that is left is material that unknown enthusiasts concealed at their own peril. The KGB even did that – demagnetised musical recordings of musicians who were in some way at fault in the eyes of the state of workers and peasants. In late 1982, the Melodiya record label recorded a double album of all the Bach concertos. It was my first digital recording. The album is still popular today.

In the spring of 1980, Richter and I held a series of joint Handel concerts in the drawing room of the Yusupov mansion. After Zetel's article came out in *Sovetskaya Kultura*, I was suddenly no longer mentioned in the press. It was as though Richter had been playing alone. If I was mentioned, then with contempt, with the desire to humiliate.

"Also taking part in the concert was the pianist, A.G."

I tried to take no notice.

Unexpectedly, Boris Grachevsky phoned me. He was the author of a regular, humorous TV series of short films for children, called *Yeralash*. He offered me a role in one of his little films.

"Andrei, you like and appreciate humour, don't you?"

Well yes, I do like a joke. Boris had thought up a silly story about a barmy Young Pioneer (communist Boy Scout!). This Pioneer runs around arresting everybody. In the final scene he bursts in on a concert given by Gavrilov, straight into the telly, and talks to me as I sit on the stage. He asks me to help him catch a spy. I carry on playing a complex passage of music and shout in irritation at the Pioneer, "They've caught him already, they took him away. Stop making such a fuss!"

I was on my way back home from Mosfilm studios one day. I looked and saw a crowd of people standing by the front door of the flats. There was a dead body beside the steps. My first thought was – is it a coincidence? Or is it a sign for me from THEM? A body by the entrance is their language. Their poetry.

In the autumn of 1980 I had to spend a lot of time at the conservatoire as I needed to finish off all the loose ends that had accumulated over a number of years.

If I was thrown out of the conservatoire, or if I completed successfully, I was still threatened with conscription into the army and deployment in Afghanistan. I understood that such a "clean" method of dealing with me was immensely attractive for Big Brother. I considered the option of post graduate study.

I met with two delightful, kind people in the conservatoire – the head of the department of Marxist-Leninist Philosophy, Konstantinov, and his faithful friend Kiselyov, lecturer in Dialectical Materialism. They were both genuine philosophers, perfectly aware of all the Soviet balderdash, and drank like fish. They both wanted to help me. In their own way – the Marxist way. They proposed my candidacy for elections to the Central Committee of the *Komsomol*! Just as the entire musical world was cheerfully trampling me underfoot, these, seemingly dyed-in-the-wool communists, were embarking on an unequal battle for my life!

The whole affair came to nought. Letters flew from activists to the district and city Party committees. They demanded that

"Gavrilov's disgraceful candidacy" be removed from the election. They got what they wanted. Karpov was elected to the *Komsomol* Central Committee. A few days later I found out their names. They were my old friends, male and female, dating back to our school days. My kind Marxists hid their heads in shame.

Thank God and Bach – I managed to pass all my exams without too much difficulty, and to be accepted for post graduate study. Soon the Minister of Defence signed a decree releasing two winners of the Tchaikovsky Competition from serving in the Red Army – Gavrilov and Pletnev.

In December I was called by a cultivated lady and invited to the KGB club to take part in a closed concert for the senior officers to celebrate their official "KGB Day". She hinted that I might be able to use this invitation to turn my fate around through 180 degrees. I even believed her. Although I already knew by then the main, standard Russian wisdom, "Don't believe, Don't be scared, and Don't ask for anything!"

I remember that first I drove Richter to his Beethoven concert, and then I went straight to the KGB club, a light blue mansion with plaster moulding in the lane just behind the main Lubyanka building. I would imagine that it still belongs to the glorious tribe of executioners of their own people, as it is a very handsome, expensive building. Anyone who wants to can check it out.

There is a buffet, with salad, brandy and caviar. My sweet lady, who is already in very advanced years but with delightful manners, smiles and waves at me in friendly greeting.

Her grey hair has been neatly set, and dyed to look golden blonde. She has powder on her little face, a pretty petite nose, blue eyes, a little beret, a lively and intelligent face, long gloves up to her elbows and a beautiful blue dress with a print of white tea roses – she is a charming society lady!

I play my first programme. Applause. Everybody is happy. I chat to the officials. I am waiting for them to bring me something like a safe conduct paper, and to apologise for all the inconvenience caused. I am ready to forgive them all instantly and kiss the lot of them. These things happen! Nobody presents me with any safe conduct papers. They feed me and pour me brandy, wholeheartedly.

The time comes for me to leave the party. I am on the point of looking at my benefactress – she holds out her little hands, glittering with tiny diamonds, in a helpless gesture and nods her head at me in encouragement, as though saying, "Just have a little patience, your long awaited freedom is not far now." Stool pigeon.

I went home. It was a frosty December evening. It would soon be New Year. I should have been happy, but I wasn't, I felt sick at heart. Once home, my metaphysical sickness materialised as something terrifying and real. I started to feel ill. Very ill. I felt dreadfully nauseous, my chest was being crushed until my ribs felt like they were about to crack, my heart one minute would stop and the next would leap out of my rib cage. I couldn't stand, so I sat down. Then I couldn't sit, and I fell onto the carpet in my room. I was suffocating. I crawled to the door of the balcony. I wanted to open it and breathe. I couldn't.

Huge yellow stars were flashing and going out in my eyes, and it seemed that my blood was boiling and bubbling inside me, like champagne, and my breathing kept stopping. I tipped over on my side and lost consciousness. The last thoughts that flickered through my head were, "Aha, so this is what it's like. It isn't at all scary. It's even nice. I feel so sorry for Mum."

I came to my senses in the night. About three o'clock. I crawled to the telephone and called an ambulance. A melodious girlish voice sang down the receiver, "All right, we're on our way, open the door you Dipso."

Two beautiful saviours turned up in the form of girls in white coats. They were intending to pump the stomach of an alcoholic drowning in his own puke. They looked at my wealthy surroundings, at the paintings, the grand pianos, the gold records on the walls and grew quiet. They reported back to the station that it was a serious case and stayed with me through the night. Svetlana the doctor was a charming brunette, and Vika the nurse was a 19-year old blonde. Vika looked like Marilyn Munroe, only about 100 times prettier. The girls measured my blood pressure. 280/150. They injected me with magnesium.

"What's the matter, pianist, a bit over-tired? Played too much? You need a rest! Otherwise you'll end up playing yourself into an early grave. You mustn't even walk. We'll undress you, put you to bed and take some blood. You should really go to hospital, but we'll treat you here, we'll keep an eye on you, you lie here at home."

The next evening Vika came running to see me and said that my blood was "weird". It was ordinary blood, although it had as much filth in it as a dustbin at a chemical plant – mercury, heavy metals and some other vile chemicals.

I told Vika everything that was on my mind. The sweet girl shook her head and burst into tears. She still came to see me for several years after that.

Scriabin Sonata No. 8

During his depression in late 1980, early 1981, Slava managed to persuade me to learn Scriabin's Sonata No. 8. I had managed to get out of it for three years, but I didn't have it in me to refuse poor, sick Richter.

"Go on, go on, Andrei, otherwise I shall die and never hear the piece the way I should like to hear it, and you can do it!"

I agreed, but was rather down in the mouth about it, as I had no desire to immerse myself in this incredibly complex opus. Slava politely placed the notes on the grand piano in his living room. There was no escape. I started quietly pecking away at the crazy parallel fourths that flew in all directions like a meteor shower. Slava chuckled and "encouraged" me. I would go to the piano, and there would be a half-bottle lying on the music rack, or a cute soft toy.

I learned the wretched sonata and for some reason Slava sat in the bathroom all the while. There was a tiny corridor dividing the bathroom from the living room. He splashed around in the water and provided a commentary, messing around. Several times Slava told me that he had tried to learn Sonata No. 8, but had been unable to. He dreamed of playing it, but was terribly afraid of it, just as he was of the Rachmaninoff Concerto No. 3. He had put aside the Scriabin sonata. But now he was dreadfully curious – would I be able to conquer this musical Fury; would I have the courage to perform it in a large hall?

I chewed away at the text day by day. Richter quacked approvingly from the bathroom. What was he doing in there?

Eventually I played the sonata all the way through. In Slava's living room. Slava listened to the "premiere" from the bathroom. Then he congratulated me on my work.

"I look forward to the premiere in the Grand Hall of the conservatoire!" announced Richter and gave me a sly glance.

I had no objection. I started preparing for the concert. My cognac-mercury poisoning was making itself felt. Sometimes I was overcome with unexpected convulsions, I would feel horribly faint for no apparent reason, and then end with an attack of nerves. Slava kindly parodied my falls and convulsions. Old Slava had a rather peculiar sense of humour.

In May I set out to play my new programme round the cities of the Golden Ring. I arrived in Ivanovo. There was a festival taking place, called something like Red Carnation. Or possibly something even stupider, I can't remember. My concert was such a success that even the reviewers were not sure what to do. In one review it said, "We held our breaths, listening to the concert and not sure who was in front of us, a new Richter or a Cliburn!"

Once again that curly-haired boy was remembered outside the confines of the Moscow Ring Road!

Along the road from Ivanovo to Kostroma I felt that the symptoms from my December poisoning were coming back. My breathing kept stopping, and it seemed that my chest was about to split and my heart to explode. I broke off the concert tour.

My Moscow premieres of the Scriabin Sonata No. 8 were timed for the end of the season. I gave two concerts one straight after the other on 2 June 1981 in the Tchaikovsky Hall and on 3 June in the Grand Hall of the conservatoire.

Richter phoned. As always it was Nina Lvovna who dialled.

"I'm coming, I'm coming to hear the sonata!" said Slava in a cheerful voice.

I asked Nina, "Should I come and pick Slava up in the car?"

"There's no need, Andrei, Slava is getting dressed and he'll walk there."

I waited and waited for Slava, but he never turned up. I even delayed the start of the concert by ten minutes. I asked and asked Zakharov if Richter had come.

So Richter never did make it to the Grand Hall of the conservatoire. He did not want to hear Sonata No. 8 played by someone other than he.

I asked for the lights to be turned out in the hall while I played the sonata. I could feel a terrible tension in the room. Demented ghosts were soaring in the room, summoned from non-being by the "spirit incantations" from the instrument's endlessly repeating guttural groans. The space in the room was filled with demonic forces. Time was choking in the sounds. It kept breaking off and capering with the tempos. The worlds were wavering like cobwebs in the wind.

Hearts were obeying the monstrous pressure of the music and threatening to break out of their rib cages and hop around on the floor like bunny rabbits. A cosmic sensuality seemed to have flooded the hall. The public was moaning.

My chest was aching again after the concert. I decided to go to Alik Slobodyanik's place. I arrived at Yugo-Zapad. I rang the doorbell. Alik's wife, Chizhik, opened the door. Alik was not at home.

"Oh, Andrei, do come in!"

Chizhik bustled about. I sat on a stool in the kitchen. Then one of my fits started. It felt as though the dull thumping inside the crown of my head had made the upper part of my skull break away and float up to the ceiling. Orange stars appeared before my eyes. A moment later the stars burst...

I fell off the stool onto the floor of Alik's kitchen and blacked out. When I came to I saw two distorted male faces looming over me. It was a doctor and paramedic from an ambulance.

"Immediate hospitalization! Blood pressure is 310! The patient is in a critical condition!"

They injected me. I found the strength to refuse hospitalization. They made me sign a document. I signed it with difficulty as I couldn't hold the pen in my hand.

In the morning I opened my eyes and raised my head. The ceiling and window slid off to one side and my throat started a spasm. Retching. My head was spinning. I couldn't get up. Chizhik and Vitya Tretyakov's girlfriend, Natasha, took me away from Alik's place in their enormous American car that was big enough for me to lie down in. The girls dragged me to the car as though I was a wounded soldier on the field of battle. They carried me into the flat on Nikitsky Boulevard in the same way. They put me to bed in the bedroom and went away.

Fira in depression

The Angel from the Philharmonia

Balding, small of stature, with a pleasant rounded face that always showed a radiant, childish smile. Kind light blue eyes. In winter he wore a thick grey woollen overcoat and in summer a shabby raincoat. That was how I remember Volodya Friedman, a saintly man who worked at the Moscow Philharmonia. He would appear when only saints can help – when actors and musicians were running out of money. He gave work to performers. He lent money. Nobody ever repaid the money and he never reminded anyone of their debts.

Volodya tended to "appear unto" musicians on the days leading up to public holidays, or on the holidays themselves. He would arrive in a minibus and invite people out to several concerts at once to provide opportunities for earning a bit of cash. I must have met everyone in Volodya's minibus: Sasha Maslyakov and Larissa Golubkina, Alla Pugacheva and Andrei Mironov, Misha Kazakov and Gennady Khazanov and many, many other artistes in Moscow.

Volodya phoned up on the eve of 7 November (which was of course October Revolution Day).

"Andrei, we're off today to the Central House of Writers, the Hall of Columns, the Central House of Art Workers, to the dacha of Marshall Grechko, the Soviet Army Theatre and we'll finish at the Ministry of Internal Affairs."

Volodya gave us the possibility of earning five or six "wage rates" in one day. To earn 100 or 150 rubles for a few five-minute performances.

We got in the bus and started our "tour". We went to the dacha. There was a glassed-in veranda. The furniture was heavy and imposing, like Sobakevich's furniture in *Dead Souls*. There were guests at the colossal table. The Minister of Defence of the USSR, Marshal Grechko, was presiding in their midst, and he looked at us hostilely through his rectangular glasses. The Marshal was treating his swollen guests to a whole sea of grub, drink and their favourite artistes.

We climbed out of the bus like prostitutes. We awaited our turn. Girls in bikinis twirled hula-hoops and bent in half right in front of the table. They thrust their haunches at the audience, who ate them up with their eyes. Everybody was happy, eating and clapping their hands. Performers generally worked at these dacha shows somewhat lazily, with more freedom; why bother exerting yourself in front of the Sobakevichs? Volodya used to draw up all the contracts and tick all the boxes in the Philharmonic accounting documents.

When the rulers of Soviet culture put me on a no-exit diet and everyone turned away from the disgraced musician, Volodya did not. He offered me work twice as often as usual. His forays and stop-offs became pretty well my only source of income.

As we travelled along in the minibus, the actors told tall tales, while others started affairs. In the Central House of Art Workers some elderly women who used to work in the field of culture were waiting for us. We played a concert. In the Soviet Army Theatre all the military brass had gathered and were craving music; in the Hall of Columns the union workers were bored without art; in the Ministry for Internal Affairs the police officials were exhausted in expectation of their performers. We finished late at night. Volodya conscientiously took us all to our own front doors. He got nothing from these forays himself; he lived on his own tiny salary from the Philharmonia. But he adored his artistes!

When I came back to life, thanks to the Alkhimovs, I started to earn good money, and Volodya started actively to help others. One day Alik Slobodyanik came to see me in my house in Odintsovo and said, "Volodya Friedman is dead. They opened up his flat and there was just one ceiling light, and even that had no lampshade."

To Dyutkovo

Richter stayed in good physical shape by going on long brisk walks. In his time he had walked to Moscow from the shores of the Black Sea. He would stop for the night wherever anyone would let him in, like the seminarists in Gogol's story.

One day, he and I set out for the village of Dyutkovo. The weather was sunny, but not hot. It made for easy walking. We left Richter's dacha in Nikolina Gora, which Richter had been granted, thanks to the tireless efforts of Nina. Slava did not like the dacha, but he was made to go there "to fortify his health". It was a small, weather-beaten rural timber house with comforts and primitive heating. Richter and Dorliak were incapable of arranging even the most basic of home comforts themselves. I never once saw a hammer or a nail in Slava's strong hands. Richter did not feel at ease at the dacha. Everything was too rural. He wanted to get back to Moscow, to his spacious, élite apartment on Bolshaya Bronnaya Street.

Nina provided us with hastily-made sandwiches in polythene bags which we fastened to our belts, and said, "Off you go, boys, take care!"

Why were we going to Dyutkovo? Slava never went anywhere without a reason. He needed an objective – an ancient park, a church, a monastery. Today he had two whole objectives: The Savvino-Strozhevsky Monastery and the Taneyev Museum at the composer's house in Dyutkovo.

Tolstoy and his wife, Sofya, who was in love with Taneyev, used to walk to Dyutkovo to visit him. As we know, Tolstoy's reaction to his wife's feelings for the composer was *The Kreutzer Sonata*, in which Leo took revenge for his outraged honour. He stabbed his wife with a dagger for playing the piano in a four-hand duet with Taneyev-Trukhachevsky. How could one not go to such an exotic place!

We walked towards Zvenigorod. Sometimes we walked along the road, sometimes along paths that followed the narrow, clean Moskva River, and sometimes we stumbled upon men and women relaxing at their dachas in various states of undress. It was my first hike through the countryside around Moscow, and I looked around with curiosity, and enjoyed the walk.

The sun was warm, and we chatted as we walked. There was never any problem finding things to talk about. We prattled away like a little mountain stream. We exchanged jokes as though we were lightly tossing a ball to each other.

We laughed and played the fool. Slava was fond of a daft student game that Slobodyanik and I used to play, where you were not allowed to call the person you were talking to by the same name twice. Richter often spent time with us, as he liked both Alik and me, and he enjoyed our jokes. Slava was not quick off the mark in his speech, but he was very attentive, and he always remembered the amusing names that we called each other. When Alik and I met we would greet each other something like this:

"Hi, Pafnuty!"

"What d'you need, Porfyry?"

"I don't need anything from you, Grigory. How ya doing yourself, Savely?"

"I told you, Callistratus, everything's hunky dory."

"What are you still drivelling on about, Syoma? I wouldn't expect anything else from you, Zinovy, you stupid Vasya, you."

Of course, it was all total nonsense, but Slava would roll around in hysterics. Slobodyanik and I would be talking with very straight faces.

Slava would ask, "Andrei, have you seen Porfyry recently?"

I understood that he meant Alik Slobodyanik, and I would reply, "Yes, only yesterday Sigismund was in marvellous spirits and was groping the piano."

He and I never discussed music in the way musicology experts would. Slava couldn't bear that. Everything that had anything to do with theorising on a musical topic irritated him dreadfully. He could even reject and lose forever someone who started theorising, even if they were a nice, interesting person. I also hate pointless, empty theorising. I believe that it is only possible to talk about music in general terms, expressing and emphasising something important, or overall, that you would like to get across to the person you are talking to. Slava would simply be driven crazy whenever he heard any of the musical terminology that musical seminarists stuff their clever conversations with. One time, we were sitting in Nina's half of the flat. We were being fed in the small dining room that adjoined the studio-living room that divided the two halves of Richter and Dorliak's enormous flat that occupied the whole floor of the élite block. The conversation turned for some reason to Nilovna. Nina started singing her praises. I snorted quietly to myself, put my fork down on my plate with its piece of sausage still on and looked at Slava. Nina seemed to feed Richter exclusively on sausages from the Central Committee supplier, while he so loved variety, poor thing. Slava pulled a hilarious face. His grimace expressed extreme disgust and gentle bewilderment; Richter borrowed his wonderful mimicry from silent movie actors. Nina had been a chamber music singer in the past, and she was in ecstasies about the prima donna's throat. She formulated her awe by saying, "But Slava, what an apparatus!"

She'd have been better off saying nothing of the sort. Slava choked on his sausage and brayed like a donkey (usually he laughed very quietly).

"What, what, what? What sort of apparatus, Nina? Do tell. An apparatus? Is it big? Where is it?"

Nina blushed, turned her back on us, slender as a girl, and with heels tapping on the floor, barely able to contain her own laughter, but not succumbing and not admitting defeat, she went into her bedroom so that we shouldn't see her embarrassment. Every time that Richter was on Nina's territory with me, rather than alone, he would cheer up and become rather frisky. He even dared to tease Nina openly. It was his revenge against the all-powerful "homemaker-browbeater" by the "little boy" who was dependent on her.

Once, Nina was hurrying to the conservatoire and left him a quick note and put it on her half of the dining table, "Boys, fretter in the fridge." We worked all night and hadn't thought about food at all. After midnight we started to feel a little tired. We went to the table. I read the note out loud. We did actually want some red wine with feta cheese to nibble. Slava looked at me and asked, with jovial inquiry, "What do you think, who did she have in mind?"

I spontaneously replied, "Nina Lvovna must have meant F. She's asleep in the fridge, worrying about the freshness of her face and her voice. Nina Lvovna doesn't want us to disturb her."

Slava giggled. Nina Lvovna came home. Slava looked at her innocently, and asked, "What's the matter, Nina, didn't you want us to wake up F?" Nina Lvovna jumped. Slava coldly continued, "You're the one who wrote that she was in the fridge!"

Nina Lvovna gave me a disgusted look.

We strode as far as the monastery hermitage without a rest. We wandered around the Savvino-Storozhevsky Monastery on the Storozhi Hill. The Bolsheviks wrought havoc here after the revolution – they opened up the relics, chased away the monks and stationed a military command in the monastery... When Fira and I went for our walk, there was still a sense of decay reigning over the monastery. We admired the old churches and went on our way.

We turned off towards Dyutkovo. We found ourselves in an age-old forest, went down the hill to a hollow that was hidden from the sun, like a magical fairytale kingdom, and we could see our little village down below. We found the museum. It was a small, wooden house with a padlock on the door.

It was closed! Even so we stood beside the old house, in deep shadow from the enormous trees, and it felt wonderfully good in a Russian sort of way, and we were filled with elation, to the tips of our fingers. Slava kept his head and went to look for the custodian.

He found her and brought her back. She was a forbidding woman, but took pity on us when she found out that we had come on foot from Nikolina Gora specially to visit the museum. She opened the door for us, shaking a bunch of huge keys that were probably left over from Taneyev's day.

It was roomy and fresh inside. There were no real museum exhibits in the house. The walls were hung with photo portraits. With difficulty, we managed to recognised Tolstoy and Taneyev. Pictures cut from magazines had also been put up on the wall. We started to look at them, and the custodian silently followed us. Everyone possible was hung up on the walls. There was Gilels from a double spread in an ancient edition of *Ogonyok*, and there was Gilels again, Vlasenko, Oborin, Zak, Sofronitsky, Cliburn,

Cliburn, Cliburn, it was a whole iconostasis. It was the late 70s outside, but here there were hundreds of Cliburns, who one might think might have been forgotten long since. No, he hadn't been forgotten. The public still loved that sunny American boy. I was suddenly struck, as if by a thunderbolt. There was no picture of Slava! We scoured all the walls – there was no Slava! I looked at Richter. He had gone green. The custodian was looking at us with suspicion and mockery. Slava rapidly lost all interest in the museum. We went outside. The woman called out after us, with a sneer in her voice, "Aren't you going to look at anything else? Shall I lock up?"

Slava smiled his most ghastly smile. If you want to know what kind, look at the famous photograph: Richter presenting the golden medal to Cliburn as winner of the first Tchaikovsky Competition. The corner of his mouth is pulled down, with lips pressed tightly closed and some of his teeth visible in the corner of his mouth. Like a snarling dog. You can delight in this same smile on the cover of the Beethoven Triple Concerto with Karajan, Oistrakh and Rostropovich. At the time, Rostropovich had forced Richter to be in the picture. Richter was furious that they had not rehearsed, they had made a bad recording, and he was also mad at Karajan, who announced that the rehearsal was nonsense, and the main thing was to take a picture.

All the same, these two smiles were nothing compared to the one that Richter sent to the custodian of the Taneyev Museum. He wore it on his face like an important burden for another good half hour, deep in excruciating thoughts. He did not look at me at all. I was guessing to myself what would happen now. We raced off like motorbikes. We wanted to leave this ill-fated museum behind as quickly as possible.

Traitors! They had hung up pictures of everyone except Richter! Gilels, Cliburn, Oborin, Sofronitsky, and VLASENKO! Once Dyutkovo was hidden from view and sank into a hollow, Slava turned his massive head towards me.

"Andrei, what do you think; did she recognise me?"

I had not expected that question.

"Erm-m-m?"

That meant a repeat of the question with intense irritation. I shrugged my shoulders. Had she recognised him or not? She seemed to have done.

"And him!"

Slava looked at me, breathing heavily like a sprinter after the 100 metres.

"That, that curly-haired one, what did he ever do for them?"

I lost my temper. What was the matter with him, was he out of his mind? Did it really matter in the slightest? There was no call to sink quite that low. He could at least have the decency to be embarrassed in front of me. He'd lost face here, like they say in Asia, and lost it so badly that he couldn't even find it the next day.

Yes, Gilels was blow number one, they had tried to squeeze him out, but there he hung. Blow number two was Cliburn. That was a heavy knock down. That was who the public outside the ring road really loved; not who they were told to admire. And this was at the peak of Richter's fame! He had everything, but even so the public loved an American. Blow number three. Slava was not even on the wall! That was a thorough knock out. One last little kick up the backside. The woman either didn't recognise him, or deliberately pretended not to, in order to demonstrate that he was not king everywhere!

So had she recognised him or not?

His face seemed already to have stuck to the TV screen, he was shown so often. I would imagine that Slava will still be waiting for an answer in the afterlife. Did she recognise him? In those years I was often witness to the way in which passers by let poor Slava know that they had recognised him, but didn't like him. That always hurt Slava. Now, though, everybody loves him. Oh, Rus, how you do love the dead!

We arrived back at Nikolina Gora. We did not stay the night but drove back to Moscow, to Bronnaya Street. Slava was gloomy (that's what comes of meeting the public!), and we sat in his entrance hall on his enormous trunk. Slava loved this trunk in the way Winnie the Pooh loves his pots of honey. Two people could easily have slept on top of the trunk, and a further three inside.

We sat and sat, not looking each other in the eye. I got ready to leave. For some reason I just couldn't get my arm into my sleeve. Slava held my coat for me and bitterly commented, "Sofronitsky once held my coat for me. I was very embarrassed, and he noticed and said, "Don't worry about it, put your coat on. Rachmaninoff once helped me put my coat on, young man… How do you like that?" What an idiot, hm-m-m?"

Savvino-Storozhevsky Monastery

Taneyev Museum in Dyutkovo

The Gonzaga Theatre

Slava dreamed of playing our Handel cycle in the Gonzaga Theatre at the Arkhangelskoye Estate. The algorithm for bringing such projects to life was always developed down to the minutest detail by Slava. A project that was dear to his heart was carefully timed to coincide with some Soviet festival or celebration. First of all, Slava would voice his wish to "the right ears", as though in jest. Then Nina would take the reins as she rushed around the various big fish pushing the idea through. Sometimes that was sufficient for the system to kick into action and for the people from the Ministry of Culture or Gosconcert to start bringing Richter's thoughts to life.

"Oh, him and his crazy ideas. Anything to keep him quiet…"

That was exactly how the cultural top brass in the Soviet Union spoke about Richter, with a sigh and the intonation of kind parents. It had taken Slava many years of painstaking work and abasement to become like a baby fed by seven wet-nurses.

After our debut in Tours, and the recording by EMI, Slava wanted to "indulge himself". In his own way he really did love Russia, he adored Moscow Region, and he was fond of Arkhangelskoye. He was perfectly aware that the theatre was one of a kind in the whole world. It had been built by Yusupov especially for a visit by the emperor from designs by, and with the personal involvement of, the Italian interior designer Pietro Gonzaga. A perfect "celebration" was coming up for the project to be tied to, and that was the approaching 1980 Olympic Games in Moscow.

We started to promote the idea. We visited the theatre and then kept going back. We frightened the local administration in Arkhangelskoye. We badgered Moscow bureaucrats as well. Although it was not really possible to play anything there – if you so much as sneezed it would all come tumbling down. The staff at the museum estate demonstrated for us some dusty stage scenery of palaces, classical landscapes and pastorales that had somehow miraculously survived, rolled on a special cylinder, as well as some ingenious broken machines and mechanisms that had been used for special effects in the early 19th century. We were promised time and again that the theatre would be restored "for the Olympics". Richter was in seventh heaven! And I was right up there with him. However, within six months it became apparent that we had been duped. The project had been approved at the highest level, though. So now they proposed, ever so politely, that perhaps we could play in the mansion itself, in the large drawing room that was to the left of the "ceremonial" bedroom. In the palace's so-called Oval Room. Slava, very unwillingly, agreed. He had set up the whole project only because of the enigmatic setting of this theatre of illusions. How many times the bosses had tricked their "baby"!

We were issued with rooms on the first floor of the Yusupov estate. So here we sat, Richter and I, on the windowsill of the Count's chambers, with our legs dangling out the window. We kicked our heels and warmed ourselves in the sun. Slava always turned into a happy child in any comfortable, exotic situation.

Having forgotten all about Gonzaga, Richter ran up and down the marvellous staircases, placed pot plants all around the grand piano and fussed around with his "special" lamp for chamber performances, when the notes are on the instrument's music rack. We always played chamber music with sheet music, as that was how it was done at the time when the music was originally written. Richter considered it in very bad taste to play baroque music off by heart, and he was right! It doesn't look nice, and it destroys the style. The lamp stood on a long, bronze leg and had a yellowish shade. Slava placed it up close to the instrument. I always borrowed this lamp from Slava whenever I played Bach. The lights in the room were turned off, and Richter's lamp, with its wonderful soft light, illuminated the pianist and the music on the piano.

Despite the fact that this was my first travel-ban year, that the area of my liberty had been catastrophically reduced, and that the repressions against me were only intensifying, the hustle and bustle in Arkhangelskoye blew away my misery and even brought me hope that this concert might be a step towards rehabilitation for me. Playing there, in a pair with the USSR's principal pianist, I automatically became part of the cultural programme for the 1980 Olympics!

Of course, no music lovers, and no Olympic guests came to the concert. The audience consisted of Soviet journalists, a few committed musicians who were loyal to the regime, and "music critics" with articles pre-written before the concert for various *Pravda*'s and *Izvestiya*'s; and they had all "sold their souls to the devil three generations ahead", as Mandelstam would have it. The whole rotten top of the administration of the Ministry of Culture was at the concert, headed by Demichev, the minister. At the first concert (of four) I recognised with horror Nilych's deputies sitting in the front row – Kukharsky, Popov, Ivanov and the newly reappointed first deputy, Yuri Barabash. This latter was extraordinarily reminiscent of Voinovich's hero, Captain Milyaga. When reading *Chonkin* I always delighted in his composite characters, the most composite of whom seemed Captain Milyaga – he is a polite sadist with a cute face. Milyaga! What a striking contrast between the bestial cruelty of this man with his "sweet" looks and subtle manners. That could never happen in real life! Oh yes it could. At my very first meeting with Comrade Barabash, my jaw dropped – there was Captain Milyaga sitting opposite me. In all his glory! Good looking, smiley, neat and blond. Wearing a pin-striped suit. Fair hairs up his nose, a handkerchief in the breast pocket of his jacket. He was a sadist who was intoxicated by his own power. Before him the post had been filled by the somewhat crude, but humane, Vladimir Popov. It was he who let me go on my European tour in 1979, not alone, but with my mother.

Barabash, incidentally, even humiliated Popov. He occupied his office, telling Popov that it was going to be redecorated. Barabash summoned me every single week to his office and ordered me off to play in some closed, free concert or other, hinting that this would then open up the path out of disgrace for me. It was all a shoddy lie. He would come to my concerts, sit in the front row to be amused by how I was trying to earn myself a breath of air. He smiled with his loathsome smile, like a corpse.

During the rhythmical parts of the concerts in Count Yusupov's drawing room, these Soviet establishment scum were all tapping their feet and wriggling their leaden backsides on their regency armchairs. Their ugly mugs glowed with the bliss of concentration camp guards. Their whole appearance was giving out approximately the following message:

"We'll do what we like! You play well, and we are tapping our bossy feet, calling out Encore and Bravo. We even rise to our feet at the end to honour you like you're one of the bosses. But let you out of the cordon? No, we're never going to let you out. You're going to sit here until you die. If you start making a fuss, we'll snuff you out!"

Our playing in Arkhangelskoye was inspired. It was our best cycle. I managed to achieve everything that I had thought to. Slava played flamboyantly and without inhibition. After we had finished the cycle, Richter admitted to me for the second time that my Handel sounded better than his. "If in Tours you still had some rough edges, here, here you showed a level beyond which it is difficult to play."

He said that, and then he scowled and sulked. Possibly because the devilish host were rustling their bat-like wings. The sneaks were whispering in his ears. The rumours flew. Richter had lost! With the top brass all watching!

Recently I heard that the Gonzaga Theatre has been restored, and that they are going to open it 30 years after Richter and I had our unsuccessful attempt to draw attention to this little marvel. I hope that Slava is happy, wherever he is, that subsequent generations have put his cherished dream into practice. Much of what is shamelessly being done now in his name was loathsome to Richter when he was alive. He did not like memorial house museums, competitions, celebratory concerts… Slava is not present in any of that.

Slava still remains in comfortable palaces where it is possible to sit on a beautiful window and dangle your legs; he is strolling among Greek statues, but not in a museum – in the watery wastes, in temples and on mountain tops.

Poor Richter! Even after his death he is still hostage to Soviet ambitiousness and to the myths that he created about himself. But he wanted that to happen. "The Lie of Richter's Life" has materialised.

And although he hated everything that the crowd respects and loves, he did everything possible and impossible to become an idol for the grey masses. Richter knew that memory in that quarter was more durable than any other!

The Gonzaga Theatre at the Arkhangelskoye Estate

Audience view of the Gonzaga Theatre Stage

Depression

The three of us were sitting in the flat on Bronnaya Street – Slava, Nina and I. We were discussing recent deaths.

"Were you at Vysotsky's funeral?" I asked Nina.

"Yes. Marina looked dreadful, completely done in! Although there wasn't as much raw suffering on her face as there was at the funeral of Odile Versois in Sainte-Geneviève-des-Bois in June."

How did she manage to get everywhere? She'd even been there! She had noticed that Marina was not grieving as much for the husband she loved as she was for her sister. She had noticed and was relishing the fact. It had never occurred to her that Marina, having buried her young sister just a month before her husband died, had been unable to pause for breath. Marina's soul had died, and she had been turned to wood by grief. Nina could not possibly understand that, she knew no more about real love than the Little Red Hen did. Slava said nothing. He was rolling little balls of bread around the table with his huge fingers, covered in reddish hair, and drumming out something from his repertoire. He would soon fall into his autumn depression. It was time I was thinking about how to pull him back out of it. The year before last there had been the ball. Then Richter went to Europe. You have to work hard there, whether you want to or not. There's no time for depression.

Richter's depressions were only dangerous on the territory of the USSR, where he gave himself up to them with a deranged passion, weeping, slumping into a morbid stupor, and reacting to any attempts to draw him out of his condition with hysterical wailing. He could not even be frightened by the prospect of Nina leaving for Petersburg. He didn't care. Nina knew this so did not use her tried and trusted weapon. She phoned me.

At the time, an article had just come out in *Izvestiya* about our Handel concerts, written by Zetel. It turned out that Richter had played "confessionally", while Gavrilov had first of all set out to play non-confessionally. He had then pricked up his ears, the little rogue, heard how confessionally his senior comrade was playing and looked for the "confessionality" switch in his brain, turned it on and also started to play confessionally, to general delight all round. At the end of the article the author had written that Richter held the "young divinity" in his hands like the Heavenly Hosts.

The young divinity at the time happened to have overindulged in red wine and sausages and weighed about 120 kilogrammes. No easy task for the Heavenly Hosts.

After this article, musicians were prone to greet Slava and me with mocking cries of "confe-e-essionally!" It seems that this ridiculous epithet then took firm hold in the lexicon of music critics, having originated from the light touch of Isaac Zetel.

By the end of October 1980 Slava had descended into a deep depression, as though into a profound coma.

"Andrei, dear, please come round. Slavochka is very poorly!"

I went to Bronnaya Street. I went into Richter's bedroom. It was dark. Thick curtains were pulled tightly shut. Slava was sitting in an armchair, not saying a word. I sat in the chair opposite. We sat like that for about five hours, in silence. I succumbed and dozed. I was woken by a weak, slightly whining voice. Slava was obviously making a tremendous effort to talk. "You were asked to come. You see, Andrei, you need to help me, and also HIM."

Slava gave a queasy smile. "Him" referred to Nina's nephew Vitya, a terrible drunkard. I squirmed nervously on my armchair. I so adored and respected the Maestro that I was incapable of refusing him even when he didn't ask me for anything directly. I now understand that Slava and Nina brazenly exploited my dedication and readiness for self-sacrifice. As well as having to entertain and drag old Richter out of his depression, hard as that may be, and capricious as he was, I also often got lumped with this wretched alcoholic nephew, accompanying him on his wanderings around nocturnal Moscow, and making sure that he didn't get into too big a mess. This was because the nephew did not only foul up and wreak havoc wherever he could, he also used to hide behind Richter when things got unpleasant, and disgrace his name.

Slava moaned and whinged like wind in the chimney, "She won't let you go just like that, you take care. You know how many times I have tried to escape from this hell!? I spent nights at the station, I phoned friends, I begged them to help me. I wanted to leave them for ever and set up on my own. I arranged to meet my friends, and they always brought her. They always betrayed me!"

Having said this, Richter waved his huge hand hopelessly and turned away. I was unconvinced by these complaints of his. How does that work – you want to leave and you can't? You, a Hero of Socialist Labour, winner of so many prizes, earning more from one foreign concert tour, despite the money taken by the Commies, than a Moscow professor could earn in 30 years of teaching, you the Commendatore, the Maestro, are unable to leave this house-keeper-snake with her sponger nephew and set up an independent life?

In actual fact Slava made no real attempt to "leave them", he just imitated rebellion and acted out pseudo-Tolstoyan flights from home. He personally asked the friends who had supposedly betrayed him, to call Nina; so that she would come for him as soon as possible to wipe his nose for him and take him back to Bronnaya Street. I looked at Richter in his depression and thought, for the n-th time, what a huge, powerful man, and what a coward and slave!

But in the direct, masculine meaning of the word, Slava was no coward. He could easily start a fight. Once he had got the better of a huge drunken sailor in a bar. The sailor was harassing women, and had got so wild that he'd started displaying his manhood to them. Everyone was cringing and keeping their heads down. Slava grabbed the sailor by the collar, dragged him out of the bar, and threw him in the gutter. The sailor shook his head around with such vigour that he broke Richter's right thumb, and Slava had to spend virtually a whole year conducting.

Sometimes Slava inspired genuine admiration in me. I saw him as a Shakespearean hero, as Pericles or Plato. I loved that Slava so much it made my chest hurt, and I love him still... But Richter grovelled in front of Nina and in front of the Soviet authorities. He gave himself up, hook, line and sinker, for "creative freedom", while in actual fact he sold out for a bowl of lentil soup...

The more I thought about the mysterious phenomenon of Richter's "metaphysical cowardice", the clearer the connection became for me between freedom and music. Slava's music, despite his technical mastery, was Soviet forced labour, prison music. It lacks the most important – there is no "esprit", the heavenly, feather-light freedom of Chopin or Mozart. There is no humour, no irony and no love. There is no sparkling champagne, no enchantingly intoxicating, noble cognac. What sort of music is it? Richter's music is the music of the convict. A convict with a musical mining pick in his hand. Living in a privileged apartment.

There we sat, still in silence... How long would these performances keep on playing in Richter's theatre here on Bronnaya Street? I was gradually beginning to get fed up of it all. Previously I thought of Richter's suffering as high drama. Now it seemed like a vulgar farce for one actor. One vampire actor whose acting grinds down his audience. Who sucks fresh blood from the obliging people around him and injects into human souls the rot that has accumulated in his own. In order for him to "work" more, with greater ease, to roll his granite musical lumps around the world and crush the worm-like people with them.

"Shall we talk?"

"What about?"

"Let's talk about your number one favourite topic."

Slava smirks half-heartedly.

"Yes, it is topic number one – however much you talk, you always come back to it. Did you become aware of your sexuality early, Andrei?"

"As far back as I can remember it was always girls I wanted to fondle!"

"What about boys?"

"It's difficult to say. We played various games of doctors and nurses, strip-poker type games... Child sexuality is very blurred. But I was aware of desire, as far back as I can remember."

"Aha, me too. Such green sperm."

Richter wiggled the fingers on his right hand as though he had sticky sperm pinched between finger and thumb and grinned, "They say green to mean immature, don't they? Isn't that what they mean?"

"I don't know, probably it's more to do with the first leaves of spring. You probably started early?"

"Yes, very early."

Richter stopped talking, sank into thought, then raised his head with a frown and said, "You know what, Andrei, when I was a boy in Odessa there was a vile old prostitute with no teeth who always used to stand near the Opera Theatre. She wore a sign round her neck that said "I'll give it to anybody!" How disgusting, eh?!"

So it transpires that is what left an impression on you at a delicate age; your imagination was working brilliantly already back then. As impressionable as the devil, you imagined everything. You felt disgust, enough to last your entire life.

Richter continued, "My first strong childhood crush was a man, the actor Vladimir Gaidarov. When I saw him first in a film called *The Tragedy of Love* I was nine years old, and I was completely bowled over. God he was handsome!"

"I've never heard of him."

"The film was shot in Berlin, and they say that the bombing destroyed all the films and of course there are no copies left in Russia either. I would so like to look at him again! I've never, ever seen him since then! I didn't even watch it all the way through that time."

"I'll have a look. I've got a friend who works in film."

"Really?" Slava looked at me beseechingly.

"If there's a copy, we'll find it! See you tomorrow!"

"Ah, is it time for you to go and see HIM?"

"Yes, I've been asked to pop in. To see how they're getting on, how Manya is."

"Oh, she's a pretty woman."

"Not to my taste," I interrupted, and ran off to Nina and Slava's old apartment, also on Bronnaya Street. It was now occupied by Nina's nephew, Vitya, with his latest wife, Manya. Manya had the figure of a broom handle, and the character of a slob, a rather stupid, gossipy woman of no culture. The main pastime of Vitya and Manya was loafing around. Coffee, cards, alcohol and five packs of fags a day. This was what kept them going. Nina paid for this lifestyle out of Slava's pocket. Vitya was the son of her brother, who had died at an early age and had been an actor at the Vakhtangov Theatre. Vitya's mother was an alcoholic and had hooked her son on drink while he was still a teenager. Vitya was the one weakness of Richter's iron lady friend. She was prepared to do anything and everything for him. Her alcoholic nephew trod the boards at various Moscow theatres with roles of "dinner is served," until he was thrown out. Nina would then abase herself in front of another director. Vitya would be taken on and subsequently sacked. At the time Vitya was working with Efros. For Richter, Nina's nephew was a sort of ongoing nightmare from which there was no rescue.

That night I had to spend all night with the bloke, through till morning. Vitya drifted wherever the wind blew him, like a bit of fluff. First of all the wind blew us to the House of Composers. We spent a little time with the vile informer Drogobych... Vitya whispered in my ear, dousing me in alcoholic fumes, "He can help us find out the details, mate! About your case!" I looked at the unpleasant old man, at his fat, stupid young live-in partner and thought that he had to become an informer to avoid being locked up himself. Naturally, Drogobych knew no "details". We dropped in to see Zurab Tsereteli. Vitya was given a couple of bottles of fortified wine there. By morning I fell into bed at home on Nikitsky Boulevard in a state of total exhaustion. My respect and love for Slava, however, stopped me from sending them all to hell. I started looking for Gaidarov. I got the whole of Moscow's film world on the case. They found some Gaidarov! In Belye Stolby!

Slava and I arrived at the famous film archive. They sat us in a screening room. Slava was shaking with impatience as he anticipated an encounter with his first love! The film was nothing special. Gaidarov had smouldering good looks. A moustache, expressive eyes. He was slightly reminiscent of the young Marlon Brando, although in a slightly sugary, Soviet version. Slava was in clover. He remembered every single scene. What a memory! He hadn't forgotten a thing in 55 years.

"Now she's going to lean against the tree."

Sure enough, some woman or other would then lean against a tree in a state of artificial exhaustion.

"Now he's going to jump out with a whip."

Indeed, Gaidarov, future performer of the role of Field Marshal Paulus and recipient of the Stalin Prize, threw a smartly-dressed lady onto the snow from the porch and then chased her down the street cracking his whip and wildly rolling his eyes. Tears of emotion flowed down Slava's cheeks.

A group of people burst into our screening room. They took one look at us and closed the door again. No doubt once they were out in the corridor they tapped their foreheads. Two people sitting in an enormous auditorium. One, an old man in tears. The other, a student geek. Both watching some old rubbish on the screen. We went back home completely satisfied. Slava had finally watched the film of his childhood all the way through. I had kept my promise and dragged Slava out of his dark lair into the light of day.

The following evening we went to Bronnitsy, to look at a church. I didn't like the place – a close friend of mine had lost her mother here in a car accident. A blizzard was blowing. We needed to go along the narrow Staroryazansky Highway, covered in snow. I was afraid that someone might crash into us. We arrived. I parked the car opposite the church. But Slava did not even get out of the car. We went home. A terrible snowstorm! We spent the night dozing in armchairs. Late the following evening we were chatting lazily about different composers. Slava engaged in his favourite game of "grading" geniuses.

"Andrei, what do you think; who gets a straight A?"

He went through his list, "Bach, Mozart, Schubert, Mussorgsky, Debussy."

Nobody else made the grade. I thought it was a strange crowd, although to be honest the "straight A" characters varied from time to time. Mussorgsky was often thrown out of the "top set".

"Well, really, he only ever wrote one and a half operas!" Sometimes Schubert was excluded, occasionally even Mozart! But to my amazement Debussy was unfailingly included among the "straight A" composers.

I asked him about something that was occupying my thoughts at the time: "Slava, how do you think Verdi managed to write his best, and also his only comic opera (Falstaff) after his wife and daughter died?"

"What's so surprising about that? Of course! There was nobody left to bother him and distract him from his work!"

I held my tongue. I still couldn't get used to my friend's extraordinary habit of explaining many of life's anomolies from the perspective of his own personal experiences and feelings...

Slava suddenly said, "Let's go visiting!"

"Visiting who?"

"Mikhail."

That meant Slobodyanik. Fine. Of course it would never occur to Slava that it might not be appropriate, in the middle of the night, to go bothering people no longer in the first flush of youth. We rang Alik's doorbell, and the door was opened by his wife Natasha, known to all as Chizhik. Then Alik came along, with a cigarette in his hand and a grin on his face. Blessed Soviet life! What a joy; Richter had come visiting. Bottles were fetched, sausages were cooked, salads were made. It would appear that Slava's depression had vanished without a trace. But that was a deceptive impression. I could see that he had only made a few steps towards the exit from the black shaft of his depression. There was still plenty of work ahead before he was pulled all the way out and set on a podium in some small provincial town in Germany or France. We sat for a while at Alik's house. Slava grew bored again. I asked quietly, "Where shall we go now?"

"To Verochka's."

That meant to Professor Vera Gornostayeva.

Once Gennady Rozhdestvensky was sitting next to Gornostayeva at a concert. Someone was playing the violin concerto by Sir Edward Elgar. Vera suddenly gave a start and asked, "Gennady, what nationality is Elgar?"

Without batting an eyelid, Rozhdestvensky replied, "Greek."

"No, really?"

"Greek. You know, Vera: El Greco, El Gar, El Registan – they're all Greeks!"

"Oh, of course," said Vera, "Why didn't I work that out myself?"

Once in the car, Slava said, "What's the matter? I like Vera, lots of people laugh at her, but I've always liked her!" It's true that everybody made fun of Vera, as she took herself so seriously. Once she had been reading the "preamble" before one of my concerts on television, and she had called the Ravel concerto "congenius". Nobody had been there to ask her what on earth she was talking about.

We arrived at Vera's house. Dead of night! Everyone was in a flutter at the arrival of the Maestro. That was enough for Slava. The visit was a short one. We went on – delighting or tormenting our hosts in equal measure.

The following day we set out for the countryside, to see an old acquaintance of Slava's. He was not at home! The women in the house would not let us in, and sent us packing. I wanted the earth to swallow me up. Slava was red as a boiled lobster, and flounced out of their house in a rage. He huffed and snarled all the way back to Moscow. However, I understood that Richter had needed this humiliation.

He had been waiting for it, and yearning for it! Humiliation for him was like an invigorating cold shower. Just like the beating! Slava was on the road to recovery!

A few days later the nephew arrived unexpectedly on Bronnaya Street. He went into the dining room in his snow-covered overcoat and Astrakhan peaked cap. Then and there, without even taking off his cap, he started enacting a scene of "vilification of Slava for his maltreatment of Nina." He declaimed in a theatrical, drunken voice. His chief complaint was that "dreadful, selfish Slava was driving poor Ninochka out of her mind by cancelling his concerts and sitting in his precious depression, and that his behaviour would soon drive her into an early grave!"

It was not difficult to see what he was driving at. For three months the money cow had not given a drop of milk. Vitya was shouting that he "would not let that vile scum destroy his aunt." Vitya pronounced the "I will not let" slowly and threateningly, wagging his finger in Slava's face. Vitya's speech was accompanied by wailing sobs. The whole scene was taking place around the dining table. Slava stood at one end of the table, with me beside him, and at the opposite end stood Nina, with her arms crossed mournfully across her chest. Vitya leapt at Slava like a fighting cock, and then leapt off again, terrified by his own daring. Slava stood calmly where he was. He was leaning on the table, making no comment, just clenching and unclenching the muscles of his jaw. He looked at Vitya with quick-tempered menace.

Unable to withhold Slava's gaze, Vitya went for the dénouement. He grabbed a kitchen knife and threw himself at Slava in true theatrical style. In response, Slava leant back slightly and said, "Well, well, come on, come on, the crescendo!" He gave a malicious laugh.

Vitya did not stab Slava with the knife, but burst into a storm of childish tears and threw the knife on the floor, burying his face in Auntie Nina's bosom. Nina embraced Vitya like Jacob embracing Rachel.

"That's enough!" said Slava, "No more!"

Two weeks later Jacob and Rachel (with an antabuse implant sewn into his butt) took Slava to the European border and gave him a kick up the backside. Don't come back without some money! The 1980-1981 depression ended in early March.

Flat on his face on the tarmac

I have never liked Liszt, even as a child. His whole artistic world is anathema to me. Incidentally, his concertos are always performed crudely and forthrightly, without any of the real unforced sparkle, grace and genuine elegance that is present on the stave. Furthermore, performers "traditionally" take outrageous liberties with the tempo. In his best pieces he is, for me, "not fathomless and not cosmic". His music is theatre. It is romantic, intelligent, talented European theatre. Everything is pretence in his work. Everything is toy-like, decorative, moderately scary and moderately beautiful.

Chopin is metaphysical by nature. Even though he may not be the sharpest knife in the drawer, he did not hang out with devils and angels and he never slaved over Dies Irae. He wrote music like a man. Without any pretensions at universal purpose. Yet he succeeded in encompassing everything! Liszt, on the other hand, "publicly" strove towards grandiose themes, to great problems of good and evil and other high-falluting romanticism. But he never really attained the heights.

It would be inappropriate to label Grieg's technique as "cheap". He is original, simple and fresh. Many non-pianist composers display similar problems. Even a good pianist such as Beethoven is guilty sometimes of an almost caricature intensification through use of tremolo, frenetic arpeggios and so forth. This seems to arise through his lack of skill as a pianist, and technique as a composer... despite his volcanic temperament! Liszt was a virtuoso pianist with sophisticated technique as a composer, but he was not greatly gifted at formulating complex musical ideas with simplicity.

Mozart composed a lot of slapdash hack work. Why? Because he had to work on dozens of pieces for different patrons at the same time. Mozart was poor, and he was coerced into creative work at an early age, just like Michael Jackson. If you were to leave only the pure musical gold, then almost half of The Magic

Flute would have to be thrown out, and Requiem would be left with just three or four extraordinary numbers.

Beethoven had a much more serious attitude to his gift, and spent his whole life moving in the same direction, developing one and the same theme. It was only at the end of his life that he found what he was looking for. Of his 32 sonatas I would "leave" the six to eight where he virtually takes flight and leaves the sinful earth behind.

The most misunderstood composers are Mozart and Chopin. They were misunderstood by their contemporaries and by their descendants. It is a big mistake to play Mozart in a tranquil manner. He was a neurotic man, charged with cosmic energy.

Chopin talks with us in his music, and we neither know how, nor wish, to listen to him. We only want to be sweetly stopped in our tracks and moved with emotion… I can clearly hear his "non-verbal words". It is by no means always a lament or a solace. There is the roar of cannons, acidic black sarcasm, whispers and cries, prayers and anguish, groans and joyful laughter, playful flirting and the howl of orgasm…

Before public performances Chopin would warm up until he found the "note of blue", he would improvise for hours. He used a variety of musical means to depict different pictures and states of mind, laughter and tears. He had fun as he played this fascinating game.

***

In all the time I knew him, I only heard Richter swear twice.

We were sitting at my place on Nikitsky Boulevard one night, with me in the armchair and Slava on the windowsill. He was swinging his foot, which always presaged some sort of mischief or monkey business.

That night Yakov Milstein had died suddenly. He had a doctorate in musicology (his dissertation was on *Franz Liszt and his Pianism*), was a professor of piano, a celebrated performer, a most honest musician and a great pedant.

Our first encounter at my exam on the history of pianism ended in concealed enmity between us. The topic of the exam was the subject that Milstein had spent his entire life agonizing over. I pulled out the question card entitled "The principal differences between the études of Liszt and those of Chopin." It was a hackneyed question requiring an equally hackneyed answer. One needed to talk about the different objectives that the composers had posed themselves as they created their études, and so forth. I asked permission to answer without taking time to prepare my response. Professor Milstein smiled with warmth and wisdom and said, "Take your time, young man, the question is not that simple."

I stood my ground and did not leave the table where the question cards lay. There were five professors sitting round the table, who had come to watch my external exams out of curiosity, which is sometimes a positive quality and sometimes anything but.

"Answer, young man!"

I blurted out a gabbled answer, "The main defining difference between the études of Chopin and Liszt is that some of the études were written by Chopin, and the others by Liszt."

A dumb show followed.

"You are taking too many liberties, young man! Come back in a month's time."

I was given a failing mark in my grade book. My grant was stopped!

The marvellous and very intelligent head of this particular subject, the rather deaf Professor Nikolaev looked at me in a strange manner, but said nothing. His eyes could barely be made out behind his thick glasses.

Nikolaev was deaf, and had been deaf for a long time for previous generations of students from the early sixties. Students took advantage of the wonderful professor's shortcoming. By the end, instead of answering during exams and oral tests they started telling completely irrelevant stories. One day Nikolaev had an operation which restored his hearing to an excellent quality. Nobody realized, of course. In an exam, some joker such as Ashkenazy or Krainev started giving him an animated commentary of the recent match between Dynamo and Spartak. Nikolaev listened calmly, thanked him for the fascinating account, and failed him soundly.

That day, after my ill-fated speech about the pianism of Chopin and Liszt, Nikolaev the sweetie-pie was sitting late in his office while I was wandering round the conservatoire, cursing myself for my big mouth and mourning the loss of my student grant. I could see that his door was ajar. There was Nikolaev rummaging around in some papers...

Suddenly his face broke into a radiant smile...

"Come here, Andrei, give me your grade book."

I handed it over. Nikolaev crossed out "fail" and wrote "excellent", and without a word, but still with a smile on his face, handed me back the document. It was the act of a legendary professor that truly characterized the conservatoire! He instilled in me greater respect for the conservatoire than the whole board of honour with all its gold leaf names of the geniuses of Russian music on snow-white marble...

Back to Nikitsky Boulevard.

Yakov Milstein had written admiringly of Richter in the Soviet press and in his methodological books. It could be said that Professor Milstein was a walking encyclopaedia who was devoted to serving Richter, of whom he was very fond, and whom he admired. When Richter prepared a new repertoire that required profound insights, then Yakov Milstein would help him with advice and accounts of all possible editions and revisions, theories and the history of how the themes arose, the musical thoughts of the composer and possible "hidden programmes" – he expounded specialized and exclusive information that could only be known by an authoritative musical theorist. He also accompanied. It would have been impossible to find a more professional and unselfish helper.

That same ill-starred evening, Yakov Milstein was accompanying Richter as usual on a new piece in Richter's repertoire, and was helping him with invaluable advice.

Then he left Richter's house on Bronnaya Street on a cold, frosty night, went home, and dropped down dead somewhere opposite the conservatoire, face down.

Slava was sitting on my windowsill, swinging his great foot backwards and forwards...

He fixed me with his gaze and asked, "Have you already heard about Milstein?"

"Yes," I said, "I heard, it's awful."

"Aha," says Slava, "He snuffed it, the old c*nt, flat on his face on the tarmac. I killed him."

He looked at me with malicious mischief. I was dumbstruck with shock. This also caused undisguised delight for Mr Musician, as though he had just eaten a delicious sweetie.

What did those words mean?

The bravado of a brilliant Maestro? Along the lines of – look how well I played! I make professors drop dead in the snow. He loved to boast about how many people had died at his concerts. He even dragged me into the macabre competition.

Perhaps he and Milstein had some old "Stalinist" scores that were never settled?... Or maybe there was some gay back-story between the colleagues?... Milstein lived with his wife and family and was extremely private about his personal life. Slava hated closet gays of that sort.

Most likely the main factor was how Yakov Milstein regularly made criticisms and recommendations, which Richter never forgave anyone. One day Slava was playing the last Schubert sonata at home, and Milstein said, "Too slow, the music gets lost."

"That means it needs to be EVEN slower," was Slava's harsh reaction.

These strongly-worded rebuffs were a sign of his extreme irritation.

Milstein's reticence, his obsessive pedantry, his tremendous knowledge and even the very fact of his help all matured in Richter's murky mind to furious hatred...

The new carpet

In 1981 Richter often lost his temper. It was the year when much that was inside of him died, when his feelings turned into habits. He was more conscious than ever of the agonizing sense of his own powerlessness before the Soviet machine, whose hostage he had become once he was the cultural symbol of the USSR, a Hero of Socialist Labour and owner of an exclusive apartment with a studio for his work, built by special order of the Politburo.

He was more conscious now, even, of this powerlessness than he had been in Stalin's time, when he was fighting and winning back the right to life. Now, having attained the highest position in the cultural hierarchy of the USSR, he felt imprisoned in a golden cage where there was no potential to develop his still-powerful nature. He had driven himself into the "dead end of the fulfilment of material desires". It was from this time that he started to die as a personality, as a musician and as a man.

I felt like an Untermensch who had been buried alive. I had a travel ban for life on the basis of a decision made by the government in 1979. By 1981 I had taken on the features of a political enemy, subject to annihilation. Slava knew what a threat his friendship with me could be. Someone who simply had a travel ban could just about still be a friend; but it was unbearable to spend time near a political dissident, which was what I had been transformed into by Andropov's punitive machine. Richter tried to stir up the situation by throwing one last stone into the water – he took a personal risk and agreed with East German Gosconcert on a string of joint concerts in various cities across the GDR that had some connection with Handel or Bach. It was a well-thought out step. The GDR was loyal to the USSR. Gosconcert in the GDR was headed by a certain Frau Gonda, and was the central point of informers and spies of Moscow. Even so, the leaders of the communist USSR took a long time to reply.

The time was drawing near for the tour "organised by Richter". There was about one week left before the first concert, and I was rather dispiritedly practising. I really didn't want to perform, even if a positive ruling was made about my leaving the country. Richter was in West Germany at the time, storming away as best he could. He was using his own private channels. This was Slava's last stand. Nobody took the slightest notice of him. Then Nina Dorliak joined in the process. She set off for the only address that would work – to see Comrade Suslov. Going to Andropov or Brezhnev was pointless, as it was they who were my persecutors. It really did make sense to approach an influential communist ideologist who might be able to convince his comrades of the total safety of the undertaking and the usefulness of calming down "our comrade" Richter. Nina came back from Suslov with an answer in the affirmative. She let out a deep sigh as she lowered herself onto the chair in the entrance hall, and announced to me in a categorical tone, "I told Slavochka that this is absolutely the last time!"

She made it blatantly clear to Slava that if he started to grumble she would immediately pack her bags and leave for her relatives in St Petersburg. Nina did not like to make jokes. Richter understood that without her he would turn into a derelict tramp. Dorliak wielded total power over Slava, and she held the reins in controlling his life. She was in charge of everything: his travel plans, his tours, his well-being and health. Without Dorliak, Richter turned into the little boy Slava who was granted a Moscow resident permit some time in the distant past.

Over the many years of living with his iron lady, Richter had attempted on several occasions to stand up for something of his own that did not match the line taken by his unsentimental common-law wife. Every time, however, he had capitulated unreservedly. Richter recognised that all the material well-being he had was due to the tireless efforts and immense political talents of his partner. Any argument with Dorliak would have taken from him the main thing for which all these dreadful sacrifices were made – the possibility of making music without being distracted or worried by the need to earn a daily crust. Dorliak defended Richter from external irritants, much like the concrete sarcophagus over Chernobyl. That was the whole meaning of their alliance. Wrecking that would have meant self-destruction for Richter. But living in her vice-like grip was a torment from Hades for the unhappy Mephisto. It was the classic situation of an artist who had established the ideal conditions for his creative work, but had lost himself.

After the positive ruling from "the comrades at the Politburo and personally, Mikhail Suslov", I was bundled onto a plane with my minder and his bottle-glass spectacles; his bleached eyes fixedly followed my every movement. He appeared bleached all over, somewhat crumpled and mucky. We arrived in Halle, where Handel was born, Luther was baptised and where, for some reason, an old bronze statue stands outside the church where Handel was christened with the inscription "From the Grateful English." We spent the night in the hotel. The following day Richter was due to arrive, having finished his tour in Western Europe and travelling, as always, by car. I went down to the hotel foyer at the appointed hour, with my minder following along behind in his crumpled, dirty suit, his bottle-glass specs and his ugly moonish face. The door banged open and Slava walked in – large, loud and lively (he was different in public in the Soviet Union). He was dressed in his favourite uniform – a dark blue blazer with gold buttons and grey trousers. We embraced under the wary gaze of my freak and several of his GDR clones, including Frau Gonda, who was accompanying the Maestro. Slava grew uneasy, and, while still playing the role of hail-fellow-well-met, he threw a glance at the photograph on the poster for the hotel sauna which showed a blonde German girl of quite voluptuous proportions lolling ecstatically in the bath, and asked in German, "Goodness, are we still in the FRG?" The GDR minders responded with putrid, servile laughs. I understood Slava's hidden meaning – Richter found the whole situation pathetic and vile, and was resorting to giving vent to political sarcasm. It was unheard of! It must be remembered that one of the principal features of Maestro Richter's official image was his generally recognised apoliticism, like a Holy Fool. He pretended that he did not know what the Central Committee of the Communist Party was, or the Politburo or KGB, and that he had no concept of the difference between East and West. His joke about the naked German lass on the picture was a manifestation of the secret rage that he was unable, or no longer wished, to conceal.

This concert tour of ours was sad and ridiculous. We both knew that it was our last. Our heated discussions about art, history, literature, sex and God knows what else were mere subterfuges intended to distract us from the subject that was really troubling us. We did not want to talk about the end of Slava's life on the big circuit. We did not want to talk about my position. Slava held himself together better than I did, concentrating on the concerts and studying documents and artifacts from the time of Bach and Handel. I was only occasionally distracted from my lugubrious thoughts, often smiling for no reason or shaking my head inopportunely. The vile snoop left us alone only if Richter slammed the door in his face. We secluded ourselves in Slava's room so that we could have at least a small chat without the all-seeing bleached eye and all-hearing ear of our Soviet Big Brother.

We arrived in Berlin. Here also, our playing was bad and lacklustre. Slava's unnatural animation, which ran counter to reality, was oppressive in its helplessness. Berlin's Apollo Hall had just undergone restoration and the floor was covered with new carpeting.

Slava and I were backstage before our entrance. The hall had fallen silent. Suddenly something absolutely appalling happened – a revolting little man in a cheap grey suit, with a lisp and a pushy manner grabbed Slava by his lapels and muttered something in his ear. If anything like that had happened in the USSR, our Hero of Socialist Labour would have refused to give any concerts for a year, or would have fallen into a never-ending deep depression, just to spite everyone. I could hear the horrible little man whispering and spraying spittle everywhere.

"I am the cultural advither at the Thoviet Embathy, and my name ith Thukath-ty, delighted to make your acquaintanth."

Slava was shaking with rage, but obediently listened to the end of the tirade. What a monstrous humiliation! Slava did not sock Mr Zhukasty in the teeth, however. Instead, with the Soviet habit of many years, he tucked his tail between his legs…

Zhukasty made his way into the concert hall…

Richter was vigorously shaking the hand that the cultural adviser had been holding as though he was trying to flick off any trace of the touch. A shudder of disgust coursed through his whole body. We finally went out on stage. I was playing first. Slava was turning the pages for me. A penetrating and unpleasant smell from the new carpet floated up to us.

We took our seats, and Slava placed the music on the rack. I noticed a dangerous glint in his eyes, the white horses on the waves that preceded a volcanic explosion of long-suppressed rage. I started my suite. Slava leaned over towards my ear as he turned over the first page and whispered, "Do you know what that carpet smells of?"

I carried on playing, but sent a quizzical glance in his direction. At which point Slava pronounced loudly and clearly, "An unwashed pr*ck!"

Titan

Richter executed some of Schubert's pieces very well. This was because Richter was consumed with melancholy. He was wracked by sorrow. His whole life he thought about leaving, about parting with the earth and its delights. He did not believe in immortality in any guise. He tearfully bade farewell to the land of the living because he would no longer be in it, he, the genius Slava Richter. His great strong body and his music would no longer be there. Herein lay the key to his Schubert. In his music Slava found a form for his own anguish. He played it superbly. But where Schubert demands warmth, humanity, sacrifice and love, Richter-the-executant hacked and thrashed at the keys... It was only his natural bouncy effervescence that got him through the music...

***

Although I was close friends with Richter for five years I know little of the intimate side of his life.

Slava had a very exulted attitude towards sex, and lived only with male semi-prostitutes or with strange, flighty men from the artistic set in the West; I could not understand where they were on the spectrum – bisexual or not, gay or straight. Half-crazy extremist girlfriends were for ever interfering between him and his long-term sweetheart, an actor who was gay one minute and straight the next – a product of the vile Euro-arty scene. Slava showed me photographs of him, which he kept at home on Bronnaya Street. He was a good-looking, athletically built young man. No muscle-bound Hercules, more like Apollo with soft, perfect contours.

Of course Slava was permanently surrounded by a buzzing crowd of "boy-fans" of various ages who were ready to gratify him in any way possible. They were all aiming to get stuck in. But Slava was looking for love, not sex. There were only a few steady, long-standing liaisons in his nomadic lifestyle, just two or three in his whole life.

According to Slava, he was not a woman-hating member of the gay community.

"No, Andrei, quite the contrary, I like women very much, their quintessential being, and their bodies, but I give preference to male relationships."

I remember that not long before we parted forever, Slava and I went to the Pergamon Museum in Berlin. He asked me to close my eyes, and he led me by the arm to a spot from which the Ishtar Gate and the Processional Way can be seen simultaneously. I opened my eyes and was flabbergasted. Slava did everything like a real stage director, not letting the impression be blurred. He showed me the perspective of the extraordinary Processional Way, and then turned me abruptly round by the shoulders and astonished me with the deep purple Ishtar Gate, which the Greeks called the Gate of Semiramis.

The tall walls of the gate were covered in stunning blue glaze. I imagined the heady nights of Babylon being this sensual, sparkling and shimmering as they covered the orgiastic mysteries dedicated to Ishtar, the Luciferian Astarte. Mythological beasts stood out against the blue tiles in monumental relief: the lions of Ishtar, the sirrush dragons of the supreme deity Marduk, and the auroch bulls of Adad, the powerful storm god. I remember that I was bowled over by the aggressively raised tails of the sirrushes, and the snarling fanged maws of the almost-white lions. In ancient Babylon a gigantic stepped Ziggurat rose behind the Ishtar Gate, the Tower of Babel.

At that moment, standing beside the silent Slava in the museum, I understood another vital aspect of Richter, possibly the most crucial – I saw him as a lion, a dragon, a bull, a tower and a Ziggurat. He should have lived in the astounding world of Babylon, at the side of King Nebuchadnezzar, not in Brezhnev's Moscow. After that we went to look at the Pergamon Altar. The Greek marble sculptures seemed pale after the colourful extravagance of the monumental Babylonians! How fascinating it would be to catch just a glimpse of them in their original, brightly-painted form. Slava retreated into his inner world for a while. He was contemplating the male figures of the battling gods and Titans, unsurpassed in expressive power. I also started to admire the frieze, without really intending to. I found the torso of a giant on the wall against the staircase, with his back turned to the viewer. The amazing power of the sculpted muscles, the slim hips and curved, firm buttocks all testified to the mastery of the sculptor, and emanated the particular tragic strength of the Hellenic period, which was in some way similar to our own rotten era...

"Nice butt, isn't it?" Said Slava, noticing how impressed I was and deliberately lowering the tone of the conversation so as not to spoil the beauty with meaningless words.

I thought again, as I had so many times before, that his rightful place was not at the piano in the Palace of Congresses, but there, in the ancient world of myths, among the Titans and the gods. He was entranced by the beauty, strength and brutal cruelty of antiquity. He was fond of telling me exactly how the gods had killed the Titans with the help of Dionysus and Hercules.

How they had pierced them with poisoned arrows, battered them with thunderbolts, perforated them with red-hot iron and flayed them.

Was this fascination with cruelty the secret of his sexuality, or was it the whimsical caprice of a genius who was bored and tormented in his own "chicken" Soviet existence, scorning our "bland civilization without any balls", where he saw himself as a "helpless rabbit", and where he was forced to play the role of the saintly pianist, the Holy Fool and Hero of Socialist Labour?

Sometimes Richter exploded, as though solar flares of mad rage were flying out of him, seemingly without justification. However, there was justification – for him, the powerful ancient Titan, robust and endowed with an inner core as tough as a sword, the man who should have been fighting in the Colosseum with other gladiators such as he, or sitting on the tribune as an emperor, for him it was sickening to play a "soppy Soviet dishrag" in real life.

He wanted to be loved for being the spiritual gladiator that he was. It would appear that he never found a worthy sexual and spiritual life partner. It is possible that he looked for such a partner in me, but I loved my pretty women.

By the end of his life Richter sunk to a low level, hiring rent boys in the Soviet Union at "three rubles a go."

It's such a terrible waste. He came at the wrong time. He was two thousand years too late for his own era, or goodness only knows how early.

Several journalists used to throw the question straight at me (seemingly expecting that I would blush and that they could then write it up in their gutter newspapers): "Were you Svyatoslav Richter's lover?"

I answer once again that no, I never was. There was never any sex in our relationship, although we were so sexually "charged" that it infected those around us. One particularly impertinent interviewer (from some far-right Italian paper) asked me if Richter ever came on to me, if he didn't ever want at least some *"sesso orale"*. In justifying himself this particular man noted that the kiss between Richter and Gavrilov had seemed too intimate when parting after the joint Handel concert in France.

Richter never came on to me, in the way that some petty, active gays do. Slava was a proud man. He hoped until the last day of our friendship that I myself would attain "supreme wisdom" (his words). He used to say in a patronizing, prophetic voice, "I am convinced that after the age of forty you will become homosexual!"

He waited for that to happen with poorly-disguised impatience. There was no "excessive intimacy" in our farewell kiss; we were both having a laugh. Richter loved pretending to be someone he wasn't and never intended to be. Acting and a desire to fool around, bordering on the disruptive, were integral features of his personality. Of course, most of all he made a fool of the Soviet public. Sometimes he would he so furious that he openly mocked them.

He would throw back flowers that were presented to him at concerts, especially if he did not like them or if they were wrapped in cellophane. The poor women and men, who had no idea what was going on, shrank away from him in horror. Richter would escape from his concerts via the back door while the inflamed public were yearning for encores. He would refuse to play any, just to spite them. He broke off concerts for no reason and told nobody.

He would hide while the audience waited for him in the hall, and he would be sitting at home with me, drinking tea and red wine with no agonies of conscience whatsoever.

Slava loved making fools of the French. He might start leaping around the stage like a mountain goat, or walking like a ballet dancer, wiggling his butt, or he might, as at that time in France with me, mimic glamorous intimate relations which never existed at all. The French public were easily taken in by clownish tricks of this sort...

About 15 years before he died, Richter suddenly "caved in".

He stopped caring. Then, in his calculating, German, resolute manner, he stopped having anything to do with sex, in order to leave more time and energy for the piano.

"You know, Andrei, I have so little time left, and I don't want to waste strength and energy on all that nonsense any more. Well, yes, that's it, Schluss, I've had enough!"

Immediately, that very month, he started playing less well. He never made it back up to his former level. Although he did renew his sexual life several times after that, it was somehow artificial and lacking in inspiration...

A right one

Least often of all in our long conversations Slava and I spoke on religious themes.

I was christened at the age of six. In our family it was only my mother who was a believer. She was prone to premonitions that, strange as it may seem, actually came true. Sometimes I was drawn towards the church, and sometimes I turned away from it. The existence of a concert pianist is that of the high life. We are like sportsmen, or call girls, with no time for religion. The profession itself is all consuming, as is the company we keep. Although, of course, in our business there are extremely religious people, they are often comical and slightly deranged.

When I started going out with an extremely religious girl I started to detest religion. She would exhaust herself fasting, faint with hunger, go running around with candles the night before any religious festival, and she would pay for notes "for health" of her friends and "for repose of the dead" to be read out by the priest.

She went to confession, took communion, asked advice from the "holy father" about intimate matters. She would wear a scarf to cover her hair and be terribly serious, religiously instruct me, kiss the icons, weep with genuine emotion before reliquaries filled with ancient bones, and generally emanate fanaticism. But I loved her as the healthy, cheerful and sceptically inclined girl that she really was if it hadn't been for all the priests, the fasting and that rubbish before Easter and Christmas.

Slava and I both loved Russian churches. Slava knew many of the famous Russian monasteries and churches. We would go in to Nikolsky Cathedral on Komsomolsky Prospect in winter, both huge in our fur coats. Slava would cross himself like a bear, which we would both find hilarious. We liked to listen to music at Whitsun. Two choirs calling to each other. It was beautiful and exhilaratingly daring. On that one day our lugubrious, Byzantine church was all covered in green leaves and living shoots. At other times it was always dark and sad. Only once did Slava speak openly on divine topics. He spoke at relative length, which was not typical for him. We had got onto the subject of poetry. Slava said, "You know, Andrei, I don't understand poetry at all, I just do not understand it! Only Pushkin, with him it is all easy to understand, pure genius! But all the others, no, I can't understand them, and I don't need them!"

"But music is so closely connected to poetry!"

"I don't know, I think that music has most in common with theatre. Almost every work of music is a little like theatre, and every performance by a musician is all the more so."

"What about religion, all that messianism, eschatology, our dear Scriabin, Pyotr Ilyich?"

"Oh yes, Tchaikovsky..."

At this point Slava quoted his couplet about Tchaikovsky:

>The valet was Tchaikovsky's lover
>But he kept it under cover.

He really loved deliberately stupid couplets. He would often declaim his particular favourite gems to me:

>Pavlov was so very cruel
>He shocked his dogs and made them drool.

>Malyavin spreads his paints so thick
>The canvas looks just like a brick.

Some of Richter's absurd couplets had a slightly more political edge to them, despite his public image of a man who noticed nothing but music.

>Hitler, Goerring, Goebbels, Hess
>Do not deserve a Catholic mass.

>Sholokhov claims *The Quiet Don*
>Don't believe him, it's a great big con!

There was one about Ashkenazy's continuing absence from the Soviet Union.

> Where's Vladimir been so long?
> He wasn't here and he's gone!

Once Richter was trying to spawn a ridiculous couplet about the non-Jewishness of Tarkovsky and had composed the first line:

> If Tarkovsky was a Jew...

He couldn't get any further. I helped him:

> He wouldn't be Andrei I tell you!

"That's it!" exclaimed Slava, and thereafter often repeated this particular couplet where appropriate and where not.

"Scriabin, well yes, there is more of all that there, like in your sonata, with all those various ladies with cigarettes."

Slava did a comic impersonation of "neurotic erotic ladies" smoking "dangerous" cigarettes. After my concert in Tours, Slava always referred to the Scriabin Sonata No. 4 as "your" sonata. Personally, I could see no ladies with cigarettes in Sonata No. 4. I always imagined brightly resonant dancing bells smoothly stealing away from me with each bar, filling an enormous space as the music progresses, and enlivening a dark blue cosmos with their exchanges of chiming rings. At the start of the sonata I imagined golden stars falling in a sort of "erotic exhaustion". As the music increased to a crazy pace they filled the rhapsodic, effervescent, brilliant-blue cosmos with golden solar flares, and an ecstatic boiling foam in the finale.

"Yudina was religious, and it comes through in her music, it makes her convincing even if she does play everything topsy turvy"

"Well, Yudina was a right one."

Slava loved this expression, and often used it about people whom he viewed as hopeless idiots, of which there were many in the musical world. A right one.

He frowned rather distastefully and continued with his German accent that came and went.

"Religion, God... Come off it. What is it all about? I have so many times wanted to believe, and I could believe, passionately! But how is it possible to believe with no proof at all? No signs of any sort! How many times have I prayed feverishly, begging for contact! Give me a sign, call like a cuckoo seven times, knock on the ceiling or the wall, give a roar of thunder right now when I ask you! Never! Hot once! One tiny little proof and I would have believed beyond the wildest dreams of any zealot!

But how is it possible to believe when he is forever silent?! Whether you believe or not, he still says nothing! Well, I dismissed the whole thing out of hand. If it's a no, it's a no! Who to believe in when there isn't anybody there? At least the devil is discernible, in actions and in evil deeds. In that case I'm in favour of the devil."

As I left his house and walked home on that frosty evening I went via the Nikitsky Gate. A light snow was drifting down from the blue-black heavens. It was pure Scriabin. It was so divine that no answers were needed. There it was, the main answer – to breathe, walk, look, love and play the piano. What happiness! Heaven on earth. How could Richter, who had spent his whole life among God's answers; among Chopin, Ravel, Haydn and Rachmaninoff, how could he fail to see the answers, to understand the signs? What was it that he really wanted? That the Lord should cuckoo like a cuckoo, or bark like a dog in the circus? Specially, by order of Richter, Stalin Prize laureate! But it never happened, so he went into a sulk.

For some reason I particularly loved him when I was convinced of what an utter nincompoop he was. A right one!

Astronaut

Dostoevsky. Pick up the Karamazov's, open the Legend of the Grand Inquisitor. You'll sink into a reverie lasting a hundred years...

Dostoevsky's language is deliberately clumsy and uneven, not fluid like Tolstoy, and not pretty and elegant like Turgenev. This is because Dostoevsky does not describe reality, he creates it, he leads his reader into it and helps attain an ecstatic, crazy, borderline state. In order to achieve this, the reader must be shaken up on a road of verbal potholes...

In this state the reader is liberated from the eyes of ordinary life, from rational motivations. The reader and author together find themselves in the "epileptic" space of inspiration, the discovery of a new evangelist – Dostoevsky... The unearthly, inhuman features and laws of this world allow the reader to experience at first hand, to sense with a spiritual body, the pain of the victim and the salacity of the sadist, the horror of the murderer and the bitter grief of the righteous man who proves his guilt; to be at once the devil and God and nailed to the cross and the Eternal Jew and a monk and a petty bourgeois and a "holy prostitute" and a Holy Fool. It is a shame that so few know how to read him...

***

Usually I did not change the tyres on my Mercedes. This was because I had special all-season rubber. In January 1982 there was so much snow in Moscow that I did have to change my tyres after all. I went to the well-known garage No. 7 at the end of Prospect Mira. The garage served the diplomatic corps and the whole of Moscow's élite who drove proudly round in imported cars, and was as full of KGB as a worm-eaten mushroom is full of maggots.

German specialists would regularly consult with the pampered mechanics from this particular garage. They were masters of their art and ripped off their clients with tariffs that were far beyond the prices asked in Stuttgart, home of the Mercedes plant. I was fortunate in that I was friends with Pasha Ivanov who worked in the warehouse at this élite garage. Pasha's story was a tragic one. His girlfriend had run a man over, and Pasha had taken the blame on himself, claiming that he had been at the wheel. He was prosecuted. Pasha spent a long time behind bars and when he was released his girlfriend had vanished into thin air. I also knew several ethnic Germans who worked at the garage. They were good, reliable people. They had been waiting for years for permission from the Soviet authorities to leave for West Germany. We understood each other perfectly, both Pasha and the Germans; my Mercedes was always in good running order, and trips to the garage were always an enjoyable way to pass the time.

I arrived at the garage and immediately remembered Vladimir Vysotsky whom I often used to meet here before – very well-toned and strong in tight jeans and boots on a heel, wearing his short leather jacket. Despite not being very tall, Vysotsky always stood out in the crowd. He was forever surrounded by mechanics who were fans of his, and the notorious garage extortionist jackals. I always felt sorry for Vladimir because they constantly and barefacedly fleeced him at the garage. Vladimir's pride, his light green Mercedes that Marina had bought, stood dejectedly beside its owner, who was always bashing it against other cars or the various obstacles waiting to ambush the unwary driver in Moscow's mean streets.

In order to have my wheels changed there was no need for me to bother my friends. I gave my car to the first garage mechanic I met and went to have a chat with Pasha. In half an hour I got my car back, fully equipped with heavy winter wheels, and I raced off towards Prospect Mira. Unfeasibly huge snowflakes were falling from the sky, like in the duel scene from *Eugene Onegin* in the Bolshoy Theatre's production, and I went into a slight daydream, admiring the blizzard, and missed my turning, finding myself already on the overpass. I swung off onto Rizhskaya over the railway tracks, put my foot down hard on the gas and suddenly took flight…

It was like those American cartoons. The hero flies high up above the ground, then looks down into the abyss with stupid eyes round with shock as it dawns on him what is happening. I'm flying along, coasting when I see about fifty metres above me an unidentified flying object floating majestically by, somehow painfully familiar.

Then another one. It takes me a while to realize that they are my wheels spinning off into orbit. The shock was so great that I am still unable to say with any certainty whether or not my car did a somersault in the air. I flew high and, as it seemed at the time, for a considerable time. Fortunately I had quite a soft landing, on all fours. I felt myself over, I seemed to be alive. I climbed out. I looked at my Merc. The car was standing on four discs; there were no wheels. People who had witnessed my flight started coming over towards me.

"Are you alive? You were f*cking flying! Like an astronaut!"

People were laughing. I also burst out laughing. Everyone was alive, I hadn't hit anyone, and even the Merc seemed unharmed. They helped me find my wheels, which had flown off in different directions. Two wheels were lying on the other side of the road, in the path of oncoming traffic, another was on the railway tracks, with the last one not far from me. I called Pasha from the nearest phone box, and asked him to come urgently. In twenty minutes Pasha was at my side. He chased away the rubberneckers, and then looked at the wheels and the discs. He turned white as a sheet, looked at me reprovingly and said, "Andrei, all of your spikes have been sawn through! Are we going to call the cops?"

"No, they'll just saw through everything else, shoot us and say that was how they found it!"

"Spikes" are what mechanics call the bolts that fix the wheels in place. Pasha summoned some backup. We loaded my car onto a breakdown truck and went to celebrate my miraculous escape.

Cadaver

Slava was irresistibly drawn to talking about cruelty. I remember one day we were having a discussion about Gogol. Even here, Slava could not resist the temptation.

"Andrei, what do you think – in Taras Bulba, where Ostap is being tortured, do you remember, where his bones are cracking, and it seems that everything inside has been broken, and Gogol suddenly writes, "… and then such terrible tortures began that the Cossack women lowered their eyes." What do you think they were actually doing to him?"

I had nothing to say in reply to his question. Torture held no interest for me whatsoever.

If I look back at the long conversations that Richter and I had at night, it often seemed to me that it was not Svyatoslav Richter talking to me, but Svidrigailov, the Duc de Blangis or Count Dracula himself.

We sat opposite each other in armchairs in his flat on Bronnaya Street. Outside the windows was the restless night of Moscow. In Richter's apartment, all was quiet. It was dark as Slava did not like light. Richter was whispering, and I was not sure if he was talking to me, or saying things for his own benefit, pulled by an irresistible force…

"Andrei, could you ever murder? I think that you could! I would so like to be able to murder. Oh, it is so difficult for me that I can only kill flies, while you, you can. You have that within you, the ability to murder – what bliss!"

"Slava, what nonsense. I have killed a pig, that's true, in the Caucasus. We were going for a picnic. We loaded a live pig into the boot of the car and went up into the mountains. Two of the friends I was with refused to kill it. One Armenian friend held down the pig and I hacked off its head. We got totally covered from head to foot… We washed it all off. Made it into kebabs and barbecued it. That was my murder."

"How? You cut its throat with a knife?"

"Well, yes, what else could I do?"

"Oh, how tempting that must be!"

It's just as well that Richter only killed flies. Or was it only flies, after all? His principal weapon was not a knife or an axe, but a grand piano. Music.

One day I was talking about Richter with a celebrated Viennese musician, a luminous character and clever man who was born back in the 19th century. He said the following to me: "Andrei, I beg of you not to be offended, but it is not only your Richter, but also all the other musicians from the USSR who are cadavers. What they are doing to music will cost us dear, as a cadaver is imbued with an ineradicable strength, tenacity, inhuman endurance, cunning, and a fundamental desire to rule the world – all this with lifeless substance but a perfect form. It is killing music."

In actual fact, every note of Chopin or Mozart performed by Richter is a dead note, a poison that kills the soul of music and the souls of those listening. Grieg's Piano Concerto. What music! But when Richter performs it is not music at all, but a sportsman putting the shot! Tchaikovsky's Piano Concerto No. 1. Like a dung beetle rolling and rolling its meaningless balls and thumping, thumping, thumping forte at the keys while obediently reading the notes in the score like an ignorant sergeant major reading an order. Instead of Tchaikovsky's lyricism there is the dull tossing of a meaningless collection of notes. Richter plays Haydn's scintillating Piano Sonata in E flat major, full of humour, light and levity, as though it is a dreadful Gogolesque deadman hurling hefty gravestones around a macabre cemetery. All this while performing with a fanatical conviction and furious energy that smash the bones of his audience…

In a few, extremely rare cases the inner deadness of the musician was appropriate for the composer's musical objective. It was fascinating to observe how enthusiastic the musical "Meister Tod" became in this evocative instance. To see with what dark rage he crushed in his playing all that was living, and transformed the fragrant, cheerful, joyfully-ringing world, overflowing with succulent flower heads, into rotting, graveyard carrion; into himself...

Richter was capable of sitting for three or four months in rooms that were darkened with tightly-drawn curtains. This was prone to happen when his own evil spirits started to prevail. Richter was tormented by a gnawing revulsion at the world and at himself. If even the smallest ray of sunlight accidentally slipped through the heavy drapery of his curtains into the room, then his face would distort with a furious, sickly grimace, and he would groan or let out a bestial roar. He roared and groaned like no human! I got the impression he had grown fangs and giant claws.

Sometimes he would swing his head and howl, "Ooooo-aaaaa-ooooo."

He howled like a terrible infant werewolf, two metres tall. It was repellent, unbearable.

In complete darkness Slava would make no sound. The silence of the grave was disturbed only by the sounds coming from Nina's half, of the flat of her clicking heels as she energetically rushed around.

I would sometimes be taken ill in the stuffy darkness of Slava's lair, and I would experience something like a heart attack when I would fall to the floor, still conscious, and thrash around as though in agonies. Instead of offering me any kind of assistance, or calling an ambulance, Richter would cheer up and watch my suffering keenly. Sometimes he even clapped his hands and said "encore."

Slava was a film fanatic. One could conjecture that it was film that served as the principal source of his artistic imagination. In the early period of our friendship he often acted out scenes for me from films that had impressed him. They were endless scenes of violence.

"And then, can you believe it, Andrei, he puts him in a dentist's chair and…"

At this point Richter's face took on a sweet expression of inspiration, like Dracula at the moment he bites the sleeping artery of the girl. Slava got up, as huge as a cliff, and advanced on me threateningly. A dreadful dentist's drill appeared in his enormous fist. He demonstrated as he narrated…

"The drill slow-ly drills all of his nerves in each tooth by turn."

After shows of this nature Slava would look at me attentively, checking whether I had enjoyed his performance. He would then immediately demonstrate and recount further scenes.

The hero of the film is in love with himself and doesn't know how to love himself still more, he has tried everything...

"He goes up to the mirror in the bathroom, naked, and puts IT on the golden washbasin, takes a knife and slow-ly cuts it off right at the root. The film ends there. It's perfect bliss!"

The great pianist's face bore a hideous, lustful smile. He retold me *A Clockwork Orange*. It was only the scenes of rape and beatings accompanied by Beethoven's music that attracted him. That was Richter's Beethoven! It seems that Richter noticed none of Kubrick's black humour and murderous sarcasm. He told me about Pasolini's film, *Salò, or the 120 Days of Sodom*. Here it was the cruellest and most sadistic scenes that attracted him, with the swallowing of needles, the gouging out of eyeballs, the rape of boys and mass murders.

"*Salò* is the best film! Yes, and that scene with the shit, they eat it, yes and the vile old prostitute stuffs her face with shit on a silver spoon from an incredibly beautiful dish. And it was the man jumping around in front of her who did the shit. Yes, yes, yes, that is our life, that is true realism."

That was the commentary provided by Richter on this monstrous film. It all made me feel physically sick.

Despite being obviously drawn towards killing and death, Richter was surprisingly sensitive to all things alive and genuine. I have never known anyone who could respond so rapidly to anything alive. It was a matter of contrasts. The deadman wanted to be alive! Sometimes he would give a leaden groan, "Andrei, I cannot lo-o-ove, I cannot fee-e-e-el, I am a sto-o-o-one, a monster, a distorting mirror..." The Soviet propaganda machine kept this true face of Richter's skilfully hidden behind a mask of a slightly ironic, lofty, otherworldly grand master of the piano. Richter spent his whole life working tirelessly on establishing this image. It was his main creation, his principal lie...

In Brezhnev's time everything was rotting and disintegrating – from the Secretary General himself to the last clearing in the forest polluted with every possible toxic chemical and radioactive waste. If Richter had not belonged to the tribe of Dracula cadavers, but had simply been ALIVE, spontaneous, free and bright then who would have let him onto the Olympus of Soviet music? How would the attitude of his masters have been then, the senile Soviet cadavers?

You, dear readers, will possibly be thinking as you read these lines, "Well, Gavrilov's exaggerating here, he's painting a devil where there isn't one really!" You are wrong, dear readers, there is a devil. Let us ask the children. For those of us who studied at the Central Music School, Richter's playing was torment, it was deathly dull and dreary as a wet weekend!

We loved music and felt it deeply with our childish, pure souls. We would listen enchanted to baroque music; Gould entranced us with his two-voice inventions and concertos by Bach; tears streamed from our eyes as we listened to Mozart. Youngsters pick up on all things living and real and instantly identify falsity and cheating. For little musicians, Richter was worse than castor oil or cod liver oil. The moment we even heard his name we would try and hide as far away as possible. When we were a little older he roused only curiosity in us – he was so big with his blue blazer with gold buttons, his loose change jangling in his pockets during concerts in the small hall at the Central Music School... We were fascinated to watch how he "broke" the piano. Not with the brilliance of the passages, like our fellow students in the senior classes, but with his whole body, like a chiropractor sawbones. Richter had an absurd gliding walk, after which he would bow and wiggle his backside. Our older schoolmates would make fun of his grimaces. Very few people actually listened to his music during his concerts; there wasn't really any music, it was more a theatrical performance of the evil witch and giant, of Richter the bone doctor. Richter never once smiled at a single little kid. Children didn't like him.

Richter's art starts to have an impact on a musician during adolescence. When childhood spontaneity starts to disappear, and for a long time nothing comes to take its place. During that period, young musicians start to imitate authoritative figures. In the early 1970s hoards of "little Richters" appeared, not only in the USSR, but everywhere, little mutant copy cats. It was these people, for the most part, who defined the style of musical performance for the next forty years.

I also drank from the same chalice, and I fell under the monstrous weight of this mechanical zombie giant. He sucked me into his orbit like Jupiter attracting a little planet. It took me thirty long, agonizing years to exterminate the Richter within myself.

It is only now, fourteen years after Richter's death, that I have sensed for the first time that the world has grown weary of Richter's music, has grown weary of pacing through the waterless desert and weary of the heavy footfall of the Commandatore... The world wants to love, to cry, dance and delight in music. It is long overdue to cast off the shackles of pseudo-intellectual, heavyweight, fakely theatrical, falsely significant and pretentiously romantic performing style of Richter...

Hiding in the loo

Richter cast aside his friends in the same way every time. While a friend was of use to him and presented himself for his vampirical delectation then all was well. When Richter felt, however, that there was nothing left for him to suck out of his friend then the friend became "uninteresting" to him.

The passage of time demonstrated that Slava had no real friends, and could not possibly have any. There were some suspiciously vivid friendships which were often terminated because Slava grew weaker and "lapsed into a state of contemptibility." He could not endure a genuine friendship among equals. He either howled and moaned, played the Holy Fool, calling himself a weakling and a shit, or he locked himself in the loo and refused to open the door.

For decades Richter would travel out to country homes without being invited, he would make visits in Moscow, also without an invitation, to "friends" who surpassed him in intellect and strength of character. These individuals treated him with disgust and aversion, often humiliating him. Several times I was an unwilling witness to scenes of this sort. Richter the masochist enjoyed being humiliated. He wanted to be denigrated again and again. It charged him with a diabolical malice. It justified and fed his latent vengeful sadism – the hidden driving force behind his character and his music.

For a relatively long time Richter put up with (and hungrily sucked dry) "slave friends" who never stopped toadying. The slaves flattered Richter, they flattered him in filthy, vulgar and crude ways. They captured him, took him to one side, rolled around on the floor at his feet begging him to spit in their faces, whispered the sort of things in his ear that would make any normal person nauseous, but they worked unfailingly on Richter. There was something of the "Comrade Stalin" about him. Slava loved to creep up on tiptoe to the spy hole in the door to feast his eyes upon his humiliated "friend" and revel in his subordinate state, his pitiful grimaces.

Sometimes Richter was wracked with conscience. For example, with the artist Vladimir Moroz. This intelligent and talented man perfectly understood how to entertain Richter. He was a master in the matter, and his fantasies, projects, masquerade balls and playful games had Slava in ecstasies. However, as a "friend", Moroz had one important shortcoming: he did not know how and did not wish to grovel. Neither before Slava nor before Nina. Once he told "the stupid bitch to piss off" in Richter's hearing. She immediately exploited the situation and placed the choice before Richter of "either him or me."

"Of course you, Ninochka."

Moroz was banished. He came to a sorry end, locked up in prison for many years. There was even mention in the national papers of "the renegade, corrupt hard-currency speculator, Moroz, who wormed his way into favour with a famous Soviet musician and exploited his patronage." Need one even mention that Slava and Nina never lifted a finger to help Moroz…?

Throughout the years of our friendship there was a prevailing chaos and lack of understanding in the band of toadies that surrounded Richter. Someone would burst into simulated floods of tears of jealousy, someone else would pull mean tricks and spew out venom, while Fira revelled in it all.

Once he told me, "Andrei, Kapelka was here today, and he was crying and whispering to me… So that means it's all over… All over… Now there is only Gavrilov, while I… It's all finished, isn't it?"

Richter recounted this all while providing a marvellously accurate imitation of the unfortunate man. Then, transforming himself back into Fira, he gave an unpleasant laugh… Kapelka's wife, Geya the cellist, had staked her life on making sure that Kapelka was never kicked out from among "Slava's friends", and was beside herself with rage. Kind-hearted folk passed on to me the soothing words she had spoken to her inconsolable husband, "Don't be upset, Kapelka, my sweet, I shall just kill that worm, that Russian pig, and then you will be the only one for Slava…"

Poor Kapelka met an unpleasant end. It seems that he died of bone cancer and turned from a flourishing, handsome Jewish violinist to being a dwarf just 70cm tall. Geya, meanwhile, swore to ostracise me till the day I died. She found many willing helpers. They lied and slandered, stopping at nothing. Our Soviet superman Richter could not withstand the pressure. His delightful housekeeper, Nina, again posed her sacramental question, "him or me".

I never concealed my irony, and mocked certain of Slava's character traits to his face. I sometimes called him "Baldy" to his face. I would parody his playing among my young friends. They would beg me, "Play like Richter!" I would chose a tender sonata by Scarlatti and sit like Fira, with my legs pressed into the piano, my body tall and looming over the keys, and then start to bash the notes like heavy cannonballs. My friends would fall about laughing. They would then race round to Bronnaya Street as fast as they could to see who could be first to inform of my public horseplay. Eventually my endless teasing, parodies and scathing tales caused his patience to run out.

Are you laughing, little boy? Played better than me in Arkhangelskoye and now boasting about it, are you? I wanted to give you the world, and you laughed at me...

In the spring of 1982 Richter bumped into my mother as she was on her way back from shopping at the market. He let fly at her, hysterically frothing at the mouth and squawking as he called me names. Mum dropped her bag of fruit in the Moscow mud, she was so terrified. It was the first time she had seen her idol without his mask.

A couple of months prior to that... At a prearranged time I had gone up in the lift and rang Slava's doorbell using our prearranged signal. I heard rustlings and a suspicious commotion behind the door. Then there was silence. Richter had locked himself in the loo.

Richter's protégé

There is an opinion present in the Russian press that I made an international career for myself as "the protégé of Svyatoslav Richter". This is one of the defensive myths of the pro-Richter clique. In actual fact it was not like that at all. Winning the Tchaikovsky Competition opened the doors of the best concert halls in the West for me. I made my own career, achieving success through my own long, hard work. My career started in 1974 in Salzburg, when the international musical press literally exploded with eulogising articles after my performance. It was not until 1979 that Richter and I first appeared in the West together. That was in a small auditorium in Tours, in a tiny chateau. By then I had already given hundreds of concerts, and had made triumphant tours twice all around the globe. It was already the FIFTH year of my international career. The broader musical community paid almost no attention whatsoever to our first joint performance. The musical public finally found out about our collaboration only after EMI made a live recording of a joint performance and the FRG film director, Johannes Schaaf, made a documentary commissioned by the second channel on West German TV. This happened in late 1980, one year after our modest debut performance together. I was an international star at the time, even though I was sitting in a Soviet mantrap.

My status of "Richter's protégé" was an invention that was initially only circulated inside the USSR, but by the end of the period of my travel ban it had been exported to Europe as well. This was facilitated by publications made to order in the Western musical press. The experienced hand of a stage director can be felt here, carrying out a special order. Someone is still feeding this myth to the present day. Richter never pulled any strings for me. He never said a word in the right ear on my behalf. But he was perfectly capable of instilling in his fans and conservatoire pupils, and in the minds of Western and Soviet musical bosses, the idea of my "apprenticeship".

Richter was dangerous when he feared for himself, and for his status and career. He often engaged in underhand manipulation. He could also strike openly, head on. He acted swiftly and harshly. It was considerably more difficult to tussle against his intrigues than it was in our musical battles. He knew no compassion. He needed to close the topic of any competition between Richter and Gavrilov, so if he shamelessly slandered and defamed a friend's career in the eyes of the international musical community then that was no problem for him. It was done "through formal and informal channels" by Richter, Dorliak and their gang.

Slava himself, in private conversation, tête-à-tête, admitted his musical defeat. On two occasions. He moaned to me about his mortal wound, about the pain that I had caused him by simply appearing in the music world. But everyone else, the whole world, was not supposed to know the truth. For everyone else, "Gavrilov was Richter's protégé."

The Enigma

The French film continues the worst traditions of Soviet propaganda – it lies by holding back. It misrepresents. It lies with Richter, about Richter, and it lies about his epoch.

The titles of the film end with the attractive short slogan, "He is a free man." At this point any honest, thinking person should stop watching the movie. Richter, just like all residents of the Soviet Union, was not free from the revolution all the way through to perestroika. Seventy years of his life. No, the romantics will object, no, that is where Richter's strength was manifest! In the prison state, in the years of repression and stagnation, he maintained his mental liberty; he spiritually conquered the Soviet tyrants and obscurantists!

Yes, there were heroes of that type who retained their inner freedom. There were. But Richter was not one of them! Just take a more careful look at Richter's dead, terrible face before the camera. It is not the passage of time that did that to him – men who have retained their inner freedom and elevation of spirit take on the appearance in their old age of the saints and wise men of yore! Old age and sickness kill the body, but not the living, independent spirit! Listen to the documentary musical material and you will hear not the music of Richter, the "unbeaten Titan", but the terror, bitterness and spite of a musician who has sold his soul to the Soviet devil. His very energy is not the energy of life, good and beauty, but a deadly emanation of evil. It is no coincidence that Richter so loved the infernal, rather stupid and heavy-handed Wagner.

Richter's career began approximately one year before the start of the Second World War and reached its first peak ten years later, when he received the Stalin Prize (1950). Richter gave concerts all through the war. He never fought. Unlike almost all the other Soviet Germans he was never deported. What curious felicity against the nightmare background of Hitler and Stalin! Furthermore, in October 1941, the "Soviets" shot his father. Even earlier than that, his mother had refused to be evacuated so that she would be in the German occupied zone and could leave with the invading forces.

From the perspective of the official ideology of the Soviet state, Richter's father was an enemy of the people and his mother was a traitor to the Motherland. Richter was the son of an executed enemy of the people and a traitor, and he then gave concerts as if nothing had happened.

HOW COULD A PERSON LIKE THAT NOT ONLY SURVIVE BUT BECOME THE LEADING PIANIST IN STALIN'S USSR?

The film provides no answer to this question.

A free man? What kind of freedom could possibly be meant? Richter was THEIR slave, and loyal cur. Otherwise he would not have survived a single year after his father's execution and his mother's treason.

I cannot pass up the opportunity of quoting here the monologue pronounced by the wife of a Soviet minister. "Can you imagine? They are building a special apartment for that presumptuous madman. It takes up a whole floor of the building and has sound-proofing, right in the centre of Moscow! They have decided to indulge that brazen homo. They'd better watch they don't overindulge him! We have all expressed our outrage!" This woman put into words the attitude of the Soviet élite towards Richter, but not of the upper echelons of power. Members of the Politburo, starting in Stalin's time and extending all the way to perestroika, supported Richter as one of their own. Why?

Anyone who watched the film and was unfamiliar with the history of Stalinism would reach the conclusion that, yes, well, there were difficulties, the civil war, repressions, but generally everything went as it should, and the great pianist Richter made himself a path leading to the very top by means of his talent and hard work. There is no question that there was hard work and great talent, but with the three minuses that Richter had (an executed father, a traitor mother and German ethnicity), no talent could possibly have helped. There was something else. What?

Or who?

During one of his deep depressions, Slava twice repeated one and the same phrase to me, through gritted teeth: "A young lady conceived a passion for my concerts, so I am told, and it seems that this saved me from much unpleasantness." Richter was referring to Svetlana Alliluev, Stalin's daughter, who was fifteen in 1941. Despite her young age, Svetlana was already spending time with Kapler who was developing her in cultural matters and taking her to interesting concerts. Judging by her later reminiscences, Stalin loved her very much indeed, and she told her father about her admiration for Richter's playing, and Stalin whispered something to somebody. Richter received protection that was invisible, but the most reliable in the whole of the USSR.

When I first saw this film I grew sad and pained for Slava, for music, and for the truth, at the end of the day. Richter was not always in a state of depression. I remember another Slava as well, a carefree idealist who loved life, as he was in Europe where he seemed to forget about the Soviet shackles. Slava captivated us when we were young musicians with his energy, his dedication and the strength of his spirit. That Richter is nowhere to be seen in Monsaingeon's film, instead there is a hopelessly weary, bug-eyed and mean old man, exhausted by life; an ageing Dr Mabuse or Fantômas...

I would so have wanted Richter to have revealed something human in himself before he died. To have started to speak sincerely. To have shared some innermost secret that he had collected and crystallised all his life in himself and in his music. No, Richter did not do that. Because his innermost secret was evil. The Sphinx did not start to speak. Because he did not want to give himself away. As a result, we find out nothing from the film except for generally-known facts from his biography.

What about the viewer? The viewer is scared to even glance into the abyss in which the Maestro's life really passed. It is much more comforting to feel sorry for the elderly musician, being moved by his caprices of genius, bandying sweet musical names around like fruit drops.

Let's suck them with Richter – Schubert! Now something about your childhood Wonderful! The conductor Samuil Stolerman? What? He shot his wife! Marvellous! What? What, Maximilian Schmidthof sent a note to Prokofiev? They found his body in the forest? Excellent.

The old Dracula recounts these two deaths with undisguised appetite.

Slava ends his dead monologue with the terrible words, "I do not like myself." If you don't like yourself, why did you live like that? Tell us, make our day. There is no humility and wisdom here, only despair. Or perhaps an inflamed narcissism horrified at the proximity of the grave?

The old gay accompanist from Jitomir pinned his reproach on himself in conclusion – reproach to all his admirers. To the whole world.

The whole time I was watching the film the feeling never left me that Richter had been forced to make the picture, that he was indifferent to it or secretly hostile! Slava told me several times that he would rather die than start to "pour out my soul to some idiot." Then this film appeared, long and boring, almost a home video, while Slava loved the talented, the elegant and the grand! What happened? Who broke him?

"Yes, Andrei," said Slava during our last meeting in 1985, "I really know so much that is fascinating and intriguing. I have met so many marvellous people.

"I was at the heart of amazing events, and I should like to share with the public what I know. But the moment this thought comes into my head, I immediately remember my favourite joke about Rabinovich. There is a funeral procession with a coffin, and in the coffin sits Rabinovich. People ask him, "Rabinovich, why the funeral, the procession and the coffin; you aren't even dead?" Rabinovich replies, "Who cares about that?" The point is, Andrei, I immediately remember these words: who cares about that? And any desire to share anything evaporates. Everything that I have seen and experienced is interesting only to me and the people who were with me there and then."

Despite this the director managed, by some means known only to him, to sit Richter in front of the camera. Money? Or a little refined blackmail among friends? Richter was also reading something from a piece of paper.

I will provide a commentary to a few of Slava's phrases.

"He perished in Odessa, the Soviets shot him."

This was about his father. Slava was unable to tell the truth, that he never forgave the Soviet authorities for this, and never would, because he was a coward, and because he knew that "to live after death" he would need to be laid to rest in THEIR earth, at Novodevichy Cemetery, beside the executioners. When Richter pronounces these words he snarls like a wolf. Almost all the rest of the text is read by Richter in a dead monotone, as though he is carrying out orders.

"They were intending to leave together, then suddenly mother says no, because it would have been impossible to take that gentleman!"

"To leave" for evacuation. "That gentleman" was Kondratiev, whom Richter's mother had brought into the home while his father was still alive. Richter loved his mother intensely, and equally intensely hated her. In the late 1970s Slava spoke of Kondratiev with desperate loathing, making him shudder.

"Can you imagine, Andrei, as well as becoming a false father to me he also became my false teacher. He used to write inscriptions on all sorts of rubbish "To Svetik from his teacher"! Eh? How do you like that? What-the-hell kind of teacher was he? He was a talentless blockhead, the conceited brute. Incidentally, it was also he who wrote that famous article against Shostakovich after *Lady Macbeth of Mtsensky District* that was entitled "Muddle Instead of Music", I saw it before he sent it off! Do you know, he had three balls! Yes! And it would seem that this made him an attractive lover! When I went to the church, to my mother's coffin, he started feigning that he was "mad with grief" and rushed to the organ and started improvising some dreadful nonsense. I escaped from the church.

God, how vulgar it was, how vile, how degrading and disgusting. I felt sick. I was unable to bury my mother, he took even that from me!"

The following passages are about me.

"He is so lucky to be always pleased with himself."

To my face Slava constantly said to me, "Andrei, you are always so unhappy, so sad, you can't live like that! You must get some pleasure from life, from everything, even from going to the toilet! You are impossible in your permanent dissatisfaction with the world and with yourself in the world."

"If would be even happier if he was more modest…"

To me he used to say: "What right do you have to set yourself such aims? Do you want the material to transform into the ideal after your concert? There was a man who wanted that with his mystery, and he came to a nasty end. Always remember, Better is the enemy of Good! There is no need to set targets that are too high! You need to resign yourself to destiny!"

"That is a sign of good health."

A sadistic comment. Slava knew perfectly well that by 1980 I had already been poisoned by KGB agents. I still suffer to this day as a result.

"People often mistook Gavrilov for me… and vice versa."

He is talking about our joint Handel cycle here. Straight after the advance copies of the records came out Richter invited his friends round and organized a guessing game after playing the LPs. He asked them to guess which one of us was playing one or other suite. Everyone was confused and kept getting it wrong. Slava was furious because he had counted on their phenomenal musical ears enabling them easily to determine who was where. Realizing, to his astonishment, that this was not the case, Slava undertook to convince everyone of the outrageous idea that any similarity in our interpretations was entirely "spontaneous". In the space of two decades he succeeded in instilling this idea into a great many people's minds. This was typical of Slava. Methodically, coolly to achieve the goal he had set himself. Water dripping on a stone.

Slava never told the truth – that after I had played "my" suites to him for the first time he rushed off in agitation to adjust the sound and character of his own suites "to sound like Gavrilov". He spent about a week faking them so that his tone would match that of my interpretation, and in his thoughts he wished me dead. By the time the recording came along, he had adjusted everything so conscientiously that now even I can't tell who is where…

Monsaingeon has edited the Soviet footage in a slovenly manner. At the start and end the sorrowful cadences of Schubert's sonata sound, beautifully performed by Slava.

I listened especially to this whole sonata – it is only the sad beginning of the second part that sounds good, but in the crescendo Slava is already thumping mercilessly at the piano, and making the "childish mistake" of not holding the long notes of the melody, thus destroying the atmosphere of solitude and mourning. There is no video footage of Richter performing this. Therefore, we hear Richter playing the Schubert, but see Richter playing the Chopin Etude No7, op 25...

Many of the other pieces that are aired in the film do not thrill the ear, but rather unmask Richter the performer. They demonstrate his affectation; they offend with their sham pathos, the frowning Soviet Wagnerianism! His inherent theatricality looks old-fashioned and comical on the screen, rather like actors in silent movies with their googly eyes and ridiculous gesticulations. The picture of the fourth étude in Chopin's Op. 10 is a hilarious, provincially theatrical mise-en-scene. A crumpled handkerchief tossed on the piano... A bad actor from a silent film seems to slash at this filigree étude with a sabre. The public are in raptures – look at his fingers go! It is possible to play it twice as fast... But in this étude Chopin did not set himself a sporting challenge. This music is close to the finale of the Funeral March Sonata. There should be a dry, clear dialogue of malignant forces heard here. But Richter, the pushy cavalryman pianist, energetically tramples the listener underfoot...

The director moulded and moulded what materials he had available; he sewed his "documentary" quilt from his multicoloured scraps. He has shown us a mummy that tells lies about itself and its own past, and which languishes in repulsion towards itself.

Music did not help Richter, it did not become, as he had hoped and believed, the justification for the compromises, capitulations and meanness that he made on the long journey of his life. It became a mirror of his personal degradation.

***

Richter and I spoke hundreds of times about his much-discussed interpretation of a musical work. For many years I sat beside him at the piano and closely observed how he worked on the text and thought about his creative method. The sole conclusion that I reached over many years of shared music-making with him was that Richter had no creative method – he played by relying on intuition alone. He learned and played the text many times over, persistently, mechanically REPEATING thousands of times every phrase to be learned by heart, instead of ANIMATING it... His essential Commendatore quality, his aggressor's instinct did not permit him to submit his hands and brain to be governed by Chopin or Schumann...

He took their music from them, denied them their voices, and would not allow them to speak through him... That was his fundamental artistic weakness; it was the "secret" of his human and musical limitations. This explains the lack of subtlety, the false, dead "perfection" of his playing... Richter had absolutely no desire to enter the painful reality of the great composers. He wanted to remain in the elegant hall of an ancient palace, in a museum, in the world of his élite apartment, on the stage... He did not wish to leave for one moment the role of chief pianist of the USSR, the mysterious, demonic, quirky and extravagantly capricious guest of the West. He did not want, and was incapable of resisting, the resilient existential pressure of his powerful, active body. Richter never left his body, he was never transformed! Whatever he performed, he was always Richter playing one thing and then another... Under the fingers of Richter the spiritualist, not one single composer ever sounded sincere, or retained his undistorted original form.

The real, bloody world in which geniuses were not tilting at windmills but battling against concrete manifestations of evil and inhumanity frightened and scared him away. Richter did not want to become Chopin coughing up blood, so he "cured" Chopin, clothed him in sturdy flesh and set him marching... Under his fingers, Beethoven, Schumann, Ravel and Prokofiev all marched...

Richter turned away squeamishly from the world where geniuses lived and worked, just as he turned away from the Soviet world beyond the boundaries of his own flat... Too often the groans and prayers for help could be heard from there. Richter was a man hardened by Stalin, and he did not look to where the screams came from. He also did not offer his hand to the misfortunate. He tried to take cover in "music" in the way that a hermit crab hides in a cosy shell. But the genius always looks THERE, where the blood is flowing, where mankind is oppressed, where his dignity is trampled, freedom revoked; the genius is compassionate and joins the struggle. The music of genuinely genius composers is faith, pain, protest, requiem, compassion, tenderness and love...

Sviatoslav Richter at the age of 22 (1937)

The third year of the travel ban

"My dear chap," said my cardiologist to me. He was Nikolai Paleyev, an optimistic and intelligent man, "You have to pay the price, you are an artist with great talent, but you need to pay for everything, especially talent."

Paleyev was able to convince me that what was happening to me was not the end. I believed him. I was sent to Gurzuf to a rest home. It did not help. The moment I left the ward and tottered down to the sea I would have a seizure. They would haul me back. I spent a miserable week in Gurzuf and then went back to Moscow. I barely made it back home.

I decided to learn to walk again. I was unable to move without the aid of a stick at the time, and I refused on principle to use crutches. Some kind friends let me stay at their flat in a village next to a CSKA training base. There were gyms, swimming pools and courts. Every morning at 8 o'clock I would drink a glass of milk and hobble down to the sports complex. It made me think of Polevoy's *A Story about a Real Man.* His hero crawls and crawls, then nibbles at a fir cone...

About three weeks of agonizing training more or less restored my ability to walk. It's true that I walked slightly wonky, but much more confidently than before, and without my stick. I swam, skipped rope, stood by the wall with my tennis racquet for hours whacking a ball, climbed the wall bars and never let myself slacken. My seizures started to occur less frequently.

From the end of August 1982 I went to stay with Slava in Nikolina Gora. One day I asked him, "Why do we only ever do things related to music, only arrange festivals of musical? We also like eating – let's organize a festival of food! Let's arrange our own Grande Bouffe."

Slava was enthusiastic. We spent a whole week painstakingly getting ready. Slava prepared the only dish he knew how to cook, which was a cold beetroot soup. I sautéed vegetables, made dolma, barbecued kebabs, fried pancakes and cooked appetizing spicy Armenian dishes. As a consequence, everyone who took part in Gavrilov and Richter's Grande Bouffe gained weight. Nina refused to participate in "this disgrace". She avoided our collaborative feasts and kicked up a real fuss. Slava cowered and hid.

By mid-September I felt that I could return to the city and start working. The seizures had apparently eased off. I soon found the strength to whizz over to Petersburg and play another Bach concerto there with Alexander Dmitriev. Richter had great difficulty in arranging our last joint Handel concerts in the GDR. It was then, in 1982, that Slava and I parted company forever.

The Soviet world was absurd and aggressive. For absolutely no apparent reason the directors at the Philharmonia started pestering me.

"You, Gavrilov, are not engaged in any sort of community work!"

Absurd demands must be met with absurdity. I had a think, and engaged actively in community work – I organized a Philharmonic football team. The directors were so amazed, they were unable to think of anything to say and so they shut up. That was all I needed. I enjoyed kicking a ball around, and it helped in my fight to stay healthy.

I worked hard and prepared another three Bach concertos, as well as Concertos Numbers 2 and 3 by Beethoven. I was preparing and playing a new concerto each week. Always playing it all the way through! Concerto No. 2 with Sasha Dmitriev in Petersburg, and the following week No. 3 with Yuri Temirkanov in Moscow. Packed houses everywhere, television... Bootleg recordings of these concerts are still being sold all over the world.

With the aid of Hideko and my agents in the West, I bought an excellent video recorder and started to collect cassettes. My friends enthusiastically visited my home club. Bashmet, Gergiev, Ovchinnikov, Toradze, Tchaikovsky, Naumov and many others first saw and heard at my house many things that were hidden behind the iron curtain. Sometimes I put on themed presentations for a selected audience. About the music of Penderecki for *The Saragoss Manuscript*, about Bob Fosse's fear of death as illustrated in his film *All That Jazz*, where he managed accurately to show his future death from a heart attack, and about the music of Janáček.

It's extraordinary! A great many people helped me in my fight for life. Actors, ballet people, singers and even some bureaucrats. Only none of my pianist colleagues. When I was virtually being buried alive by the KGB, many of them did not even bother to conceal their delight. My Japanese friend Hideko tried to help me. We even got married. We hoped to loosen the grip of the Soviet Union by doing so. I am now amazed at my own naivety, but at the time I genuinely hoped that I would be let out of the USSR with my wife. Hideko and I had barely had our fill of laughing at the farcical Soviet nuptial procedures when Big Brother made the next sneaky move. My wife and her family were given 72 hours to leave the USSR. They were all accused of spying.

The KGB told me, "Andrei, you need to divorce Hideko immediately so that we can help you." Hideko was not allowed to enter the country, and I was forbidden from leaving it. There was nothing we could do. I sent Hideko a telegram, "Need stamp from your police." My angel Hideko arranged everything. Which is why my divorce certificate, issued by the registry office in my local Moscow district, bears a scarlet Japanese stamp.

After this blow I desperately wanted to go to my homeland, to the sea and the Caucasus. I checked my Mercedes before leaving. Everything seemed OK, but the wheels were obviously not going to last a journey down to the Caucasus. I sent a telegram to my agents in the FRG. In two weeks my wheels were at customs. I couldn't collect them, though. Why not? Just because. I couldn't and that was all. I remembered that one of my former spooks had at some point been in charge of customs on the Moscow railway. I contacted my spook. A week later, on a rainy summer morning, with brand new wheels, I was turning right from my Boulevard onto Kalininsky Prospect to head south, avoiding possible bottlenecks on Varshavka.

At my side was my indispensable assistant, Aida, an uninhibited girl from Bosnia with a strong personality, a sharp mind and a fierce temper. On the Prospect we noticed a familiar face. Vadim Sakharov, a wonderful pianist, was standing on a traffic island with a look of deep concentration on his face. He was gazing at the grey skies of Moscow and looking fed up. He was holding a string shopping bag in one hand. There was a white loaf of bread and a brioche in the bag. He noticed us and waved us down. We stopped. Vadim stuck his head through the window.

"Where are you off to, ladies and gentlemen?"

"To the Caucasus."

Vadim opened the door and calmly sat in the back seat.

"I'm coming with you. Anyone want some brioche?"

The romance of the Soviet Union! Where else would this be possible! Neither Vadim nor the bread got back to the house. By evening we were sitting in Rostov-on-Don in the Ocean Restaurant, chomping on succulent grouse and fried fish from the river Don. We were washing it down with beer.

We stopped in Pitsunda at the ranch of some Armenian friends of mine. The suffocating KGB muck that seemed to me to have infused my whole body and troubled my breathing, thinking and living was being blown away by the sea breeze here, where I was free. What joy, even if for a short time, to forget about THEM. To connect with the Sun, the sea, the damp salty air and finally to wash off the toxic powder that the poisoning Moscow so generously sprinkled over each of her ants.

We were pampered by life in Pitsunda. Fishermen invited us out to fish with them and the local police took us up into the mountains to mess around with guns. They escorted us with a whole cavalcade. It was their tribute to a fellow native who had not forgotten his roots. I looked fondly at my Mingrels, my Armenians, Georgians and Abkhazians and thanked them in my soul for every moment of the magical life that they were so generously giving to us! Everyone was together back then. They drank and loved and were friends and neighbours. Who could have imagined then that in just eight years a bloody war would break out, and that half of Abkhazia would be destroyed and burned, and that thousands of people would be slaughtered; that Georgians would be thrown out of their own homes, and then turned forever into homeless refugees? That Georgians would kill Abkhazians and Armenians. That Russians and Chechens would be invited in to kill Georgians. And that at the end of the day an independent Abkhazia, recognized by nearly nobody in the whole world, would find itself under the dusty boot of the Russian soldier who had not yet had time to sell the golden cutlery and toilet that he had stolen in Georgia.

We watched football on TV in Pitsunda. The World Cup. Italy played divinely that year, unfortunately for the last time! The Italians outplayed the wonderful Brazilians, and then the powerful Germans with Beckenbauer, Grabowski, Müller and their other stars.

The trip did not pass without a miracle as well. I saw her first on the seafront, near the Pitsunda "high rise blocks". She was young, beautiful, strong and confident and she proudly tossed her head with its pony tail. She was a golden girl. I felt as though I had been hit on the head, and I told myself, "I won't let that girl go. Whatever I have to do!"

This beautiful stranger was walking along the seafront surrounded by young men. I didn't even notice them because I had fallen head over heels and was already dying of love. It is possible that readers will be under the impression that I am some sort of macho, or a lady-killer, as they say. Unfortunately that is far from the truth. I had never even tried to chat up a girl in the street...

In the meantime, my fille inconnue had vanished. What an idiot! I should have rushed to throw myself on my knees to kiss her feet! Back at the ranch, I told Aida about the beautiful vision. My trusty Bosnian friend immediately grasped the situation and promised to help. We went to a bar to watch the next match. There was dancing in the bar, but I was miserable, remembering my sweetheart. Sober Aida tugged me by the sleeve of my T-shirt and pointed.

"Is that her? That girl's got class, and no mistake!"

I recognized her and bulldozed my way over. I swept her away from some Abkhazian boy. That evening we went skinny dipping in the warm, Abkhazian sea, alight with golden luminescence...

Subsequently my golden girl, Ilka, came to my aid several times at critical moments in my life. Despite the fact that there are mountains and oceans between us, we are still the closest of friends.

That autumn I recorded all of the Bach concertos at Melodiya studios with the Moscow Chamber Orchestra, as well as double concertos (for two pianos) by Mozart, Bach and Mendelssohn with that year's winner of the Chopin competition, the wonderful Vietnamese pianist Dang Thai Son.

I also trained with my star-studded football team. Gergiev and Ovchinnikov were the forwards, Toradze was defending. I was centre back and on-the-field coach. I set my team the objective of winning the Moscow Theatre Troupe Championship. The leaders in the field at the time were teams from the Bolshoy Theatre and the Mayakovsky Theatre, where my old friend Armen Dzhigarkhanyan worked. We achieved our objective, and in the spring of 1983 we won the championship final against the Mayakovsky Theatre team – not without brilliance, though I say it myself. We won even though our team was missing Gergiev, our unstoppable striker. The day before the match our team had been training till late in the evening at the Borodino stadium. I personally drove all of my players home after the session. The last person I took home was Valery Gergiev. I took him to the Hotel Moscow. I stopped the car by the pedestrian underpass. I embraced Valery and wished him a good night.

"Valery, please, I'm begging you, go straight to bed. Take care!"

I hadn't even had time to turn away when Valery tripped on the first step of the subway and tumbled into the abyss. I watched, appalled, as my favourite striker somersaulted down the horrendous concrete staircase... Gergiev came to the match on crutches, and took part only as a spectator.

The Moscow evening newspaper wrote about our triumph. I am filled with more pride by this report than by the countless musical reviews of my piano-playing. Armen provided his own sardonic commentary of our victory: "Andrei, your team deserved to win, and for my own freaks I humbly apologise to you and your team." Armen's players, not expecting defeat, and certainly not a score of 6:2, had refused to shake our hands and had turned their backs on us defiantly and left the field.

My divorce from Hideko brought no positive change to my situation. The KGB had lied to me. Quite the opposite had happened. Hoards of goons now followed me, all actors in the people's theatre of the KGB. I was invited to play at the prestigious Moscow-Paris exhibition at the Pushkin Museum.

I played a programme of French music. The ambassador came up to me and thanked me tediously and at great length. I couldn't resist it and mentioned my own problems. He instantly vanished into thin air.

One day I headed off to the US embassy to watch *The Shining,* Cubrick's famous film. I went even though I already had the tape at home, but I really wanted to spend some time with the enemies of the KGB, to spend even two hours "cradled by foreign wings" and watch this electrifying film on a big screen. I walked up to the embassy, and had even forgotten that a group of about five humanoid "people's goons of the Soviet Union" were traipsing after me. When I was about 20 metres from the embassy entrance the "people's artists" acted out their macabre show. Initially they apparently "had an argument". They immediately simulated a "fight". A few times they fired shots, supposedly at each other, but actually at me. I set off at a run, zigzagging up the road to avoid being hit. It's a good thing the marines on duty didn't open fire in response, which is perhaps what the "actors" were counting on?

Sometimes I succeeded in complaining to Western diplomats about my fate. I didn't realize immediately that nobody would help me. The West was of course thrilled to tease the "Evil Empire", but had no intention of taking any serious measures for the sake of some honky-tonk piano player. I was of no particular use to anyone. Except possibly as a red rag to the Soviet bull. The Western security services needed major spies or dissidents for their reports and bonuses. I knew no secrets, however, except for those hidden in notes and sounds.

Aida and I celebrated New Year in 1983 by getting married! Aida moved out of her horrible conservatoire student hostel to live with me. I warned my Bosnian wife how badly it might end up for her. Aida reacted to that by saying, "I foster no illusions about the

My-Gods... They might kill me or expel me, might they? Then let's go and get married!"

"What do you mean, My-Gods?"

Aida told the story. Her Bosnian grandmother often reminisced about the liberation of Yugoslavia by the Red Army in 1945. The Soviet soldiers raped everyone regardless, Russian, foreign, old and young. The moment the gallant "liberators" appeared the girls would rush out of their homes shouting, "Girls, into the forest, the mountains, the My-Gods are coming, the My-Gods are coming, ru-u-u-u-un!" Forty years later, Aida's grandma could still see these terrifying images in front of her eyes; she could still hear the cries and screams, and experienced the same horror at the prospect of the "My-Gods".

Once again I believed and hoped. Maybe we could quietly slip away via Yugoslavia? We couldn't. But Aida became the messenger between me and my Western friends, who supported me as best they could...

On 10 November 1982 Brezhnev died.

Aida and I hungrily watched the telly. We picked up on portents of things to come. Incidentally, never before or since has anyone been shown for so long – an endlessly long time – on television as I was then. From morning till night, dressed in a glorious white tux, I played the funeral music personally for the USSR's chief, Secretary General Brezhnev. The Soviet functionary freaks were of the opinion that any classical music would suit for a funeral. Those Bach concertos have such exhilarating finales! There I was on the screen, playing jolly, sparkly dance music from the 18th century for the gobsmacked Soviet public. I was practically doing a jig on my seat as I played.

The Sovs reckoned it would be a good idea to have all the sirens of all the factories and everywhere else going off during the funeral. I was at football training at the time, chasing a ball around with the other guys from the Philharmonia. Suddenly a bunch of blokes ran up to us, fists waving, eyes flashing, and threatened to call the police.

"The people are burying the leader, and you are playing football?!"

I wanted to come up with some bright riposte, but one of my friends ran up and advised, "Play it safe and leave; the police really are on their way." I decided not to stir up the hornets' nest, whistled to my team and we all scattered to our various homes.

I got there just as they dropped Leonid's coffin. They did it with such finesse that a tremendous crash could be heard from every television in the land.

The coffin with ropes

I am unable to boast of extensive experience in touring around the USSR because I almost always tried to find any excuse to get out of such tours. Sometimes at night I still dream the typical nightmare of the touring concert musician as I run to a rehearsal in a freezing cold hall to a hungry, dozy orchestra. Alexander Slobodyanik told me how once when he was on tour the plane he was travelling on made an emergency landing because of "insufficient fuel" in a desolate spot in the middle of a field near Taldykorgan. The pilots wrapped up the engines in covers and disappeared. All around was virgin wasteland, a field covered in the first snows of winter and a blizzard blowing.

Somewhere in the distance, just about within walking distance, was the district centre, but not the town where Rosconcert had sent Slobodyanik. It must be noted at this point that the difference between Gosconcert and Rosconcert was a dramatic one. Gosconcert was the gravy train for privileged musicians who were permitted to travel, and by whose hard work the state of workers and peasants brazenly earned hard currency. Rosconcert was the tool for sending musicians round the Soviet provinces. It was a factory for introducing musicians to the multifarious members of the USSR's family of ethnicities. According to Slobodyanik, he was rescued from a cold and hungry death in the Kazakh steppe by a travelling circus of midgets. He even performed happily with them until he eventually reached a town with an aerodrome. This far-from exotic and, by Soviet measures, routine story happened not to some little-known musician, but to Alexander Slobodyanik, the unsurpassed interpreter of Chopin, whose photograph twice graced the front cover of *America* magazine because of his unprecedented popularity in the US.

He was an extraordinarily good-looking man. Richter told me that while giving a concert he first set eyes on Slobodyanik in a box in the Grand Hall of the Moscow Conservatoire. He stopped playing and was unable to continue the concert for some time.

By this time I had spent four years locked in my apartment on Nikitsky Boulevard. In order to earn a crust of bread I had to beg for permission to give concerts in different places around the Russian Federation. Rosconcert generously allowed me to play in the provinces. One winter, when it was fiercely cold, I set out for Karelia to try out the seven Bach concertos. I got off the train in Petrozavodsk and immediately came face to face with my own nightmare. The Philharmonia was a wooden structure, as was the hotel. The heating was hopeless, and the staff walked around inside in thick felt boots and fur coats. I turned up at the canteen, hoping to get hold of some hot water and two hard boiled eggs, the only thing that can save the body and soul of a frozen pianist. The canteen was closed. I set off for the rehearsal. I met the orchestra. I am still astounded by the courage and idealism of that generation of musicians – in these monstrous conditions, they were thinking only of music, only of Bach! They were rehearsing in gloves, but they played pretty well.

On the day of the concert the temperature plummeted. Minus 40 degrees centigrade. I was standing outside, waiting for the Philharmonia minibus. Later they told me that the minibus wouldn't start because it was so cold. So there I was, standing in my thin little lacquered shoes on a street covered in snow and ice. My legs were numb from the knee down. There was no bus. Fortunately, some policemen picked me up as they drove past the hotel.

They put me in the back of the paddy wagon and drove off. I arrived at the Philharmonia in my paddy wagon and saw a crowd and an enormous queue. People were standing out in the extreme Karelian cold because they desperately wanted to listen to Bach! I went into the Philharmonia and then ran to the green room in the hope of maybe warming up slightly there.

I opened the door and saw a surrealist picture before me. On the table in the empty green room stood a black coffin. A real coffin, wrapped around with ropes ready to be lowered into the grave.

It turned out that the musicians in Petrozavodsk shared their Philharmonia building with the theatre. The coffin was needed in a play by the Karelia drama troupe, some ghastly piece about

Finnish folk mores. So it was that after travelling in a mobile police cell, meeting a coffin and only just succeeding in overcoming the shivering of my icy hands, I started to perform the Bach concertos which I subsequently played on many occasions with the best orchestras in the most prestigious concert halls in the Western world.

The hall of the little Karelia Philharmonia was full to bursting, with some of the audience weeping out loud. I can still hear the voice of one girl who was soothing her sobbing mother.

"Mum, mum, calm down, stop, there are people all around!"

The audience was affected by the purity, love and immense faith of the German genius as they flowed in a blessed stream into the hall during the slow movements of the concertos.

The concert did not end for a long, long time, even though all seven concertos only last about three hours.

The audience demanded encores, and it wasn't until the end of the concert that their breath had warmed the icy hall of the polar city.

On the staircase at Lubyanka

In January 1983 I developed insomnia. I even forgot how to close my eyes. In February I caught a virus. What are those terrible viruses in Moscow? In the West neither I nor any of my friends have ever suffered from SUCH horrendous flu, tonsillitis, and respiratory diseases as in Moscow. A malignant Soviet aura? Remains of a biological weapon? There is plenty of radioactive waste in Moscow, so why not biological?

I had a temperature of 40 degrees. Ambulance. The doctor listened to my chest, tapped me all over, looked at me and shook his head... I was already completely out of it. I was croaking, trembling, thrashing in a fever, almost at death's door. Trusty Aida was wringing her hands. Beautiful Vika (from the ambulance) was unable to help in any way, and kind Paleyev the cardiologist was powerless.

I stared at the ceiling the whole time. It seemed to me that it was someone's horrible flat chest and it was breathing. Suffocating me. Suddenly, out of the blue, I saw Natasha Alkhimova standing at my deathbed. She was wearing a fur coat and hat. She placed her cool hand on my burning brow. She stroked my face, rough with stubble, and burst into tears. Natasha Alkhimova was my first true love (Buratinka's daughter Polya was my first infatuation).

Natasha was the daughter of Vladimir Alkhimov, chairman of the board at the USSR Central Bank, Hero of the Soviet Union, member of the Central Committee of the Communist Party. And who was I? A pianist. My artist father had died years ago, and my mother was a music teacher. Social inequality had stopped us from getting married. Our parents did not believe in the stability of a marriage like that, even though Natasha and I had been seeing each other almost since childhood. We lacked the necessary audacity to send them all to blazes. In the USSR it was all so complicated. Just the issue of residential registration and a roof over one's head made people slaves for life, combined with poverty and a total lack of rights.

How had Natasha heard about my illness? I still don't know; I think my mother must have summoned her. She decided to make use of this last chance. Natasha persuaded her powerful father to help have me hospitalised in the Central Clinical Hospital. Which is how I ended up in the most privileged clinic in the whole of the USSR, on Michurinsky Prospect in an isolation ward with its own little garden. Not far from Comrade Andropov, as it happened.

It was a most luxurious isolation ward! Doctors flitted here and there like bats, always ready to help. A garden, silence, air. In the space of two days the doctors at the Hospital had me back on my feet. They brought my temperature right down. Taught me how to sleep. Calmed my nerves. It was just like Dr Stravinsky's clinic in Bulgakov's book. I revelled in life. Half the day was taken up with medical procedures and then I was free to do what I wanted. There was a fantastic library. I read volumes from the complete works of Tolstoy and Dostoevsky with their letters and diaries.

A couple of weeks later I was discharged. Natasha came to collect me in her father's official car and took me to Nikitsky Boulevard. She told me that she was married with a child, a boy.

We parted in the street and I thanked Natasha for her miraculous appearance and for saving my life. Natasha left. I was wobbly with weakness. Once home I became ill again. The parquet floors and irreproachable doctors had pumped me full of imported medicines, got me back on my feet, but they hadn't actually cured me.

I thought that Natasha would never reappear in my life, and so I didn't call her. But I had underestimated her. Once she started on something she saw it through, just like her father. Natasha had several serious conversations with her father, asking him to help me. Vladimir Alkhimov adored his youngest daughter and was incapable of refusing her anything. Very soon I sensed that some sort of force for good had involved itself in my fate. Well-versed in the games played in the Soviet echelons of power, Alkhimov was a stalwart fighter and a political heavyweight. He did not rely on telephone calls, and did not make use of his "vertushka" closed telephone system, reserved for a select circle of very high-ranking Soviet officials. Like an experienced military commander he prepared every bridgehead with thoroughness. He started his work from the bottom up, with the little people. He never forced, rather he was persuasive, seeking an individual approach to everyone. He gradually worked his way upwards. When he drew nearer the top level of officials the matter was already virtually in the bag, and all that was needed from the senior figures was a signature, and they signed.

At first this irritated me – what was he doing? All he needed to do was pick up his special vertushka phone and call his buddies in the KGB or the Central Committee, and that would be it. Here he was, dragging me round the Party organisations at the Philharmonia, taking the effort to come himself, examining everything for himself, and talking to the slimeballs as well. It was only much later that I understood the full worth of his wisdom. Alkhimov was perfectly au fait with the value of the vertushka. He knew how deeply subordinates loathed the orders that came down to them via the vertushka; how intensely they hated people pulling strings, and with what ease they could sabotage any decisions, how spitefully take revenge if they were sidetracked or bypassed. He was therefore personally cleaning every latrine, pulling out every weed, and doing it so neatly that even if everyone was fired from their posts, his protégé would be removed from the danger zone by the only escape route.

I resigned myself as I started the rounds of Soviet bureaucratic torture. I had a permanent KGB shadow assigned to me. It was we who asked THEM for this as we needed them to track my every step. I was assigned the most useless person they had, a former executioner, a senile old major and alcoholic of long standing. He behaved like a child. He went everywhere with me.

When necessary he would show his ID. He sipped brandy all day long. After a week's "cohabiting" he was calling me "son". If the order had come, however, he wouldn't have hesitated a single second before taking me out for liquidation.

Alkhimov would dispatch the plan for the week to me via Natasha. For example: talks with Party and *Komsomol* functionaries at the Philharmonia. Visit to Stanislavsky Theatre to Khrennikov's premiere with presents – with a plan of the conversations and compliments. Visit to Sviridov to ask to perform his military suites for the piano (I couldn't bear them any more than I could Khrennikov). Of course all this in the presence of my senile KGB shadow. And so on in the same vein. Visit to the KGB for discussion with interested parties. Written reports about all my foreign acquaintances. I wrote about my producer, John, about my favourite agents – Walter Vedder from Frankfurt and Ian Hunter from London. I sat in the KGB club and wrote complimentary things about my friends and colleagues in the West. Nobody was asking me to lie, so I wrote the truth about these good people. Later I understood that the people from Kochuevskaya Street were insisting that everyone I had written about were spies. So I wrote disclaimers to all the slander by Ivan Ivanovich and Seryozha while drinking brandy paid for by the KGB, and in so doing I denied the charges against myself as well.

I could feel that the heap of lies that had built up over the years was gradually shrinking of its own accord and disappearing. Sometimes Alkhimov praised me, but more often he criticised me for getting above myself and being impatient. Natasha begged me not to explode. I kept my mouth shut. Slowly, without looking back, I crawled out of the Soviet Hades. I remembered the myth of Orpheus from when I was a boy. In my first year at the Central Music School, the teachers staged Gluck's opera with pupils at the school. Orpheus was sung by a beautiful violinist girl from Tokyo, Yoko Sato, who had somehow ended up at our school – there was no cultural exchange with Japan then or now. We little ones were in the choir, singing the part of the demons with great gusto, and howling a loud "No" in response to Orpheus's tearful entreaties.

After six months rattling around the lower rungs of every possible organisation, after reports on my community works and artistic plans at meetings of the grass-roots level of the organizations, Alkhimov sent me off to Shostakovich's dacha at the House of Composers in Ruza. This was all done through Khrennikov again!

Ten years after the Tchaikovsky Competition I found myself at the main dacha of the House of Composers, a destination over which Soviet composers constantly bickered for rest and "creative work"…

The events that were taking place on the musical front alarmed me. A mass exodus started up of musicians from the Soviet Union.

In June the talented violinist Vika Mullova defected with her conductor husband, Vakhtang Jordania. They escaped despite being closely shadowed by the KGB. She pretended to be ill after a concert in Finland and made her way in a hired car to neighbouring Sweden. She managed eventually to drop her shadow there and made her way to the American embassy in Stockholm, whence she and her husband were taken to the airfield in an armoured car, wearing white theatrical wigs. Two days later in Washington, Vika and her husband received residency permits for the USA.

The last time I had performed with Vika was on the day marked in the calendar as the professional holiday for the Police, in the Hall of Columns of the House of Congresses.

Vika was boiling with rage. Her beautiful big eyes were flashing with fury, and her strong, slender figure was shuddering with indignation.

We did not know each other well at the time. Even so, Vika burst out, "Andrei, it's impossible! I've won two competitions in a row, the Sibelius and the Tchaikovsky, and I'm not getting any concerts either in the USSR or abroad! This year I have two trips to the provinces. I don't know how to give bribes at Gosconcert, and I don't want to! I'm not going to put up with this!"

I settled into Dmitry Shostakovich's house in Ruza. Composers from the neighbouring houses started dropping round to see me. They told me extraordinary rumours about the wonderful pianist and my close friend, Lexo Toradze.

"Have you heard that Lexo Toradze has gone missing in Spain?"

"He's been kidnapped by ETA, the Basque separatists…"

This Lubyanka fabrication spent another four days working its way round the Soviet Union. On the fifth day Lexo turned up in America.

From there he phoned his father, the celebrated Georgian composer, wanting to reassure him. His father died of a heart attack straight after the conversation with his son.

In the course of six weeks at Shostakovich's dacha I played on the tennis courts to my heart's content, I lost some excess kilogrammes and learnt – not Khrennikov or Sviridov, but a new programme of Scriabin and Rachmaninoff. Natasha told me that negotiations were already underway for me to go to Prague, supposedly just for a concert at the embassy, but in actual fact to record Scriabin and Rachmaninoff with EMI in Prague.

The long-awaited moment came when the whole bottom rung in the Party and the secret police on my case had been cleaned out. Now I had to face the prospect of heading upwards.

To Philipp Bobkov. To get acquainted and have a face-to-face talk. Alkhimov was worried because he knew that Philipp was not a straightforward man, and I was impatient. I needed Bobkov to like me, which meant I needed to trick this seasoned expert in human nature. It was far from easy.

In early October I set out to the top floor of Lubyanka, to meet Bobkov. I had to go through those infamous massive doors, and up the same staircase that Solzhenitsyn wrote about. I was met by two young men in dark suits, and a few seconds later I was at the foot of the Lubyanka central staircase. I looked at the famous stairs and was rooted to the spot – this was the same staircase, the very one from the *Gulag Archipelago*.

I never once felt fear in all the years of explicit and implicit persecution. As I stood now in Lubyanka at the foot of the staircase before a meeting with the main persecutor of the intelligentsia I checked within myself – no, there was no fear, just a strange sense of mischievous boldness.

Bobkov's errand boys were sporty, almost balletic. They skimmed up this dreadful staircase, which had just five centimetres on each side that you could step on firmly, while there was a deep trough worn down the middle (like a bob sleigh track) by the trudging feet of prisoners. The boys were delighting in my stupefaction, and understood perfectly what was on my mind. They ran half a flight ahead of me and looked back with dazzling smiles, clicking their fingers as I limped and shuffled behind them.

Here I am at the door to Bobkov's office. I go in. The office is panelled in expensive wood, and there is a picture of Dzerzhinsky on the wall. It is a typical scene from a movie. At

Lubyanka. Bobkov gives a friendly smile, gets up from his desk. We shake hands. He looks very like a Russian version of Richter. He is tall with broad shoulders, a powerful physique, a light step, grey hair framing his face and his impressive head. He invites me to take a seat. We start chatting like old friends.

I heard that from the outset Bobkov had apparently been against any persecution of me. Maybe that is why I feel something like an affinity for him. I have no sense that before me sits the executioner of the dissident movement, a general in the KGB army. Bobkov is dressed in civilian clothes, elegant trousers and dark sweater.

"Please have no hard feelings, will you!"

"Whatever for?"

"I am glad that you are starting a new and happier page in your life."

"Thank you, I'm glad!"

"What are your plans?"

"Work, records, concerts, I want to make up for lost time."

"Good luck!"

"Thank you, I'm so grateful."

The conversation is nonsense. He is listening to my undertones and my backing vocals. He is looking into my eyes and reading what is there, or trying to. My eyes exude goodwill, calm, simplicity and obsequious gratitude. His eyes express satisfaction with what he sees. I try not to think or feel, just to exude goodwill. Any interior movement will give me away. It will leap out of my eyes to tear him to pieces along with his whole festering setup and that vile staircase. Which is why I am besotted with Denis, and soft as sealing wax. A piano and a crust of bread, that is all that I need. We are both in raptures over our meeting. We adore each other. Denis rises to his feet, wishes me success in my music and a pleasant trip. A trip! Farewell, Denis, it has been a pleasure meeting you! The dark boys took me back downstairs. The moment I walked through my apartment door the phone rang. Alkhimov.

"Denis liked you, well done!"

Before leaving for Prague I played my whole programme at home to Alexander Tchaikovsky.

"You know what I like in your playing, Andrei? That you play with such immense enjoyment!"

Alexander is one of the few who were genuinely pleased at my release. In Prague I was met by John and people from Supraphon. The reserved Czechs were pleased but said nothing. We embraced like spies in a detective story. The following day, Chris Parker flew out, the best sound engineer at EMI. There was very little time. The Czechs had found a venue for the recording in a tiny old cinema in a semi-basement space. The cinema was due to be demolished straight after the recording session. John Willan went away and left me with Richter's John: John Mordler. I was sorry as we were old friends and understood each other without needing to explain everything. Willan had managed to come out to Moscow twice as a tourist in order to see me and cheer me up. Mordler and I were working, the acoustics in the cinema were bad and the space was too small. Chris Parker was working miracles with the microphones. John Mordler was helping me, motivating me to play. We recorded Scriabin in two days. Subsequently this recording won a great many prizes, including the rarest prize, which is hardly ever awarded for solo recordings, the International Record Critics Award (IRCA). We needed to record the Rachmaninoff, but Chris Parker could do nothing with it. After the very first chords we realized that playing Rachmaninoff in this space would sound like a caricature.

The Brits gathered up their equipment. At seven the following morning a digger arrived and started demolishing our cinema. True melodrama. The Brits left for London with their tapes, and I travelled back to Moscow.

In December Alkhimov told me that EMI were coming to Moscow to record Rachmaninoff by night in the Grand Hall of the conservatoire. My John arrived in Moscow and we recorded together at the conservatoire, for the first and last time in the history of EMI.

I was working day and night in the run up to New Year. The neighbours were going crazy. But what else could I do? Alkhimov found a solution here as well. An enormous, rundown dacha was for sale in Odintsovo. Alkhimov knew that I could afford to buy it and do it up. I celebrated New Year with Aida and Natasha in the fairytale palace outside Moscow. Ten days later John Willan arrived in Moscow with Mark Vigers, a first-rate sound engineer whom we "stole" from Paul McCartney. I was gradually returning to life.

With Tikhon Khrennikov (1984)

Piano Concerto for the Left Hand

I have never understood why the experts underestimate this concerto by Ravel. In my opinion it is the best concerto for piano and orchestra written in the language of the first half of the 20th century.

The music is dark, proud and serious.

In his own way, Ravel is quoting and developing here the famous medieval hymn Dies Irae (Day of Wrath), ascribed to Thomas of Celano, which for many centuries has been used as a sequence in the Catholic mass, and used by a good half of all composers throughout history. Other resonances of this quoting can also be heard in Ravel's music (Mozart and Verdi's Requiems, and Mussorgsky's Dances of Death).

The first words of Dies Irae are a quotation from the Old Testament Book of Zephaniah:

That day is a day of wrath, a day of trouble and distress, a day of wasteness and desolation, a day of darkness and gloominess, a day of clouds and thick darkness.

That is precisely the picture that Ravel paints with his music. At the start of the concerto hollow, lifeless and uniform fourths sound (double bass), after which the contrabassoon comes in, the most forlorn and lowest instrument in the orchestra, as it plays the theme backwards, as an inversion. When the French horns join in on the three notes, B-A-G, it seems as though death itself is hanging in the air of the concert hall.

The dead world stretches out before the listener and an evil indigo cloud hangs over the listener's head.

Nobody has ever been able to hear the theme from Dies Irae in the music because Ravel "cut off" every other note from the original and left only the skeleton of the theme.

Ravel has B-A-G, B-B-A-G, D-F-E-D-F-E-D. If one adds the subsemitone to each note (as church singing often does), then the text will be: B-A-B-G-A-F-G. This is Dies Irae, and the theme is quoted elsewhere throughout the whole concerto.

I can remember that the moment I guessed this I immediately rang my former professor, Naumov.

"Lev Nikolaevich, have you ever noticed Dies Irae in Ravel's Piano Concerto for the Left Hand?"

"Where? I've been teaching this music for 45 years, and I don't see any Dies Irae there."

Then I played the theme for Naumov over the phone. He heard it and understood. He congratulated me with my discovery.

Ravel then distributes the images of death around the different instruments in an original jazz harmony. Spanish motifs can be heard, their ancient games with death.

The music constantly produces visual and sensual images. Ravel is extremely cinematographic. His music is not suitable for cinema, as it is film in sound, itself.

After the secondary theme, in which the piano melodically "weeps" and "sobs" in the same modulations as the death theme, the march is born, then grows and grows, ever stronger. The march through the desert is interrupted by a burst of machine gun fire. There is no other way of interpreting the progression of chords both for the piano and the orchestra: ta-ta-ta-ta-ta-ta – giving way to sort of crawling, dead chromaticisms. Corpses falling to the ground.

Paul Wittgenstein, to whom the concerto is dedicated, lost his right hand in the First World War. He spent time as a prisoner of war in Siberia and served on the Italian front until the end of the war. The Italian army fought a brutal war in its various African colonies. "Africa" and a black, jazz flavour are plainly present in the concerto. Furthermore, by using this exotic material, Ravel develops the theme of Dies and projects it onto his own contemporary period.

There is no trace of American jazz (as the text books assure us). Ravel creates his own unrepeatable, individual black jazz. It is Spanish, Basque and apocalyptic, but by no means originates in New Orleans.

The death theme in Ravel sounds terrifying and tempting (clarinets, oboes). Death's sweet tone cluster is sometimes tormenting and sometimes interrupted by short melodic insertions of burlesque, and I see in these spontaneous splashes of contrasting bright consonance the wildlife of Africa, the oases and birds. As a truly great artist, Ravel shows in these episodes the contrast between playful, frisky nature and the destructive quintessence of humankind.

The concerto ends not with the triumph of life, but with the apotheosis of death and non-being, the orchestra bellows with all of its instruments – the brass, percussion and strings, drowning out the piano, whose sounds blend in as one of the colours in the general bacchanalia of death. The concerto breaks off in disharmony – this is death coming on bony feet, and with a few terrifying blows it puts an end to the current of existence.

Ten years after this concerto was written World War Two started.

Tigran

Tigran was a short, quite delicately built man with a little round belly that served as a comfortable perch for his small hands. When walking or standing chatting to someone he would always comfortably tap the fingers of his hands, folded on his stomach.

He wore fashionable and comfortable shoes, neat, dark blue or grey trousers with braces, beautiful soft shirts and elegant jackets. In summer he had a lightweight, beige jacket and in winter a cosy, thick, knitted jumper. He loved trilbies and trench coats.

His face was swarthy, with a large Armenian nose and sticking out ears. Dark brown, somewhat doleful but intelligent eyes sparkled in his deep eye sockets. When playing chess he would wrinkle his brow... He seemed to me to be the epitome of comfort and dignity. Whenever I was near him I would unwittingly be put in mind of the snowy peaks of Ararat, that symbol and anguish of the Armenian people, and hear the enchanting sorrowful sounds of the *duduk*; I would remember the pink peach blossom of spring and the sapphire blue of Lake Sevan...

Petrosyan bought a house in Barvikha and lived there for 16 years, almost never leaving for his apartment in Moscow.

It was a beautiful, spacious two-storey mansion of wood and stone with an enormous dining room on the ground floor. It was a palace. Like almost all Soviet celebrities, Tigran liked comfort, and specifically comfort in the American style. He had an enormous American TV, an American washing machine, a General Electric fridge and a gigantic American car. Either a Cadillac or an Oldsmobile. His diminutive wife, Rona, drove the car. She would put three cushions on the seat, tied together with a belt. Tigran himself never drove...

He also never walked along the side of the road because he was afraid of falling onto a ditch...

Despite being so small, Rona had the energy of a booster rocket. She and Tigran would often reminisce about the time Rona dragged him to his final match with Botvinnik. Tigran was shouting, "I don't want to, I won't go, I'm tired!" Rona shoved him from behind and hissed, "Yes you will go, you lazybones, you will go, you donkey." She shovelled him into the car and took him to the match. Tigran shook his head, smiled shamefacedly and muttered, "Rona, Rona, stop giving away trade secrets."

Tigran often went to visit the Alkhimovs. As a rule, people who lived in Barvikha tended to drop in on each other regularly. They rarely spoke of politics. They swopped society gossip (did you hear that Rostropovich poisoned himself?), prattled on about their villas, discussed what neighbours had bought what, and boasted to each other about successful acquisitions for their own houses, even if it was only a gilt handle for the toilet door... They almost always talked very quietly, practically whispering... Even in the garden or in the woods. Stalinist fears still thrived in the minds of the Brezhnev élite, just as the Stalinist censors still ruled the roost in the Brezhnev newspapers, magazines and television... Back then even the trees and flowers had ears... Tigran spoke in his normal voice and didn't whisper, but he also loved to chat about his purchases...

The Alkhimovs had a bad-tempered Alsatian called Jupiter. He was a horribly stupid dog. He was like the Soviet policeman who shot at me by the Japanese consul's house on Vavilova Street. You could walk past Jupiter 100 times, and on the 101st he would definitely bite you. Tigran had known Jupiter for many years, but one day the crazy dog suddenly bared his teeth and, quick as lightning, he went for poor defenceless Tigran. Although the bite itself was minor, Tigran became terribly agitated, he went green with terror, and he was convinced that he would succumb to rabies at any moment which "of course" Jupiter had transmitted to him. The Alkhimovs panicked, as they knew Tigran to be a dreadful hypochondriac. He was incredibly scared of injections, but this time it would seem that he even asked to be injected with a double dose of anti-rabies medicine and stoically put up with all the agonies. Even though the Alkhimovs heaped a whole pile of certificates on the table for Tigran, testifying to Jupiter's good health, Tigran carried on with his course of injections. For a long time after he would look suspiciously at water, and gaze in the mirror while shaving, worried that he might start frothing at the mouth...

Tigran really adored music – classical, jazz, pop... He had a wonderful record library at home with some rare recordings that he had been collecting all his life. When abroad, Tigran bought expensive record players, tape recorders, amplifiers and speakers...

Tigran had very poor hearing, and a large, cream-coloured hearing aid always hung behind one ear. Tigran was never embarrassed about his hearing aid, constantly fiddling with it without taking it out from behind his ear while the apparatus gave out horrendous squeaks and caterwauls, and the impassive Grandmaster calmly continued his conversation.

Tigran loved to spend time alone in his study upstairs. The shelves there held gold and rosewood chess sets, silver engraved dishes and decanters, all gifts from Armenians the world over, and on the walls hung decorative weaponry with inlay and jewels. He would take off his hearing aid and turn on his half-kilowatt speakers at full whack and enjoy the music. The house used to shake so much that Rona was afraid it would fall down. Nobody was allowed to disturb him during these moments. There was only one person that Tigran permitted to do anything at all, and that was Auntie Dusya, or Duka as he used to call her; a large peasant woman who was their housekeeper and had lived with the Petrosyans all her life. She was as devoted to Tigran as Savelevich was to Petrusha in Pushkin's story. Tigran loved film, especially comedy. I can remember his delighted, radiant laughter when he watched the tape I gave him of the brilliant musical film, *The Blues Brothers*, with the great John Belushi and many of America's greatest jazz musicians – Ray Charles, Aretha Franklin, John Lee Hooker, Cab Calloway, etc. He watched the cassette practically every day...

I first met Tigran in the mid 70s, when fate introduced me to many Moscow celebrities. We only really made friends when I bought the house in Odintsovo in the autumn of 1983. Tigran really liked the way I played, and was well informed about the repressions against me.

His kind heart could not bear injustice and he sympathized with me and helped me as much as he could. He was thrilled by even the tiniest little triumph on my part, and was livid when he found out about the latest ignominious act against me on the part of our all-powerful state...

When I bought the house, Tigran was suddenly enthused – he had long dreamed of playing real billiards. Despite the impressive size of his own house, there wasn't room for a huge Russian billiard table.

Tigran often used to come and see me and give me advice on building, and tell me stories about the past. He seemed to relive his youth with me. The son of a caretaker at the officers' club in Tbilisi, orphaned at a young age, he had won the title of world champion in a highly challenging battle, and was transformed from a poor, provincial Armenian to a world celebrity and a chess legend. There was something similar in the paths our lives had taken and in our professional destinies...

Tigran loved sharing happy, good news with his friends, and entertaining them with all sorts of fun. Having turned up early one morning and discussed for the 500th time where the billiard table was going to stand, and having shot the breeze about boilers, cathodes and diodes, heating systems, thermo-ventilation and other domestic matters, he dragged me off to some far-flung shop to buy something for the house... Tigran had trusted agents who provided him with priceless tip offs on what was available where, and immediately shared his secrets with me. "Andrei, today in Khimki they've put some Swedish leather furniture out – sofas (he said sofies), armchairs (armchies), wonderful cupboards (cubbies) and wardrobes (wardries), we're going straight away!"

Tigran didn't actually have any speech impediments, he was usually softly spoken, calm and clear, but when he was gripped by the thrill of buying stuff he would get terribly excited and mangle his words in a very amusing way. When Tigran came out with these cutesy diminutives it was an indication that he was in the best possible mood. We got in the car and slogged all the way across town for the sofies and armchies... Once there, we lost no time in doing the paperwork for the purchase... If I didn't have enough money with me then Tigran would always add some of his own (when you get rich you can give it back). Thus, thanks to Tigran's spy network, Barvikha filled up with exotic imported goods. The only thing that cast a dampener on triumphs of this sort was the fact that although the houses were filling up with handsome furniture, it was all exactly the same. This was the case with other items for home use. The Bosch gas ovens, the AEG food processors, the Italian ice-making machines, the top-loading washing machines...

It was 1984. The billiard room had still not been built, but the rest of the house was almost finished. Every day, Tigran and I walked in the woods and discussed my affairs in detail. Tigran supported me, and encouraged me before each of my meetings with the top dogs: "Don't take too long over it, but also don't be in too much of a rush, the main thing is to make your moves in the right order." That was his favourite expression.

I had absolutely no idea that serene, well-balanced, harmonious Tigran, who took such care of his health and enjoyed life so much, was actually standing on the edge of the grave...

It was as though Tigran was hit by an avalanche. At first he had abdominal pain, then vomiting, then he was taken to hospital, had tests and then a diagnosis. Pancreatic cancer. He was examined by the best doctors... There was no hope. Nobody said anything to poor Tigran, as he would immediately have died of fright... Tigran believed he had "a little food poisoning" and said, "I must have eaten something, I really must be more careful."

When our good friend Arno Babadjanian died in November 1983, Tigran said, "The bombs are falling closer and closer." That was in my garden in Odintsovo, and as he spoke Tigran kept his hands on his stomach...

Everyone except Petrosyan knew that he was dying. Everyone lied to his face, and he never suspected a thing.

In June 1984, two months before he died, many of Moscow's luminaries gathered at his house – doctors, academics, chess players, musicians. It was Petrosyan's 55th birthday. Natasha and I were there. Everyone knew that Tigran's days were numbered, but made toasts wishing him good health, and invoking many happy returns of the day... The table was laden with food. Tigran was pale, thin and sad as he sat at the table...

Tigran did not live to see the billiard room completed, but he did live long enough to see my first trip to the UK, which he had been looking forward to impatiently.

Shortly before he passed away, in the hospital, the dying Tigran asked his wife, "How did it all go for dear Andrei in London?"

Rona answered, "Wonderful!"

Tigran sighed, laid his head on Rona's hands and burst into tears. He was buried in the Armenian cemetery in Moscow.

Only with you

1984 started magically. The Brits flew in from EMI and came straight to Odintsovo to see me, through deep snow, and wearing Russian felt boots and mittens. We recorded Rachmaninoff by night in the Grand Hall of the conservatoire. It was so romantic! We recorded everything over four nights. Unfortunately, the Brits were not very well acquainted with the specifics of the acoustics in the hall. The quality of sound in this recording was not optimal. Nevertheless, the disc left a pleasant impression. It was spontaneous, lively music...

At the end of February I set out for the GDR, for the second time in my life, for a recital tour with an enormous programme. After the success of our joint Handel concerts, Richter had been gripped with the idea of doing a similar tour with all six of the Bach French suites. Slava wanted to divide up the cycle with me and perform it together. However, after my musical "victory" over him in Arkhangelskoye, Richter had abandoned the plan. I learned all six of the French suites and included them in my programme along with Rachmaninoff and Scriabin. I was supposed to play them in the same place that Richter wanted to perform the French suites, in the Gold Room at the Sanssouci Palace in Potsdam.

In Berlin I was met by a small, black-haired woman called Lilian. She was my interpreter and attendant from the GDR side. The first concert in my tour was held in East Berlin, in the hall at the Komische Oper. The concert was a huge success. Articles appeared in GDR papers with headlines that were far from typical of the socialist press.

"Concert held yesterday by concert pianist with clear signs of genius."

My interpreter blushed and told me, "You are not at all how your fellow Russians described you, Richter and Dorliak."

"What did they say about me, if it's no secret?"

"Nina Lvovna said that you were a spiteful, worthless and dangerous man, and Svyatoslav Teofilovich backed her up, called you a toxic loudmouth, and said that it was best to have nothing to do with you. I don't understand what right they had to say that!"

Hearing this I was not even angry. Why be angry at the past?

Lilian and I travelled all round East Germany and ended the tour with the Bach suites in the Gold Room. All the concerts were highly successful, the audience gave standing ovations, demanded and received encores. At the end of the evening of Bach at Sanssouci, Lilian kissed me with pride and called me a "victor".

I should have been happy and rested on my laurels, but I was horrified to feel with my whole body (just like Prince Myshkin) a dread premonition of a seizure. A spasm rose up from my stomach to my throat. I was unable to breath, but I was fully conscious. A horrible torment. I trembled and thrashed and my eyes almost popped out of my head. It receded slightly and I gasped frantically at the air. I could feel that someone was holding me in their arms, like a child. Someone quite small, but very strong and sturdy. He was saying fondly, "Don't be scared, son, the ambulance is on its way. I felt there was something wrong, you were so pale when you were standing on stage. I'm Colonel Sokolov, commander of the local military unit."

That was how kind Colonel Sokolov held me in his arms until I started to breathe again.

The following day I flew back home, where I threw myself into finishing the building work on our country house. I always derived immense pleasure from drawing up and implementing plans. The team I had hired worked amiably together. Sometimes they would ask me, "Gavrilov, play us the Elegy!" I would play, and they would weep.

At the same time I was preparing Natasha for the idea of emigrating. At first she refused point blank to talk about it. Then she understood that I had no other way. She cried and wrung her hands.

"What will happen to Father?"

Alkhimov had planned my life in his business-like way first to be honoured as Distinguished Artist, then People's Artist, and Hero of Socialist Labour, to carry on Richter's work, and in the wonderful distant future to be the first pianist in the USSR. Wealth, privileges, awards.

As an honest man, but Soviet to the core, he found it difficult to imagine that I did not need all that. Natasha had more insight than her father. Nevertheless, she hoped that my wish to break free would dissipate of its own accord as soon as the disgrace was lifted from me and my material and political situation improved. As time went by she realized that this was an illusion. She resigned herself, but grew depressed and was scared at the prospect of trips that we would make abroad. After my trip to London in June she met me and whispered, "I was certain you wouldn't come back."

"Only with you."

In May I flew to springtime Bratislava to make recordings with EMI. I waited a long time for whoever was meeting me, but they didn't turn up so I went into town by taxi. Before leaving the airport I noticed a woman in cream trousers, raincoat and black hat searching the crowd with her eyes. This Madame was affectionately stroking the bonnet of her cherry-red Volga. She suddenly waved her arms and, let out a screech. She jumped up and down, hugged and kissed some people, seated them in her car and left.

Later it transpired that this cream lady had been sent to meet me, but had happened to see an old friend in the crowd, the niece of Gerasimov (the film director), with a group of friends and without a moment's hesitation she left with them. When I rolled up at the hotel, this lady was chatting with someone at the entrance. The Brits from EMI came over to me. At this point the woman realized that she had messed up big time and rushed over to us to apologise. That same evening she fell hopelessly in love with me. Her friend (Gerasimov's niece) managed to develop a crush on my producer. These crazy girls nearly disrupted our entire work, chasing after us and several times bursting into our hotel rooms. We were completely unable to reciprocate their feelings – I was still cross with the hat woman for the story at the airport, and John happened to be gay. The lady in the hat once appeared, like a mirage, near my house in Odintsovo. I gave my builders the order not to let her in.

We recorded a double album with all of the Bach French suites in the glorious Philharmonic in Bratislava. It was the first recording I had made without rushing and with no unnecessary dramas. As soon as the disc was released on the international market it got the highest rating.

Before leaving I decided to go for a walk around the old town. I met a great number of émigrés there who were actively buying crystal, leather and various other luxury items that cost considerably more in Austria than in Bratislava. In the crowd of former compatriots loading up with junk I spotted Oleg Maisenberg (Gidon Kremer's long term partner), who was just starting his professional solo career in the West. Oleg noticed me. He looked askance at me. He couldn't understand how Gavrilov, who was "locked in the KGB dungeons", had turned up in Bratislava. What's more, he was plainly discomfited by the fact that I had unwittingly caught him in the act of stocking up with vulgar crystal ware. I read his thoughts in the confused expression on his face, and smiled.

At home, our life was overshadowed by the agonizing talks Natasha and I had about emigrating. During this period it was not only us, but millions of other "prisoners in the Soviet camp" who were convincing their near and dear to leave with them. They were persuading them to take the risk and hurtle into the unknown. In the USSR an application to emigrate led to the spectre of loss of job and friends, social isolation, and sometimes even prison. By no means all arrivals abroad could expect paradise. Nobody was waiting with open arms at the other end. Every émigré experienced the pain of these conversations and decisions.

Our little family, Aida, Natasha and I, tried to resolve the irrational situation in a rational way. We needed to "break the bonds" and "retie the knot" all over again. We did not want to make each other unhappy and, strange as it may seem, we found an amicable solution.

Aida would divorce me and go to London. Natasha and I would get married in order to leave the Soviet Union together. We would all meet in London in February 1985 and decide then how everyone was going to live further. The main thing was to save ourselves from the Soviet dragon. The plan was a good one, but we knew perfectly well how easily the KGB could break plans and bones. The future remained unclear.

As was always the case in instances of emigration, what was depressing was that even if we got away from the USSR, we were leaving a host of defenceless hostages in its jaws. Natasha's son, her father, mother, sister, niece, my mother and my brother. Aida, being Bosnian, had no family in the Soviet Union, but she had her own nightmare – she was scared of travelling to London on her own without knowing the language.

Our plan started to be put into practice. After all the marital re-arrangements we sent Aida to London. She went to live in the large house of my producer, John, and started to learn English. Natasha and I prepared for a trip to Poland in October which was to be a prelude to our escape to London at the start of the following year.

In the autumn of 1984 I had to meet Bobkov for the second time in my life. I was supposed to show him my brother who had not been allowed to go to Rome with his wife in December 1979 because of me. I needed to persuade him to lift the ban on my brother. Igor froze with fear, like all novices at Lubyanka, whereas I, an old-timer, just chuckled and reassured him. Denis met us with wonderful cordiality. We did not talk about business. Bobkov just took one look at my brother and immediately worked out that Igor was not part of his remit. We drank tea and chatted about my successful return to musical life. Bobkov politely asked Igor about his artistic plans and advised him paternally not to miss anything in Italy that might be valuable for his artistic development. Soon after this, Igor went to Rome with his Nina.

Crashed and burned

November 1984. The first time abroad with Natasha. To Poland. The last KGB test before being allowed to go to a capitalist country with my wife. They tested my reliability in the GDR, Prague, Bratislava and then twice they let me go to London. Alone! Now, finally, together! Well, yes, Poland was of course not really abroad in the full sense, but we were sure that Poland would be a springboard from which we could jump into the free world. In February the following year, 1985, we were expecting concerts and recordings in London. We would be going there together! We just needed to keep it together in Poland. Eight concerts in total. It was a recital programme.

My first leap into the free world from the Soviet Union took place in June 1984. London! After almost five years of misery without being able to leave the country. I got off the airplane in Heathrow, flew through the friendly customs, passed passport control and stood on the travelator. I looked around from side to side as I went along. This is it, my world, now I am home. It was a strange, melancholy feeling. I tried to remember everything that had happened to me over the long years of imprisonment in Moscow. And I couldn't! It was as though all my memories had been wiped clean. I had woken up in London after a long nightmare. Everything here was familiar and congenial, and everything that remained THERE was alien, even though I had seen and experienced it all a thousand times, it was unfamiliar. Where was my native land? It was where my freedom was. At that moment, on the travelator at Heathrow, I felt that as an absolute truth and the only certainty! The Russia that I loved till it hurt – the Russia of Rachmaninoff and Scriabin – had come with me, not on the soles of my shoes, purchased in the infamous department number 100 at GUM, but in my heart. *That* Russia was always with me, inside me.

For five years I had held back the tears, and now, in the airport, the dam burst. Thank God, nobody saw me. Even if they had seen me they would have left me alone. A wonderful thing, English privacy and dignity.

Sunshine, black cabs, intelligent, courteous London cabbies. The Thames, the South Bank. Concerts, concerts. Queen Elizabeth Hall, the Royal Festival Hall, the National Theatre. London had not forgotten me, and the tickets had long since sold out. The excited cries of the public, the complimentary reviews in the UK national papers… A sensation. Interviews, photo shoots, elegant salons, celebrities – it all flew past me like pictures in a colourful kaleidoscope. Success!

Why did it not thrill me like it used to? And never would thrill me again. Because I was mortally injured, and would be wounded till my dying day. The years of agony had not left me untouched, and something had changed inside me. Reality seemed to have lost its power over me. Physics had given way to metaphysics – burning new questions faced me, and I would search for the answers all my life.

I came back to Moscow from London and – a strange novelty – I felt indifference. What if they bury me alive again? I couldn't care less. Let them bury me alive, torture me, humiliate me. It's all the same to me. I don't care where I am. I don't care what new scumbag is now ruling in the Kremlin. I have ash in my heart. I have burned out like the Fuse in the Bosnian film of the same name. In October I went on another trip to London. On my own again. I did not feel intense joy the second time, because me wife was still with THEM as a hostage, as were my mother and my brother.

Natasha's father persuaded the highest authorities in the USSR to lift the mark of disgrace off me. This honest man proposed himself as the "guarantor of Gavrilov's return" and was successful. Natasha and I made a plan to wait for permission for both of us to go on tour and remain in London. We intended to start a battle there against the KGB to fight for freedom of movement around the planet, and we dreamed of proving to everyone, to the Soviets, and the émigrés that the age of defection was over. We did not inform Alkhimov of our plans. This was the only weakness in our scheme. We were troubled by our consciences. The only justification for us was that we were not fighting for "boxes of chocolates and champagne", but for survival, for the air to breathe, and we wanted to open a window through into the world for Soviet performers. The "ordinary Soviet public" would come after them. We hoped later to explain to Natasha's father, and to ask for his forgiveness while also enjoying success. We succeeded in implementing the first part of our plan on our own, with the help of Natasha's father, while the second part – the liberation of the Soviet public – was performed by Mikhail Gorbachev, a great man. We also made our own modest contribution to the story.

Warsaw, Chopin airport. It turns out that Chopin is now an airport! There are Mozart chocolates, Wagner toilet paper (I saw it myself in Bayreuth in the 70s, complete with musical notes), a dog called Beethoven in the movies, a vodka called Tchaikovsky, so why shouldn't Chopin become an airport? With a runway, hangars, passengers and baggage collection... Brilliant... We got in the car and went straight to the station. We travelled from there to Poznań where my concert tour started. The embassy staff met us as though we were VIPs. Once again I was "a celebrity and the pride" of the Soviet Union. Thank you for your trust in me, dear comrades! Only I have no further need of your raptures. Because I know, on the evidence of my own health, what comes next.

Natasha and I ran for the train, dreaming of being alone at last in our first-class double compartment. We went down the steps leading to the platform. There we found crowds of people. They all had red-rimmed eyes from crying. They were almost all in black. What was going on?

I didn't immediately click that today was 3rd November, the day of the funeral for Jerzy Popiełuszko. He was a much-loved public figure, a singer of freedom and Solidarity, a preacher of the brotherhood of love and independence. Agents of the Polish Interior Ministry Security Service had savagely murdered this inspiring man. Probably with permission from big brother. The disfigured body had been thrown into a reservoir, where it was found only ten days later. Today was the day of the funeral to which, as I later discovered, a quarter of a million people went. These people were now making their way home.

We forced our way through to the platform. There were people everywhere. It was a weeping sea of black mourning. We barely managed to squeeze onto the train for Poznań. The vestibules at the ends of the carriages were packed full, in a compartment designed for six there were fifteen people. Some had climbed onto the roof of the train. Nobody was speaking. I spoke to Natasha in English, "Not a word of Russian, let's go to the restaurant car, I don't feel very well, I need to drink something." Somehow we squeezed our way into the next carriage. I looked at the Poles as we went. Almost all the passengers in the train were men. Many of them had torn shirt fronts. What faces! Their eyes were red, faces dark, some of them writhing in fury, others ground down by grief and in tears. Many of them were feverishly clutching the crosses they wore round their necks. Their knuckles were white with tension. Their crosses were cutting into the skin.

I never saw "mass expression of public love" for anyone in the USSR. Have the Russians ever loved anyone except for Stalin, Lenin and other villains? Do the Russians have a "public heart"? Or has its place long since been usurped by a prison slop pail?

In former times such a demonstration of public love occurred only once, when Mikhoels was buried in 1948. He was killed by KGB heroes who ran him over with a truck. Thousands of people stood silently in the January cold of Moscow. Although there probably were gentiles among the mourners, it was the Jews rather than the Russians who demonstrated their love and mourning for Mikhoels.

Who have ordinary Soviet people loved?

Possibly only Vysotsky. He touched a nerve. I can remember his funeral in Moscow during the Olympics. Crowds of people came out to bury Vladimir. At the time I thought they were like sheep whose loudest ram in the flock, the one with the hoarsest voice, had just died. When I was little I used to watch the chickens in our yard. If a cat killed one of the chicks the mother hen would jump on the little corpse in her distress, dig in the soil with her claws, cluck and twitch and it looked like the poor bird might die of sorrow any minute. A moment later she had forgotten all about her grief, and wouldn't even notice the chick's little body still lying beside her. How like our fellow countrymen that is!

Here in Poland it was different. Faces bore the inscription: No, Commy Comrades, you won't get away with this murder! The Poles will not forget Jerzy Popiełuszko the way the Soviet hens forget their dead. Whatever the Polish people still have to live through, they will not forgive, and they will not forget. And the fearless priest will lead his people to freedom even after death!

The train was flying towards Poznań. The night was drawing in. Some of the men were fervently praying. Others were beating their chests with their fists and tearing their shirt fronts…

"Jesus Maria! Woe, Calamity and Disaster! Alas!"

Waves of anger and weeping swept up the train.

My poisoned body could take no more, my trampled soul seemed to want to break free from my body in its agony. I was Russian, Soviet, and I had been sent here by the assassins, and I was supposed to play Chopin to the Poles in their name. I was the killer!

I went into one of my seizures. With the last of my strength I tore through to the space between the carriages, tossing large men out of my way as I went. Before passing out I managed to pull the communication chord. The brakes screeched so loudly it seemed the Moon had crashed into the Earth. My eyes were blinded by a purple light…

A few minutes later, what felt to me like several years later, I could vaguely make out the face of my Natasha. For some reason we were not on the train. There were trees all around. We were in an autumn forest! Fresh air was whistling into my lungs. I closed my eyes and passed out in my wife's arms.

I came to in the consul's car. The consul was consulting with the doctor.

"Is it possible to take him all the way to Warsaw by car?"

"You see, he's in a serious condition."

In doctor's parlance that means – you're unlikely to get him there alive. In my head buzzed the thought – uh-oh, we've got no chance of making it to London now. The tour has gone where the sun don't shine. I didn't pass the final test. I crashed and burned!

Everyone who was helping extract me from Soviet nonbeing would turn their backs on me in disgust.

I lay curled on the back seat of the car with my face buried against the back of the seat and said nothing.

C minor, Op 48 No 1

The Nocturne in C minor is one of Chopin's most powerful pieces. In the musical world the view is generally held that it was written with the influence of Liszt and his Hungarian motifs. I think that this is a mistake deriving from an EXTERNAL rhythmical similarity between Chopin's piece and Liszt's music. In actual fact there is no profound affinity between them.

Chopin's piece makes no reference to Hungary, nor to dances. In the Nocturne in C minor Chopin provides textured documentation of his grief and his reaction to the suppression of the Polish uprising by the Russian army in 1831. Many of Chopin's close friends were killed in the battles against the troops led by Diebitsch and Paskevich.

In the first section of the nocturne we hear the voice of the composer (in the upper register). Chopin is mourning his people. In the lower register the music imitates the sound of cannon fire and exploding shells, at times distant and at times approaching. The fusion of these two musical themes (weeping and cannonfire) makes a stunning impression. The listener is present in the heat of battle and also hears and shares Chopin's mourning lament.

The central section of this nocturne would make a perfect national anthem for Poland. This music is a passionate and proud call to arms in the battle for freedom.

The concluding section of the nocturne is a mortal battle before the triumphant end. In my view, the Nocturne in C minor has far more grounds for being called Revolutionary than the famous étude to which Chopin's contemporaries gave that title. Chopin succeeded, like no other, in demonstrating the horror and insanity of war, oppression and murderous cruelty.

Chopin recognized and embodied in his music not only the sweetness, but also the tragedy of being; not only heavenly beauty, but also bloodthirsty violence; not only human solitude and despair, but also human joy and the triumph of the shared just cause.

QR link to the Chopin Nocturnes performed by Andrei Gavrilov

A story with bowler hats

Before leaving for London Natasha and I went to see Richter, at the request of his trusty agent, Nina Dorliak. Having used her own channels to hear of my family ties with the all-powerful Alkhimov, she had decided to do a little fishing in troubled waters. As it happened, Nina's trusty hound Kukharsky had just been sacked and she was needing to look for new connections. She had been surprisingly quick to forget that it was she who had connived to split up Slava and me. As for Richter, he had forgotten that three years ago he had hidden in the loo and not opened the door for me when I had come to see him at his own invitation.

I had not forgotten the bad, but nor had I forgotten the good – our long, productive friendship – so I went to Bronnaya Street. Slava and I spoke as though we had never parted.

Nina immediately started trying to ingratiate herself with my Natasha. She even asked her if Alkhimov might be able to "have Kukharsky reinstated." Natasha was embarrassed. The whole thing made me sick, but I didn't show my feelings. Slava was confused by the unexpected turn matters had taken: Nina as a supplicant to my wife. After two hours of such talk, Natasha and I left.

When we parted I experienced no tug on my heart strings and no urge to wipe away a tear – by then I already saw Nina and Slava in a different light. They were two miserable people on their way out of life, in a soulless apartment, and seated at a cold table that held the same smelly sausages from the same Soviet supplier that had been there for the last twenty years.

I kissed Slava on the brow in parting, although I should have driven a wooden stake through his heart.

In February Natasha and I were taken to Sheremetyevo Airport in Alkhimov's official Chaika car. A few days prior to this I had organized a going-away party at my house. I had invited Gergiev and Bashmet as well as several other musicians, Ilka, and Vika from the ambulance. I hinted that once in London I would start to fight for our freedom – the freedom to travel and make music independently of state institutions. Gergiev and Bashmet promised to help as much as they could from inside the Soviet Union. My loyal friends Ilka and Vika gave us their blessing for our mission and supported and prayed for us for many years to come.

We arrived in London and went to the Soviet Trade Delegation in Highgate, next door to the cemetery where Marx is buried. Considerate Alkhimov had phoned someone before we left and we had been allocated a small cottage. Officially this trip came under the patronage of Mezhdunarodnaya Kniga, an organization which was part of the Soviet Foreign Ministry and engaged in robbing artists of all sorts, as legalized in the USSR. The bosses at Mezhdunarodnaya Kniga compiled a deliberately impossible recording plan for me. In two weeks I was supposed to record an incredible number of discs with exceptionally difficult programmes. Their appetite had been whetted by the takings from my latest EMI recordings, for which I received virtually nothing, while Mezhdunarodnaya Kniga received all the fees and the rights. I was not even preparing for the recordings. I had a concert planned for March with the London Philharmonic Orchestra in the Royal Festival Hall. Rachmaninoff Concerto No. 2. I wanted to play this music as a man free from the Soviet octopus.

***

I realized a long time ago that recording classical music with the aid of modern technology does not produce the desired result. Music, and generally any art, will always be locked in an inconsolable conflict with lifeless technology. The most important and magical part is transmitted from performer to listener by means that we do not understand. All recordings disappoint me.

A good CD recording of a modest, lifeless performance often sounds significantly better than the most spectacular playing.

***

The day after I arrived in London I went to the EMI studios on the famous Abbey Road. I met my old friend Yura Egorov there. He was recording Mozart concertos in Studio One. We got talking. At the end of our chat I said, "You know, Yura, I'm not going back."

Yura threw up his hands and whispered feverishly, "Lovey, what are you talking about? What do you mean? Don't be stupid, THEY'll kill your brother and drive your mother into the grave. Don't do it!"

"It's too late, Yura, I have already made my mind up, there is no going back."

On my way out of Studio One I met Sam, the exceptional doorman whom I hadn't seen for six years. Sam was a genuine Cockney who spoke in a gorgeous dialect. He knew all the studio's musicians and never asked anyone for a security pass. He was not a tall man, and on his right cheek there was an enormous growth, like an apple. Strange as it may seem, the growth did not transform him into some sort of Quasimodo figure. It rather made him interesting, unique. Sam had worked at the studio since before the war and was one of the walking legends of the place.

At the studio I discovered that my favourite producer, John Willan, had got a promotion and was leaving. Later he told me that the following week he was going to become Managing Director at the London Philharmonic. My dreams of all the records that I could have made with John evaporated. It was the second serious artistic loss I had suffered, after the concerts and recordings that never took place with Karajan. I blame the abominable leadership of the USSR for all the losses of those years. As well as humiliating me and bleeding me dry, trying to kill me, poisoning me and locking me away for several years, the worst thing they did was deny me the opportunity of making major recordings at EMI studios, still untainted by the spirit of commerce in those years. They stopped me from completing my life potential. For that I will never forgive them.

I called John and asked him urgently to come for a serious talk. An hour later he was in the EMI office. I explained the bones of the case. John listened to me, clicked his tongue and said, "And

I thought you'd never take the plunge. How do you imagine it will all work?"

"What is there to imagine? Let's write a letter to Pete right now."

John knew that I wasn't talking about Peter Andrew, a producer who had made it to the very top and was president of EMI at the time, but about the Minister of Culture of the USSR, Pyotr Nilovich Demichev. To be perfectly honest, these two Peters were both bureaucrats with a lot in common.

"What shall we write to Pete?"

"Nothing special. We'll ask him for two years for medical treatment and to get a ruined career more or less back on track. What you need to do is get protection for Natasha and me. Otherwise the Sovs will send us back home in pieces by diplomatic bag!"

"I see. We need to find a lawyer with connections at the Foreign Office. Are you absolutely certain?"

"I couldn't be more so. I'd rather die in a ditch here than forever be slave to those Soviet slobs. I can't bear to look at their hideous faces another second!"

"I understand. Shall we write in English?"

"Of course; we need to taunt the animals at least a bit. Let Pete get my letter through the UK government and then have to sit and wait until it is officially translated." John laughed out loud. As I discovered later, the letter in English particularly enraged the Soviet cultural bosses. Some of them were dumbstruck and genuinely believed that even Gavrilov couldn't be that disrespectful, and thought that the letter was a provocation. Other more intelligent officials understood me perfectly well and put their own spin on the letter: that worm Gavrilov is too ashamed to communicate with us in Russian, he thinks we are all vermin.

At this moment, John's secretary Alison Fox came into the office. She was a typical English spinster of the sort that occurs regularly in literature. Alison treated me sympathetically, as though I was a foundling, and was kind to me, although her character and manners were a little abrupt. Alison found a music-loving lawyer that she knew, with connections in the UK Foreign Office. We printed a letter in red ink on EMI headed notepaper, and I signed it. I attached an invitation that I had received the day before to teach at the Royal College of Music. As he had handed me the letter with the official invitation, the Principal of the Royal College had looked me in the eye and commented shrewdly, "I do very much hope that you will be teaching at our college…"

After that we went to see James Grey, the lawyer. James read the letter, shook his head, witnessed my signature and sent the letter by courier to the Foreign Office. He said solemnly, "From this moment you are no longer ordinary Soviet citizens abroad. You are individuals with no official status. You will be the subject of negotiations between the English and Soviet governments. You mustn't leave this office until there is a reply from the people who will take responsibility for you. Do you understand that?"

"Yes, of course. We are very grateful to you," I replied, speaking for Natasha as well as myself. Just to be on the safe side, Grey taped the conversation. Friendly banter was over, now protocol took over. All of us installed ourselves in James's large office. We were awaiting further instructions. At this point I suddenly remembered that all our belongings were in the Soviet trade mission, on Soviet territory.

"Alison," commanded John, "take Fraser and quick march round to the Soviets. Collect up all the stuff and get a cab straight back here." The poor secretary and young Scott, John Fraser, who had just started working at the studio, set off for the delegation of the Evil Empire to carry out their debut spy mission. I looked at the expressions of horror on their sheet-white faces. Natasha did not interfere in the goings-on; she kept doggedly quiet. She was obviously thinking about her son, her mother, and her father who had already suffered a stroke. I was buzzing with excitement. I tried to placate her.

"Natasha, don't be upset, nobody's going to do anything to anybody; they wouldn't dare. They only understand the language of diktats, so we have dictated what we want. And we want only one thing – for them to leave us alone for two years. England is now standing behind us. Those creeps, those Soviet scum, will come crawling to us on their knees, you'll see."

In fact, that is exactly what happened. Three years later, at a charity concert in aid of the Spitak earthquake appeal, those same

Soviets who had almost done for me in London, were now sobbing on my shoulder.

"Andrei, you are a genius. The Motherland will never forget what you have done for your country!"

A couple of hours later Alison and Fraser came back from the Soviet delegation, excited and happy. Everything had gone without a hitch; nobody saw them and they calmly packed up all our things and took them away. One hour after that we got a call from the Foreign Office. We had to leave London as soon as possible and head north to the town of Woodbridge in Suffolk, near the North Sea coast. We were told which hotel to check into, and that we should wait for Foreign Office people to come to us.

We drove to Woodbridge in a comfortable blue Ford belonging to EMI. John Fraser was driving. Alison sat beside him while Natasha and I snoozed on the back seat. We made a blunder while checking in, although we didn't notice at the time. We only found out the following day, after two representatives of the Foreign Office came to the hotel. As I was getting ready for bed I imagined how Nilych would be frightened when he got my letter through the British embassy, how his bureaucratic snout would be distorted with fear and malice, how he would rush around, start whispering, and then rush helplessly to the Central Committee or the KGB for instructions.

I fell asleep in a comfortable English bed, imagining the scenes that were being acted out now in all those Soviet festering ulcers of power: Lubyanka, Staraya Square, Kuibysheva Street and Neglinnaya. Natasha had withdrawn into herself and hardly spoke to me.

The night brought no relief to me or Natasha. We understood that our fate and the fate of our loved ones was being decided. There was nothing else we could do – the enormous bureaucratic machines, both British and Soviet, were cranking into action and countless sharp, heavy cogs had started to whirl. They were controlled by officials who were blind and indifferent to our fate, and who were interested only in their own careers and the prestige of their own governmental departments. We waited and waited and waited. It was already nearly one o'clock when two men arrived from London – one was small and compact, while the other was of average height and very thin. They were faceless, polite and civil. God, I thought, they are all so alike! Although these ones seem a bit more civilized than Ivan Ivanovich from Kochuevskaya Street. They wore bowler hats rather than flat caps. They took us to the window and showed us a number of men sitting on benches in the garden. One was pretending to read a newspaper, while another was perusing various documents, and a third was admiring nature.

"Those are Scotland Yard people, they're here because of you."

"Because of us? What on earth have we done?"

"You made such a mess of checking in yesterday that the woman on reception phoned the police to have them suss you out."

Of course, this was England! Every other old woman in the provinces was Agatha Christie. Yesterday the woman at reception had asked me, "Your passport and the address where you live." Instead of calmly removing my passport from my inside pocket and tossing it on the desk in a lordly manner, I had leaped back and started consulting with John. John hadn't known what to do. I asked him in a whisper what address to give and whether or not I should give her my passport. He got the wind up and snorted, "How am I supposed to know?" The woman had looked at me very closely – Russian fur coat, dark glasses, two days growth of stubble. Then she broke into a fake smile, gave us our keys and phoned the police. The police sent their own men.

"What are we supposed to do now?"

"Don't worry. Your attendants will return to London, and we will take you to Framlingham. It's not far from here, and there is a hotel there where our people will look after you."

Alison and John paid the bill and left. Natasha and I went down to the underground carpark, got into a Jaguar with tinted windows and left the hotel. The bowler hats laughed at the policeman. Even that was just like Russia. In Framlingham the bowler hats themselves checked us in, recommended that we not leave our hotel room, and then disappeared.

Once again we waited for the unknown. The food and the bar in this restaurant were wonderful. I ate and drank. Natasha was having a really hard time of it. She didn't drink and couldn't eat anything.

A few days passed in this way. John Willan brought his wife and kids to see us in our hiding place. John cheered Natasha up and told me musical news. Finally the small, compact bowler hat came to see us. He had news.

"Andrei, the Soviet government insists on a personal meeting with you by authorized Soviet embassy staff. What is your view of that?"

"Negative, I have no wish to enter into any negotiations with them."

"I understand, and I will consult with my own superiors again."

He left. The following day he was back.

"Andrei, the British government is experiencing intense pressure from the Soviet side because of your refusal. They are accusing us of having abducted you. Only a meeting with them can put an end to these accusations."

I realized that we had no way of avoiding it. These creeps would yell that we had been injected with psychotropic drugs. This was standard practice for the Sovs, until you punched them publicly in the face.

"Well, I understand your difficulty, and I do not wish to place the British government in the position of the accused. I am prepared to meet the Soviet representatives."

The bowler hat cheered up and said that he would inform us of the time of the meeting which would be held in James's office, in the presence of an equal number of people from either side.

"In addition to that, it is very hard to restrain the press. I didn't want to worry you about it, but the press are aware that you have disappeared, and are craving explanations from our side. A decision has not yet been made."

At breakfast the following morning I opened the papers.

"Gavrilov and his wife are the latest in the line of defectors!"

So there it was, we were already defectors. All I wanted was for us to be left alone for two years. The Soviets provoked the scandal themselves, instead of quietly forgetting about us for two years. They wanted a war, they'd get one. The following day our meeting took place.

The bowler hat came to get us in the Jaguar. As we approached the office I noticed that a guard had been put round the office. Agents were poking out from behind bushes, sitting on benches, standing in doorways, on the pavements. What had made the Brits involve such an army? Soviet cunning... Umbrella stabbings, strange diseases and the death of defectors... Traffic accidents, unfortunate incidents with an aerial accidentally hooked up to the mains, sudden disappearances, sensational returns and confessions and goodness knows what else.

We went into the office. Two English officials from the Foreign Office were sitting there with an interpreter. Tape recorders. We waited for the Sovs. I was sitting, thinking, "Come on, show your faces, my dear diplomats, because whoever comes is the spook, the KGB agent."

They arrived: first was the embassy secretary, Mukhin, a young man of tender years with a little Hitler moustache and a typical Soviet expression on his face – as though he was sucking a lemon or a dead rat. The second was the "cultural" attaché, Fedosyev, a hysterical booze artist. They were both plainly ill at ease. Those KGB scumbags have no idea how to talk to people when they aren't the ones with the power. Ever since Stalin won the Second World War, the Soviets have spoken to the whole world from a position of strength. The world rarely answers them in the same way. Once they did answer back, and the USSR collapsed.

Mukhin said nothing, but Fedosyev immediately launched an attack. He shouted in a voice that cracked with rage, "Want to be another Horowitz, do you?"

He behaved as though he was about to throw himself at me with fists flying. I calmly listed the reasons for acting as I had. In fact, my only "crime" was the letter to Pete-Nilych with the request to leave me alone for two years. I never announced that I was asking for political asylum in the UK. Fedosyev didn't listen to me from the start, and carried on yelling. Then he quietened down slightly and changed to a familiar, almost a friendly tone. Fedosyev asked, "What the f*ck more do you want?"

I replied, "I can't possibly re-establish my ruined career from there!"

"Well, yes, you won't get far with those arseholes from Gosconcert!"

"It's not only that, the main thing is that I need to be in the right place at the right time all the time now, don't you understand, not running around asking for permission."

"Yes, I see, you can't fly all round the States from Sheremetyevo, can you."

"Exactly!"

"Does Natasha agree with you? Natasha, do you agree with Andrei?"

"Of course," poor Natasha managed to force out.

Finally, Fedosyev asked the key question, "Are these blokes pressurizing you, provoking you?" He pulled an expression of distaste and nodded towards the Brits who were sitting sedately by.

"No way, they're just sitting there; they don't understand a word."

Fedosyev let out a nervous laugh. We even shook hands when we parted. A modern reader might not be able to understand why I was so restrained in my conversation with the Soviet officials. Of course I wanted to tell them all where to get off in no uncertain terms, and forget that they ever existed. I would have done just that if I hadn't been remembering, every second of the conversation, that the lives of my mother, my brother and Natasha's family were in THEIR hands. I succeeded in my main aim and the Sovs got the message that my story was not political but personal. Musical, in a way. They left. The interpreter asked me to decipher our conversation. We left for East Anglia. That day we were moved to neighbouring Aldeborough. It appeared that the recent story with Oleg Bitov was still fresh in people's minds.

February was drawing to a close. My Rachmaninoff concert was scheduled for March. The Sovs were keeping mum. International regulations stopped me from performing until my status had been determined. If the Soviets simply permitted me to live in the West, then I would get a British visa first, as a Soviet citizen, and then a residency permit. If the Sovs just laid low and kept quiet then I belonged to nobody, and would be unable to give concerts unless I asked for political asylum. I didn't want to do that. I wanted to attain liberty without politics.

Eventually our families found out about our situation. My mother took the news that we had stayed in the West remarkably calmly. She understood that my action was neither flippant nor a game. I could quite simply have done nothing else. Natasha's father was deeply saddened. To start with he couldn't even believe it. Then he pulled himself together. Thank God he suffered neither a stroke nor heart attack. Natasha started gradually to come back to life.

It was only later that I realized why the Sovs had kept quiet. They had no time for me. It all happened just at the time that the latest leader was dying, Konstantin Chernenko. There was no malicious intent in Moscow's silence, there was just an overriding panic. To be honest, I was not even surprised when the bowler hat came to see us and told us that Moscow had finally given an answer. My wife and I were permitted to live in the West on condition that in two years' time we go back to the USSR.

I immediately started rehearsing. EMI put all my discs on the market, Scriabin from Prague, Rachmaninoff from Moscow and a double album of Bach from Bratislava. Critics wrote reviews, the public were animated and invitations flowed in – the international music stage had accepted me, and I whirled off in a frantic dance. Natasha was ready to go back to Moscow. Every day she would talk with her father, her mother and her son on the phone. She was desperate to see them. I tore up her Aeroflot ticket to Moscow.

"Not now, darling, it isn't time yet, let the situation sort itself out completely, then you can go with an easy mind."

She agreed.

The agent Shelly Gold came to see me in London from New York. He was the deputy of the famous impresario Sol Hurok, and he had inherited the agency after his boss's death. He was a swarthy, tall, imposing Jew. He had a Jewish sense of humour and a mellow, unhurried New York voice. Like so many American Jews, Shelly was the son of a Russian immigrant. The first time we met he told me that he was planning my debut at the Carnegie Hall on 28 April, and an incredible number of concerts all over America. Later I discovered that I was taking the place on this

American tour of Rudolf Serkin, who was ill. Destiny was giving back to me what had been taken, as my own American concert tour had been planned for 1980, but was divided up between various young musicians (including Zimerman and Pogorelić). I immediately outlined to Shelly a concert for the Carnegie debut– An Evening of Chopin. Playing this concert in the best hall in the States had been my childhood dream. Steven Wright heard our conversation and was horrified, "Andrei, nobody has been successful playing a full concert of nothing but Chopin at the Carnegie. It will be a disaster!" Shelly said, "If you want Chopin, we'll do Chopin." He flew back to make arrangements for the tour. He went on Concorde. Shelly loved luxury. A young member of staff at EMI, by name of Anna Barry, let Natasha and me live in her one-room apartment on Portobello Road, complete with grand piano, while she lived with her boyfriend. I started to prepare for the American concert tour.

A flat major, Op 32 No 2

The Nocturne in A flat major is a penetrating piece about love. Chopin here tells us about a romantic experience that affected him profoundly. The waltz in the middle section of this nocturne is immensely painful, fragile and nostalgic. It bruises the heart of the listener. In the exposition and the coda we can again hear the voice of the composer, whose soul contains a wound that bleeds astonishing musical passages.

In order to understand this nocturne it is helpful to re-read Turgenev's First Love, *Tolstoy's* After the Ball, *Pushkin's lyrical poetry, Mickiewicz and Byron. I believe that the Nocturne in A flat major is a musical tale by the composer about his only and most intense love.*

My advice to all who already play and wish to play this piece is to look very closely at the directions that Chopin includes in the middle section. Study all the micro-pauses, all the minutest details. Then reproduce them in your playing with mathematical accuracy! Then you and your audience will hear the author's breathing. The start of the middle section is interrupted by the beating of his heart. Later the breathing is firmer, but still occasionally interrupted by the fluttering of his heart. Until the most intimate cry, a whoop of joy as the first theme recurs.

The middle section of this nocturne is a medically accurate picture of the state of mind and body of a neurotic young man overwhelmed by love. In the coda the dreams are brought to life with genius and carry the author and the listener away to a transcendental world. Any more, and the author will pass out in ecstasy.

 *QR link to the Chopin Nocturnes performed by Andrei Gavrilov*

In London (March 1, 1985)

Stalactites under the belly of the piano

In June 1985 Natasha and I flew back to London after a victorious tour in more than twenty cities across America. It was a happy period of musical triumphs and work that I loved. We only remembered about the Soviet Union because we had family still living there. We had nothing but bad things to say about the cursed KGB – my poisoning still made itself felt with sudden severe onsets. Before going on tour to the States I took out a mortgage on one floor of a four-storey house in Hampstead, and bought my first ever concert Steinway. I started to get used to a new life of luxury in England. Our flat needed some minor cosmetic work doing. I planned to get that done while Natasha was away in Russia for a week. I had promised Natasha this trip before going on tour. Her family were looking forward to seeing her in Moscow.

"I'm frightened that they'll take you hostage!"

"That's impossible, Dad gave me his word that he's made sure of everything!"

We discussed it and walked around our new home, where only the kitchen was equipped at the time, and a brand new grand piano stood in one room. We started to talk about furniture.

I sat at the piano. It was an amazing instrument! It was a joy to work at! I had chosen it myself in Bond Street at the Glazebrook brothers, the legendary directors of the London Steinway store. I played a few notes at the piano. I could feel that something wasn't quite right. For some reason the pedal wasn't working; the middle sostenuto pedal for sustaining certain notes. I love carrying out minor repairs myself. You feel an instrument better if you tinker around with it yourself. I crawled under the piano. Good grief, whatever was that? The whole white underbelly of the grand piano was dripping with bizarre brownish stalactites about the size of my index finger. A chilling suspicion crept into my mind. Poison. They had reached me here as well.

"Natka, look at this, what the hell is it?"

Natasha also crawled under the piano, had a look, was as astonished as I was and rushed into the kitchen for a cloth. We started clearing up and washing away the mysterious gunk. I noticed that the rod that joins onto the levers that sustain the selected long notes was knocked out of its green felt grooves, as though someone had knocked it or kicked it. One of the actors in this macabre comedy had probably knocked the rod with his KGB backside while crawling under the piano! Thank God it wasn't pianists doing the job! If that pedal had been working properly I would never have noticed the stalactites under the belly of the piano. A month or two later I would have quietly died, and nobody would have known what from.

I sent Natasha to Moscow and immediately called the old bowler hats. I told them about the stalactites that had grown underneath my grand piano while I had been away from London. The bowler hats believed me and came straight over just quarter of an hour after my phone call. They brought little metal cases with them. Once they had taken samples they headed back to their offices, and then called me about an hour later with an urgent recommendation to spend several nights in a hotel. While I was living in the hotel, people in respirator masks cleaned and decontaminated my piano and the whole of our flat. They explained what I had already guessed without any analysis – that the liquid stalactites were a lethal chemical compound, the poisonous fumes of which would lead to heart failure. It was a parting salute from the Soviet Union. The bowler hats said that there would be nothing to gain from making a fuss about it. I was always amazed by the defeatist position occupied by the West in relation to the Soviet Union, which was running amok with impunity. I never told Natasha about the poison, as she was scared enough of her native land without that.

When I got back home I called Natasha in Barvikha.

"Sunshine, you're coming back the day after tomorrow!"

"No."

Natasha's voice sounded deadened.

"What do you mean, no?"

"Circumstances don't allow it."

I went crazy. The bastards! The damn bastards!

"Natka, I'll get a press conference arranged for tomorrow!"

"Please don't, I beg you, don't do that. It will make it even worse!"

It all made sense. It was Natasha's turn to be taught a lesson in Soviet cruelty now. When Natasha arrived in Moscow her father immediately laid the pressure on – that's enough of your nonsense, forget your ridiculous anti-Soviet husband. Natasha stopped eating and stayed in bed in her own room. Alkhimov was stubborn, but he was no heartless brute from Lubyanka; he was a loving father. He got the message and generously allowed her to fly back. Natasha kissed her father, and he phoned someone and said, "Give her her passport!" So Natasha was due to fly in a few days and still had no passport. People from Lubyanka came to see Alkhimov. They "inspected" his study, asked humiliating questions, rummaged around in his papers. All this with no warrant and no written permission, just to frighten and denigrate a man who had devoted his life to THEIR country. Alkhimov did have a second heart attack after all. That was his last award from his homeland. When he told me, before he died, how the KGB had humiliated him ("they spoke to me like a spy and a traitor!"), I noticed that there were tears in his eyes. It was extraordinary that this old, heavy-weight apparatchik finally understood everything at the end of his life and could not forgive THEM! He came over to my side.

The attack by the KGB humiliated Alkhimov, but did not frighten him, a Hero of the Soviet Union who had drawn intense fire from the Soviet artillery in order to guide the destruction of German tanks in 1944. He approached Gorbachev, and together they managed to curb the high-handed KGB. Two days later Natasha arrived in London, pale and tottering with weakness.

Gidon

It is long time we stopped seeing ourselves as post-culture, post-twentieth century. There is no dead-end, no waning. There is no end in sight for art. If there is something on the wane today, it is religion. Certain animals become aggressive from desperation and grief before they die. Possibly we have religious wars ahead…

New things arise after a catastrophe. Just as our whole planet renews itself, so society does likewise. There will be new music. The old dogmas and habits will be destroyed as boring rubbish. In the same way a tsunami washes distant villages from the face of the earth, and streams of lava burn forests and cities.

Irreparable human losses and destruction can temporarily sober a crazed individual and a panic-stricken society. Only then do common sense, humanity and creative ardour return to the world for a short time… It is dreadfully sad, but humanity will only stop to think and rise to a higher level of development after an asteroid hit, or World War Three. Even then only if most of the population on Earth is killed. Then, possibly, spiritual values will once more take on their true, original significance, and finally the great composers and performers will be needed. In the modern world, the road ahead is closed to them.

Therefore the wider public thinks that they are absent. Nevertheless, a musician must not hope for destruction and catastrophe, the main concern today is becoming, developing and strengthening individuality. Composers and performers need to nurture themselves. Be true to yourselves. Listen to yourselves. Work and believe in yourselves…

***

I met one of the best violinists in the world, Gidon Kremer, in 1976. Gidon hung out at the time in a narrow circle of intellectuals and recent graduates. They considered themselves the "élite" and looked down on everybody else. Many of them were arrogant, idle smart alecks. Gidon by then had already split up from his wife, Tatyana Grindenko, a wonderful violinist with whom he had lived for 11 years. Tatyana had immersed herself in the Orthodox Church.

Gidon was forming and educating himself with intelligence and diligence. He was enamoured of music, and was a modest and profound true musician with an excellent grounding in the humanities and an interest in politics. His main driving force in life was the wish to experiment in art. I learned a great deal from him. We became almost inseparable friends. At one point we even lived together in his little flat near the Sortirovochnaya depot. All night you could hear the tooting of shunting trains, the loud commands of the controllers, and the crashes and metal clangs of the carriages banging together as a new engine was attached to the trains.

Gidon and I often worked at my place on Nikitsky Boulevard. There was plenty of space and my mum cooked really well. A good friend of Gidon's would come to see us as well, Alfred Schnittke. At the time, in 1978, Gidon and I were preparing a sonata by Schnittke for a concert in Salzburg.

Alfred made a very positive impression on me. He was a true Russian intellectual, with none of the usual foibles that composers have. He was gentle, polite, modest and easygoing, despite the passions that bubbled and boiled within. Alfred was very aware of the strength of his own talent and believed in himself. I have always liked people like that. It is easier and more pleasant to work with someone of that type.

Schnittke patiently explained to me how various musical images should sound in his works. He taught me how to play clusters, "glass kaleidoscope" ornaments, and fearlessly to improvise smoking, volcanic cadenzas.

I kept pestering Alfred, asking him to write something for the piano. Schnittke admitted honestly, "I don't know the piano. I only play the accordion, myself. I can feel string instruments, there is more friction there and it is easier for me to create my own style."

"What about Tchaikovsky? He didn't know how to play the piano, or strings, and look what fantastic music he wrote!"

"But he never did create his own piano style!"

I couldn't agree with him, and I really wanted to winkle a piano cycle out of him.

Khrennikov and his clique, as well as other Soviet composers were already giving Alfred a hard time by this point. It was considered the done thing to give Schnittke a good kicking. Alfred's compositions were banned from performance.

Elem Klimov's film *Agony* was shelved. The music to the film was written by Alfred Schnittke. I asked him, "What do you think, Alfred, why do you think that they won't let a film be shown that depicts the corruption of power in Rasputin's times, and the inevitability of revolution?"

Alfred thought for a moment, then replied as though musing aloud, "I think it is because it shows very clearly, in sharp definition, the mechanisms of power in Russia."

Klimov had not taken that into consideration, and it was this that had mortally terrified the bastards in the Kremlin.

We discussed the prohibition on Schnittke's Requiem, which he had wanted Alla Pugacheva to perform.

"Pugacheva?"

"She is so magnificently vulgar," replied Alfred with a delicate smile. "She does not need to fake anything or work on her image, she is vulgar by her very nature, and it would be impossible to find a better performer for the role of the she-devil!"

Pugacheva was not permitted to sing in the State Philharmonia, but Requiem was put on in the Tchaikovsky Hall. The whole of Moscow's motley intelligentsia gathered for the premiere. I was curious to hear how the symphony orchestra would try desperately to play with a rock group, whose bearded and long-haired musicians were obviously finding it difficult to read the musical text. Some Sovs were non-plussed, while others were celebratory and delighted. Schnittke's Requiem was never again performed in Soviet Moscow...

One of the most shameful pages in the cultural life of the Soviet Union at that time was the public flogging of Alfred for his attempt to stage Tchaikovsky's *Queen of Spades* in Paris. Tchaikovsky's music had been supplemented with several numbers that Alfred had been commissioned to write by the Paris Opéra. The Stalin old guard were still in charge in Soviet Music, and, as in all such cases, they found a vile musician (in this case it was Algis Zhuraitis, conductor at the Bolshoy Theatre) who agreed to sign an enormous anti-semitic article in *Pravda*.

The article was entitled "A Provocation is being Prepared!" and in it Schnittke was accused of setting out to destroy this hallowed work of Russian art. A horrendous bout of harassment against Alfred was instigated, which took many years off his life.

Meeting Schnittke in 1983 in Ruza I did not even recognise him. He was sick and pale as death. I tried to say something encouraging. Alfred waved a dismissive hand...

Shortly thereafter he had a stroke...

***

Incidentally, Fira took no notice of Schnittke or any of the other Soviet avant-garde composers. One day he and I were standing backstage at Moscow State University while Kapelka was playing Schnittke's violin concerto. We listened, standing near the open door. The music was temperamental, and Kapelka was playing superbly.

Fira shook his head, then smiled one of his many unkind smiles and said, "Still, it really is Jewish music, isn't it, hm-m-m Andrei?"

When I listen to work by avant-garde composers, more often than not I am overwhelmed with a sense of discontent.

In these musical constructions everything is too clear, arithmetical and trivial. "Clear" not in the Mozartian sense, but petty and eclectic. In this fragment it seems that the composer is thinking, pondering, and here he is suffering and grieving, and it is even obvious what about, while here there is some Russian Orthodox singing, and there some Pink Floyd, which has all been "symphony-ised" by the bittersweet deployment of the accordion and adorned with sweet little gurgles and sobs by the violins... It's pretty, and terribly "astral", but I just can't take that sort of art seriously.

It is flat music. With no depth and perspective. Easily exhausted as a resource...

With Bach, Mozart or Chopin, on the other hand, every sound is inexhaustible. The beginning of Requiem – nothing happens, the strings play an empty accompaniment, then the bassoon enters, then two French horns and then... time recedes, drawing the listener into sweet eternity. Like a river flowing...

Avant-garde music, or conceptual or post-modern music – despite all its anguish, cosmic abysses, glugs and significant pauses – is light music, wonderful, sparkling, but it does not touch, it gives your cheek a quick stroke and tugs at your ears...

I listen to it with half an ear, I recognise where the musical material comes from, I laugh and stay exactly where I am. This music does not let you rise above the mundane, nor plunge into the depths...

Listening to it is the same as going for a walk on a picture postcard of a landscape.... It's all very well, but not enough.

Playing it is too easy, there is no demand for "heart or head" when performing. It plays itself, or as Ostap Bender said about the astrolabe, it measures itself...

***

Gidon was older than me, we had different personalities and we interpreted and assessed reality differently, but musically we were as close as twin brothers. Sometimes we would prepare a new piece separately from each other. We would then meet up to play it through before performing. We would play, then we would both collapse in delighted laughter, because my piano part and his violin were so perfectly suited to each other it was like two halves of a pearl. All they needed was to be brought together and they bonded, forming a precious, shining whole. Gidon told me that he had never experienced anything of the like with any other pianist before.

Gidon often went to concerts given by Richter and Oistrakh, while I stayed at home reading. Gidon had a great many samizdat books on his shelves, and other editions that I could not get my hands on. I would jestingly ask Gidon, "Are you off to listen to Baldy again?"

"Uh-huh," Gidon would answer, and burst out laughing. He liked it when I affectionately slagged off the best Soviet musicians. Gidon secretly taped their music on a little tape recorder in the actual concert hall. I would listen to his recordings and often railed against them, especially when Baldy was playing Chopin or Schubert.

Gidon would comment, "Yes, it isn't Chopin, but it is interesting all the same!"

Gidon worked in a disciplined way and managed to achieve a great deal. He would get up early and work for three hours. Then he would head off to a public debate or something, rush off to a concert, rest and then practise some more. Gidon was constantly learning and developing himself. He also had a taste for all sorts of adventures: he flew on a TU-144 supersonic jet to Alma-Ata, he went to the North Pole in an atomic ice-breaker, the *Lenin*. Despite his modesty, Gidon really wanted to be the first and most famous everywhere.

Gidon and I both had a sarcastic attitude to the squalid Soviet lifestyle, and to the blinkered Sov mentality. We both understood that at some point we might be unable to bear it any longer, and would leave the Soviet Union for ever. I tried to discuss this issue with Gidon. Gidon kept his thoughts to himself and concealed his own ideas about the need to emigrate.

In 1979, when we had finished our joint tour in Austria and West Germany, Gidon defected. If he had told me about his plan, even the day before he escaped, then I would never have gone back to the Soviet Union on my own.

In March 1985 I made my announcement in London that I was not intending to return to the USSR. Gidon was on a flight from New York to Europe when he found out. He then came to see me.

"I wanted to jump out of the plane over London when I opened the *Herald Tribune* and read about you!" Kremer told me. We chatted for a whole day and night, sitting on the floor. We were as happy as kids and made plans.

"We'll have it all, Andrei! We can perform and work together," said Gidon enthusiastically.

My very first season after the London poisoning I was playing in Munich where Kremer was also on tour. A severe seizure started there on stage. With my last strength I hung on, I didn't fall over and I kept playing. Later, in the green room, my wife gave me an injection of camphor with sedatives and an anti-epileptic drug. Just then, Gidon walked into the room. He saw the syringes, the needles and blood and the colour drained from his face. Then he blurted out in fright, "That's crap, man!" and legged it. Our paths parted forever.

Caviar, Forshmak and Foie Gras

You grow accustomed to the good life very quickly! I was living in clover in London. I was very pro-British in my attitudes. I respected Mrs Thatcher and her British government that had stood up for Natasha and me in the battle against the loathsome Soviet Union. I loved wearing my English cashmere tweed jacket with the top button of my shirts done up and good quality brogues. When I went for a walk I took my long brolly with me. I was well on the way to becoming a stuck-up dandy, helped along by my visits to the mansions of the English aristocracy and my closeness at the time to the company of royalty and courtiers.

I was really getting a taste for it all, when I suddenly received an invitation to give a concert tour in Israel. It was 1985. There were no diplomatic relations between Israel and the USSR, let alone any cultural exchange. The Jewish state was still an "enemy" of the Soviet Union. It was tempting to become the first official Soviet touring musician in Israel. I had no concept of the country, but I was keen to touch the biblical ruins. In the middle of August I started a tour of fifteen concerts. I flew in to Ben Gurion airport.

I appeared in public as such an elegant Brit, with my cane and tweed jacket, and I arranged my face in a meaningful expression. I took off and soared, but was immediately brought crashing down to earth. A short guy with a lively, Semitic face tugged at the sleeve of my jacket. He addressed me in pure Soviet Russian, "Hello, my name's Shlemo, we're going to see the boss now. There's a reception dinner there."

I made up my mind not to be astonished by anything. After wandering around the streets of Tel Aviv, we arrived at a bizarre, large, white bungalow... It was the villa of Shabtai Kalganovich. Later his name changed slightly for some reason, to Shabtai Kalmanovich. This man spent five years in an Israeli jail for spying for the USSR, and subsequently became manager of the national women's basketball team and owner of the Dorogomilovsky market. In 2009 he was assassinated in his own car in Moscow.

The bungalow proved spacious, and Shlemo walked through a series of smallish rooms then pushed open the door to the dining room. We went in. Sitting round a large table were painfully familiar characters from a typical Moscow kitchen. Women, girls, children, men. Happy devils! They were all clapping and chanting, "An-drei! An-drei!" I started to go dizzy; everything swam before my eyes, as though I had been knocked out. The table was groaning under the incredible spread of familiar Moscow grub. Meatballs, mashed potato, herring salad, caviar, Forshmak, Foie Gras, vodka, Russian salad, chicken, fish in aspic, Napoleon pastries and soured cream so thick the spoons stood upright in it. I felt weary. It had taken me five years to escape from the Soviet Union, risking my life and the lives of my near and dear. Twice I had almost been killed. All so that I could fly back to the Soviet Union via Ben Gurion airport and end up sitting round a Moscow table. At this point Shabtai gently took my arm, with me nearly fainting from the shouts, the heat and the smell of meatballs, onion and warm vodka – that inimitable fragrance of our great country – and showed me round his house.

Shabtai was very good looking – he had a slim figure, the sort of chiselled features you might find on a medal, and a mane of dark hair flowing down to his shoulders. He walked slowly and importantly, like a goose, tossing out odd phrases that I could not always understand. He wore baggy blue trousers of very fine cotton, and a well-cut, rich beige T-shirt that flatteringly emphasised his muscular, tanned arms and strong torso. Shabtai elegantly brushed the surface of a shiny table with his fingertips and whispered in an indifferent bass, "Italy, leather." I had thought the table was made of glass or highly polished wood and looked at him uncomprehendingly. Shabtai was plainly enjoying my reaction. Slowly pacing ceremoniously from room to room, Shabtai lovingly touched the furniture and tossed out fragmentary attributes.

"Marble, Versace, coffee table, armchair, Italy, leather, chaise longue, leopard."

I looked at him curiously. I had never met anyone else like him.

"Television, satellite, Moscow, live broadcast…"

Some time later I retreated to the hotel, excusing myself with a headache and the next day's concert at the Rubinstein Centre. In parting, Shabtai hospitably invited me to enjoy myself to the full in Israel, to eat in the hotel and not to take any risks with the heat of August. The following morning Shabtai's helpers came to see me. There was Mr Paz and another one whose name I have forgotten. Paz was an enormously tall and fat Jew (I hadn't realised there was such a thing) who got out of breath and constantly mopped the sweat from his brow and neck. The crude features of his face seemed to have been hacked with an axe from a chunk of wood by a recidivist sculptor. The second one, who seemed to be in charge, could have been European. They both immediately announced that I shouldn't eat in the hotel as there was plenty of delicious food available from street vendors.

The second concert of my Israeli tour was supposed to be in the Mann Center, named after the mayor of Philadelphia whose family came from Smolensk, and whom I had met during my summer tour round America. I told my companions that I knew Mann in the hope of getting them to talk, and to win their trust. Their reaction was instantaneous – he was a bandit and a cheat, this Mann of mine, he'd ripped off half of Israel and as for his so-called cultural centre, he'd made the Israelis pay. I decided on the spot not to interfere in any inter-Jewish issues again. Remembering Shabtai's advice, I ignored his helpers' insistent requests and had my lunch in the hotel. I ordered the daintiest meals, light and expensive. In so doing I denied the helpers the money they had hoped to save on feeding me. They retaliated by begging me daily not to eat in the hotel. They muttered the same thing over and over, like robots.

The Israeli tour was not an easy one for me. I played in large halls, and the audiences who filled them were demanding, and had their own specific tastes. At first I played as I was supposed to play. The programme consisted of works by Chopin from the time of his greatest sufferings. In the music of that period, Chopin comes across as a patriot of heroic, bleeding Poland. Here was I, playing the funeral sonata – scherzo, the second movement, with executions, death, fights, the scaffold, gallows and blood. The tempo is terrifying, the contrasts are savage as sparks fly from the conflagrations, crimson smoke spreads and ash falls from the sky. I looked at the audience and saw fat little ladies in the front row staring at me with hatred in their eyes. I shrank into my stool. The women were probably important teachers. Their faces registered disgust. It was plain that they had no use for the real Chopin. They needed something sweeter, more glamorous. The next day the *Yedioth Ahronoth* newspaper scolded me – Gavrilov's really too young to play Chopin.

Another newspaper with an even worse title for the Russian ear gave me a worse hiding – Gavrilov's really an idiot and is giving us not Chopin, but some sort of action thriller on the piano. I had to capitulate. My innovative interpretations were blatantly not appropriate here. The following day I went on stage and did not rush to the piano, but rather timidly walked over, like a student from a cookery college, and sat quietly down. Everything about me was demonstrating my meekness. Then I tossed my head back in genius style, drooped my eyelids languorously and started to play. I played sweetly and melodiously, in little round phrases. I looked at the house out of the corner of my eye and saw that the ladies were smiling benevolently, whispering to each other and nodding approval. This was the "Russian" Chopin, sickly and as calm as Poland once it had been slain by Paskevich. How easy it was to be a musician loved by the public!

My two blokes were gloomy as they saw me off at the airport. I had obviously eaten them out of their caviar, Forshmak and Foie Gras. They could barely wait to see me through the customs inspection, which in Israel takes over three hours, before walking abruptly away without saying goodbye. They didn't ruin my mood, as I had been the first Sov with a free passport to give a concert tour in Israel.

When I got home to Hampstead and Highgate by tube I collapsed with over-exhaustion. My blood pressure rose. I stayed in bed until I felt better and started preparing for my first concert winter in the UK. A couple of weeks later, lying on my lovely English sofa leafing through *The Times*, I stumbled upon a report about Shabtai being arrested by London customs. He had been trying to bring a load of false diamonds into the UK.

***

Rozanov wrote about the "grandeur of the charlatan…"

Sincere and talented people treat themselves with irony and criticism, and never forget their place in the universe. The moment such people detect in themselves an aspiration for "grandeur", they laugh or grow sad. If you have noticed anything of the kind in me, let's have a laugh about it together.

There are people whose essence cannot be expressed in words… They are the salt of the earth, and there are very few of them. One such man is my friend Hilary Koprowski, inventor of the live polio vaccine. This scientist, who has saved millions of children around the world from agonising disease, is a miracle of impropriety…

I live like everyone else on this earth. An "ordinary" life. Like everyone else I try to battle against the challenge of everyday life and all the negative aspects of my own character. I take care of my loved ones. I am snowed under with work. I practise for up to 17 hours a day. Sometimes I pass out from weakness. Sometimes my fingers bleed…

Uncle Zhenya

I often spoke with Richter about different conductors.

"Slava, who do you like better than anyone else? Who do you like working with the most? Was Muti your protégé, just as you were his?"

"Yes, I really was the one who discovered him. After winning the competition. I liked him a great deal at the start, but then he turned into a bandmaster, unfortunately."

Richter fell silent, thinking back over his memories, and then said, "My best concerts were with Svetlanov!"

I hadn't expected that. Svetlanov seemed such a Russian nationalist despot by the 70s, crude, lacking in subtlety and a "musical butcher".

"Yes, yes, with Svetlanov," repeated Slava. "Despite everything, it was always rather special with him. I still like my recording with him of the Chopin F minor more than lots of others."

I couldn't make any sense of it at all. Deranged, fragile Chopin and the massive Russky Svetlanov! But Slava wouldn't give praise were none was due. Once I had broken into the free world after my enforced incarceration I looked hungrily forward to every meeting with the Western stars – Abbado, Muti, Haitink, Tennstedt, Rattle and Ozawa. I finally got my chance, and found that I was disappointed

Ozawa, for example, seemed to me to be an alcoholic with a poor grasp of music. I had waited so long for a concert with the Berlin Philharmonic. Finally Ozawa "commissioned" some Tchaikovsky from me. I arrived in Berlin. I turned up at the rehearsal in a haze of happiness (I adore the Concerto No. 1), at ten o'clock as arranged. There was no sign of Ozawa! He arrived forty minutes later, with an obvious hangover, reeking of alcohol.

"Andrei, today I'm going to work on the Blacher Variations on a Theme by Paganini so let's go through the concerto tomorrow morning, starting at nine."

I wasn't happy about wasting time, but never mind; we could sort it out the following morning. I had long been wanting to play Concerto No. 1 again. I knew where Tchaikovsky's original tempos are traditionally messed around, especially in those octaves in the first movement of the concerto that caused the composer to fall out with Anton Rubinstein over their "non-performability"; I wanted to try out some new accelerations, especially in the coda of the finale. I had a new reading of the main theme. I arrived at half past eight and started to wait. Seiji arrived at ten and was again under the influence.

"Andrei, I'll go through Blacher with the orchestra now, we didn't manage to get it all done yesterday, and the rest of the time can all go on Tchaikovsky."

I waited, simmering. I could hear the hackneyed strains of Paganini wafting through the door of the green room. I looked at my watch; two hours had passed and he was still rehearsing Blacher. There was only twenty minutes left till the end of rehearsal! Finally they called me. I rushed into the hall. Ozawa's music stand was empty. Ozawa loved to show off about his memory. He naturally "knew it all from cover to cover". We started. At the very first tempos, not the ones at which the "musical matrices" play the concerto, but the real ones, the Maestro started drifting like a chunk of floe ice. He flapped his wings but the Berlin locomotive stayed where it was. He was so hopeless, he did not know the tempos. He did not prepare the rails, he did not train the musicians, he did not explain, he did not rehearse and he had not understood what the piece was about. Without that, the musical machine would not move. It was stuck. The concert was the following day. As expected, Ozawa arrived at the finish in second place, with the orchestra in third. I was beside myself at his lack of professionalism. I started to play encores, and "with a friendly smile" I firmly planted Ozawa on his rostrum under the piano.

"Listen," I said, "the encores are for you."

I hammered out everything that I knew as loudly as I could, so that at least his head would be splitting after his drink. In the second half of the concert he played his Blacher. The critics wrote admiringly about me, but they didn't even mention his Blacher… Ozawa hasn't come within a mile of me since.

I met Uncle Zhenya Svetlanov in Munich in the late 80s, in the brand new super-expensive Philharmonic Hall there.

"How do you like the acoustics in our new hall?" the director of the Philharmonic asked the famous Bernstein at the inauguration of the hall.

"Monstrous, it hasn't got any!" – replied Lenny.

"What do you think needs to be done to improve the acoustics in the hall?"

"Burn it!" answered Bernstein laconically. They didn't heed his advice.

By then I had heard a good number of colourful stories about the stern habits of Svetlanov from various Western agents. Uncle Zhenya "changed his mind" about conducting a concert in London and disappeared. He was found on Tower Bridge with a fishing rod. Svetlanov was calmly fishing in the Thames! In the evening, once he had actually played the concert after all, Uncle Zhenya bellowed in his dreadful voice, loud enough for the whole hotel to hear, "London is Scheisse, England is Scheisse, Thatcher is Scheisse, capitalism is Scheisse!" Once, Svetlanov woke up everyone he knew in London, as well as all the guests at his hotel, with shouts of, "My wife is dying!" They forced open his door with great difficulty. The corpulent body of Uncle Zhenya's wife was lying unconscious on the floor and blocking the door. They moved her. Picked her up. It turned out that Madame had eaten herself half to death.

They brought the poor woman round. Uncle Zhenya knelt unhappily in the corner of his room and prayed. The wife opened her eyes and whispered, "I'm dying, Zhenya." Svetlanov was weeping and praying feverishly.

"Promise me one thing and I will die at peace."

"Anything at all, darling!"

"Stop drinking!"

"No, I can't promise you that!"

At a concert in the Tchaikovsky Hall, a tipsy Svetlanov lost the orchestra in a Rachmaninoff symphony. The orchestral musicians blenched and fell silent, as it was already completely impossible for them to find their way by then. Svetlanov thumped his fist on the stand in front of him and shouted as loud as

Hercules, "Stop!" It is said that plaster fell from the ceiling at his voice. Then he shouted even louder, "Twenty five, you fuckwits!" So they carried on from number 25. Another time, Svetlanov wandered into the orchestra during a concert – from delight and excitement – and fell down somewhere between the cellists and the viola players. Without interrupting the flow of the symphony the orchestra leader, green with terror, took him by the arm back to the rostrum. That was the "dragon" I was supposed to meet on stage in Munich for the Tchaikovsky Concerto No. 1. I went into the hall. My knees were shaking – I loathe arguments! Our State Orchestra was already on stage. I could recognise a lot of the musicians, and they recognised me, giving me friendly winks. We hadn't seen each other for about twelve years. Svetlanov stood on his rostrum, looked round at his orchestra like a hawk, and suddenly started to yell! He swore at the entire orchestra, and at each and every musician personally. For lack of discipline, for not playing in unison, for flat performances, and just for sitting there in front of him as though nothing had happened. I nearly crawled under my piano. I had never heard a man shout so loud in my whole life. Certainly never on stage.

"Get out!" shouted Uncle Zhenya. The orchestra left the stage for a break. Svetlanov went down into the auditorium, sat in the tenth row and buried himself in the score. I went backstage where the orchestral musicians were drinking tea and coffee. My face must have shown such astonishment that someone from the orchestra took pity on me and explained Svetlanov's behaviour, "He can't bear bad reviews, and yesterday they had a bit of a go at us in Nuremberg, so he had a good shout. Take no notice!" he said, and winked. I went back into the hall and walked fearfully up to Svetlanov and sat beside him. He looked at me, smiled his radiant, childlike smile, grasped my arm and said with a slight lisp, "Andrei, dear, have pity on an old man and don't rush the tempos too much, all right?" I nodded. We went on stage. Uncle Zhenya looked at the orchestra like Ivan the Terrible and suddenly brought the French horn into play with a light wave of his hand.

The horn energetically and joyfully blasted its famous four notes, F-D-C-B I felt that our Tchaikovsky had somehow fallen into place at once. We only stopped a couple of times during rehearsal. We played as one. The concert was that evening. The music sounded wonderfully fresh, and it was easy and comfortable to play. The main thing was that it was real Tchaikovsky. After that we often played together, and with different orchestras, in London, Berlin, Paris and many other cities. Uncle Zhenya was always quiet, kind and tactful with me. He conducted like a god. He was also a brilliant accompanist.

In the 90s Svetlanov had the same problem as all the other intellectuals who were not granted access to the Russian feeding trough of oil and gas. The orchestra had no money. The quality of playing plummeted and musicians left the country. The full collection of works by Russian composers, which Svetlanov had been recording for many years, 100 discs, was surplus to requirement. The recordings were not digital. Uncle Zhenya phoned me disappointed and sad. He was confused, as were many other honest and straightforward people like him.

"Andrei, dear, I have been offered a contract as principal conductor in The Hague, what do you think about that?"

"Uncle Zhenya, sign it immediately without even stopping to think, and without any doubt!"

"But how is that possible! After Moscow, after so many years working as principal conductor in the capital. Going to The Hague! Would it not be better to wait for an invitation from London?"

"No, no, it's just for a couple of years, and then any orchestra will be yours for the asking."

"What am I, a child?"

"It's a completely different life, the West, there are different rules. There's no other way! Nobody's taking away your achievements, everybody knows who and what you are. You can limber up in The Hague, the orchestra there is not so bad, and it is the capital after all!"

"Really? Not Amsterdam?"

"No, The Hague!"

"Well, thank you, Andrei, my dear, I shall think about it."

I read later in the newspaper that Svetlanov had signed the contract! Good for him!

Kirill Kondrashin, who escaped the Soviet Union in 1978, used to say, "I am so happy that I left the USSR, the only thing I regret is that I did not do it much earlier!" Kirill then got the job of principal guest conductor at the Concertgebouw Orchestra, one of the best in the world. He died in 1981, aged 66. That was extraordinarily early among conductors.

The same thing happened with Uncle Zhenya. His affairs had just started to take off; the first-class orchestras were just beginning to invite him, with no intrigue, no nepotism or grovelling. What happiness! Then Uncle Zhenya died. On Good Friday on the late Easter of 2002. One of the Moscow crazies rang me and howled in typical Russian jackal fashion: "He dropped dead at Easter, must be a saint!" I said, "Get lost!" and put the phone down. Uncle Zhenya was buried at Vagankovo Cemetery. The Sovs could not forgive his "treachery" in going abroad. With his Lenin Prize and his title of Hero of Socialist Labour he should, by rights, have been interred at the more prestigious Novodevichy Cemetery.

Vishnya and Buratinka

That was what they called each other – he called her Vishnya [Cherry] and she called him Buratinka.

All their houses were called Cherry House, and their streets Cherry Street. Their gate was always decorated with a glamorous picture of two appetizing, wine-red cherries on a double stalk.

The morning after an exhausting evening concert in London, Vishnya, Buratinka and I were standing by just such a gate with cherries, and waiting for the caretaker with the keys. Buratinka announced ceremonially, "Andwei, we are now going to inauguwate the fountain!"

Buratinka had ordered a fountain for the sitting room to celebrate his own return home. A present for Vishnya and himself, as though it was a surprise. The English caretaker came and opened the gate, and Buratinka went grandly into the living room like Trimalchio entering the banquet hall, looked masterfully around his home and suddenly discovered, to his own surprise, a large stain on his grey linen sofa, which was obviously of unseemly origin. He looked at Vishnya and asked mournfully, "Is this Poyka's work?"

He answered his own question immediately, "It would appear so, who else could it be?"

We went into the corner of the living room to look at the fountain. A small tiled basin for the water had been installed. The basin held a rather ugly lone stone with a hole in it. Buratinka flicked the switch and a modest little jet of water dribbled from the "stone". Buratinka was thrilled and clapped his hands, barely restraining his laughter. This cheap fountain from an ordinary high-street shop quite plainly did not deserve an ovation here in Buratinka's pretentious house. The cottage was spacious, not quite rich, and with a vague attempt at chic glamour. The ceilings in Buratinka's living room were tall, and the windows were coloured at the top, rather like stained glass windows. The furniture was a strange mixture of rather expensive and really cheap, of different styles, often with rather ridiculous glass elements. It had all been bought haphazardly, as was everything else in Buratinka's house. The cottage was not cosy, not clean and not well looked after, as is often the case with the houses of artistic people whose inhabitants are too busy worrying about themselves and have no time or desire to think about anything else. As though he had read my thoughts, Buratinka said, "Andwei, don't get the wong idea; this house is nothing, but the one we have in Pawis, that one is weally something! We even have our own woad, with tarmac!"

I nodded sympathetically. After the "inauguration of the fountain" we set out for an early lunch at the Britten Society, where Buratinka was either Chairman or Vice. Buratinka told a couple of his inevitable jokes that he had prepared beforehand. His clumsy English destroyed any last traces of humour in these hoary old Soviet jokes which were, by definition, incomprehensible to foreigners. In Buratinka's grotesque retelling the jokes about Vovochka, the standard butt of many Soviet jokes, sounded like the genuine ravings of a lunatic. The Brits laughed politely and reservedly. Plans were made and we went rushing off round the shops – they might have some sort of multi-coloured "stones or pieces of glass", we bought some coloured shot glasses. Buratinka told me, "You know, Andwei, I love coloured glass, I love it. You look at the glass or thwough it, and immediately feel so good."

That evening we performed the Rhapsody on a Theme of Paganini by Rachmaninoff together in London. Buratinka flapped his wings like an injured crow, and before that I helped him mark up the sheet music with coloured pencils to stop him getting confused. Straight after the concert we were hanging out together in the green room, with the cries of the audience still going on, and Buratinka was happy that it had all held together. He said, "Andwei, Vishnya is going to come in now and she's going to pwaise us." And he giggled.

The majestic Vishnya swept in, and with an operatic, slightly hysterical laugh, she sang, drawing the words out playfully, "Andrei-ei-ei, ho-o-o-ow many fingers do you ha-a-a-ave?!" Her eyes flashed. Goose bumps tingled down my spine...

After the concert we sat back in Buratinka's living room and drank. The conversation turned to Richter.

"Yes," I said, "Incidentally, Fira says hello."

"What Fira? Eh?"

Buratinka and Vishnya looked at each other in surprise?

"Did he weally say that to you? That must mean that he has taken you to heart, you can't get any closer than that."

I told them everything that Slava and I got up to and the fun we had – they shook their heads.

"So that's how it is. We thought he was so mysterious and lofty…"

I realised that despite their having known each other for such a long time, with musical collaborations and shared leisure, Slava had never revealed his true self to Buratinka. Buratinka only ever saw the mask. There was so much more hiding under it. In the 60s Buratinka had paraded around at one of Slava's masquerade evenings dressed as a crocodile with a belly stuffed full of *Sovetskaya Kultura* newspapers, and harped on to everyone that he "was pwegnant with Soviet culture and was about to give birth."

The name Fira came about like this. In the old days Buratinka and Slava used to compete against each other, not for real, just as a joke. They played together. Slava would go faster and faster, then Buratinka would go even faster until there was steam coming out of their instruments. Or they would both play piano-pianissimo. Slava would play piano, and Buratinka would play pianissimo. Then Slava would be pianississimo and Buratinka pianissississimo. Until the instruments would fall silent under their genius fingertips. That was how the young musicians had fun, with their blood fizzing like champagne! Buratinka said, "Svyatoslav would go so berserk, so berserk that I would shout at him. You cwashing, clashing idiot, you wotten Glasha, there's no doing anything with you!"

Buratinka started to call Slava Glasha. Sometimes he would use a diminutive form, Glashenka. Later, when Glasha was older, Buratinka added respect and distance, and Glasha started to be called by her full name, Glafira.

"My Glafiwa, you are so talented!"

Soon the Gla at the beginning was dropped and all that was left was Fira. Buratinka started to call Richter Fira.

"Fiwa, Fiwa, come here, listen, you played that so well, Fiwa. I weally wespect you for it."

Slava had acted the whole story out for me. Buratinka was stunned that Slava could have told anyone their personal secrets. Buratinka and Vishnya had had a bit too much to drink and they sat shaking their heads, worrying again and again over the "hello from Fira," whom they hadn't seen or spoken to for so long. Before passing out completely, Buratinka told me his favourite story. How he had given a present to Vishnya on her birthday. Another surprise. I'll tell his story in his own words, as I remember them.

"So, Andwei, it's soon going to be Vishnya's birthday and of course she is expecting a pwesent from me, some sort of good pwesent. And I'm thinking what could I give her? Vishnya has emewald eyes, so I'm thinking I always give her jewels on her birthday. When she was 30 I gave her 30 cawats, on her fortieth it was 40 cawats, and so on, do you see? Now I'd just been invited on a cwuise, to go for a twip, play a little music, and I met a man there, a little man who turned out to be vewy useful. He had a mine in Afwica, do you see? A mine."

At this point Buratinka and Vishnya both dissolved in drunken gales of laughter. I had the feeling that this was not the first time, and not even the fiftieth time, that Buratinka had told this story. As a matter of fact, Vishnya's eyes really were pure emerald.

"So I ask him, could he get me a stone of about 100 cawats, and he, listen Andwei, he says to me that stones like that don't often turn up. As soon as they find one at the mine, I'll call you. Thank you, I say, I look forward to heawing from you. But as a back-up and just to annoy Vishnya, I also bought a little emewald fwog, just in case; a tiny little toad from Cartier, and I wapped it up as though it was something incwedibly expensive, do you see? Well, time was passing, and the man calls me, the man with the mine, and he says there is a 90-cawat stone. So I met up with him, took the stone, popped it in a matchbox and wrapped it in a piece of dirty old newspaper. So, on her birthday I give her an eno-o-o-ormous parcel. From Cartier, and she unwaps it, unwaps it, dwumming her nails with impatience, tap-tap, and inside the parcel is getting smaller and smaller, and eventually she gets to the end and there is a fwog there. Vishnya is so fuwious, she thwows the fwog at me and starts to howl! "For me-e-e, on my birthday? Wha-a-a-at does it me-e-e-ean? Ooo-ooh, get out you howwible Buwatinka, you monster! And so here I toss the stone in the newspaper on the table, and the newspaper has been on the table for a while, and I say, look, look what newspaper is that there?

"What newspaper? What is it now?! And I push the newspaper towards her, urging her to take it. She opened up the newspaper, then the matchbox, and there was a 90-cawat emewald, polished by Cartier! She waises such a howl. My Buwatinka. She starts to cwy, Buwatinka, you didn't twick me, my sweet, my only Buwatinka! She cwies and cwies, so there you have it!

Before that I had gone to Cartier and asked them to polish the stone. I come back, run in and ask them what I owe? And they say for you, Maestwo, its fwee. So that's the stowy."

After finishing his story Buratinka's head fell on his chest and he broke into a gurgling snore, then quietly slid down to the floor. I woke up about four o'clock in the morning. My head was splitting, I felt sick and piqued. I tiptoed between the piles of stuff and the bodies of the eminent musicians lying like corpses on the floor of the dining room, and finally left the stinking frowst and went outside into the fresh air, called a taxi and left for London. Along the way I remembered...

"Oh, Vishnya, Vishnya, you were so beautiful! We schoolboys must have come running to the Bolshoy at least twenty times apiece to watch *Eugene Onegin* and see Vishnya-Tatyana in her nightdress in the letter scene. We used to take binoculars with us. Vishnya's voice was a rarity. Sopranos do not often sound beautiful, usually it is more of a shouting scream. But her voice was pure and full, and Vishnya had a natural musical culture. Talent! There was not quite enough warmth in her voice, though; she emanated coldness."

And now... The only thing that was left of the former beauty that was Vishnya was her emerald eyes. There was a portrait on the wall at their house. The artist had put green lightning flashes in her eyes.

Vishnya knew the power of her eyes. She would purr over and over again in her prima donna voice, "People are scared of me when I flash my eyes menacingly! Grown men faint. Buratinka even crawls under the table!"

Buratinka agreed with her all the way, "Yes, yes, yes, I'm tewwified, yes, yes, it's dweadful how scared I am."

Richter would reminisce about Vishnya and laugh, "Yes, she really is a wonderful singer, I loved her Tatyana. Once I was listening to her in the Bolshoy, she was singing beautifully, but somehow very bad-temperedly. After the show I went to see her in her dressing room. I don't often do that, but I wanted to on that occasion. I went in and asked – You sang beautifully, but why were you so angry? Do you know what she replied? She turned towards me in her chair, like a queen, looked at me like a panther, so stunning, and said, there are enemies all around!"

Vishnya and Buratinka reminded me somehow of a pair of hilarious fairy-tale bandits; from Pinocchio or the Brothers Grimm.

Vishnya was a woman in high society with emerald eyes and a superb voice, who had retained the manners of an operetta prima donna from Odessa. Buratinka was a cello Maestro, a walking inferiority-superiority complex.

When I watched him "in action", not on stage, but in society, I would be embarrassed to the point of discomfit, and have to hide my eyes and block my ears.

It seemed that all the energy in Buratinka's life was spent only on coercing important media celebrities who were useful to him in his constant attempts to be charming and witty. Buratinka was in fact neither, but he did know how to imitate charm and wit. He had immense strength and he was very pushy.

Buratinka always jotted down crude, vulgar jokes, racy stories and other anecdotes in a special notebook, preparing them each day for each occasion, with carefully chosen ones for each significant person. Buratinka had the thrust of a tank. People would collapse under the thrust, give up resisting and provide the services he needed, being sucked into the interests of the money-scooping machine. That was exactly how Buratinka lived, like a Soviet snow plough that scoops up snow with two powerful metal arms and minces it up with a dreadful spiral that glitters in the overcast air of Moscow in winter. Only it was money rather than snow that he ploughed. Vishnya sang, Buratinka played and wheedled people that he needed. This hard work alternated with constant drinking by the adorable couple. They wolfed down 70 percent proof alcohol. They glugged cognac and champagne. What was touching was their consistent infatuation with each other. Although Vishnya was constantly driving Buratinka crazy with her affairs, provocations, eccentric escapades and leonine passions. Buratinka loved his Vishnya to distraction, but for some reason his love never stopped him from making awkward passes at every passing skirt. So it was, paradoxically, with daily infidelities and boozing that their tragi-comic married life was cemented. But they liked it that way, and thank Goodness!

That crazy morning I left a note of thanks and farewell on their rosewood dining table, excusing myself for my unforeseen departure to an "urgent concert". I ended the letter in that way to avoid being bothered by them again. After florid and vague thanks "for everything", I blew them a "big kiss".

I never saw Vishnya or Buratinka again. Buratinka died a few years ago. The elderly Vishnya has become an important lady in the new Russia.

I remember the furiously livid look in Buratinka's eye, as though two titanium drills were boring into me. He was enraged by my diplomatic trip to the Soviet Union in 1986 to settle the status of the "new, free Soviet individual."

"Andwei, what is all this? Have you suddenly decided to give in to them? You've got yourself all weady to go? If you're going to play games like that with them you do know that we won't shake hands with you again, don't you?"

Of course I understood, what was there not to understand? The way they wanted it was to go back to their "moronic native country" as it knelt before them, to arrive on a white charger. I'm certain that Buratinka's friend Solzhenitsyn felt something similar, although with a slightly different slant on it. The Messiah (musical or scrivener) does a divine favour and returns from exile in the "cursed West" to the "foolish, filthy and blind freaks of nature" to show them the true path.

We somehow got talking about the Russian public. I can remember that Vishnya roared, "Freaks, I once put a huge cross round my neck, a fake emerald, either Chanel or Cartier, but a cheap, clumsy fake, you know, Andrei, a really blatant fake, specially for them. And some old lady started pawing at me."

Vishnya transformed herself here into a stooped old woman with mad eyes, with her hands held out as if in supplication, and started to speak in a ghastly, moronic, quavering voice, ""Maaaariiina Paaaavlovnaa, Mariiina Paaavlovnaaa, is that the cross of the murdered Prince Dimiiitri?"

"I stepped back from her, and answered, of course it is, exactly that one! What did you expect?! What idiots, eh?"

Russia had fed the creative activity of people like Vishnya and Buratinka with its "celestial naivety". In the West they earned money and worked in conditions of equality, while at home, in their own country, they were set alight by the opportunity of an ego trip at the expense of their unhappy, benighted compatriots. It was not only famous musicians who felt like that, but almost the entire Soviet ruling élite. They were excited and entranced by the distance between them – "the gods" – and "the people".

Svyatoslav Richter was no exception. Once he burst out, "Yes, Russians are of course almost all deranged, especially the musical public, hm. Do you know, Andrei, I could easily go and live in the West, but do you think it's better there? The moment they feel that they've got hold of you they start talking to you in su-u-uch a to-o-one! As equals, and sometimes even condescendingly."

That is absolutely true! You also have to rush around like everyone else, not sit on a cloud, and you can't spend six months lolling around in depression, and nobody is going to kiss the soles of your feet and wipe the dust from your heels with their beards. The main thing is that you can't humiliate anyone. That is the one thing the privileged couldn't imagine life without. They needed to see the mass humiliation, the worship! Which is why, once they'd made enough money in the West, they went back home. They returned to die in this deranged soil, once they had luxuriated in Russian folly and tail-wagging devotion.

Gorby

Who was I in the USSR? An ordinary Moscow ant and Carbonari. I thumbed my nose at the Party and the government behind their backs and couldn't give a toss about any of them. Unfortunately they became seriously interested in my modest persona. They wouldn't leave me alone. It was this that motivated my departure.

The New Russia? Of course a lot has changed, but the main thing hasn't. Russia has remained a stronghold of bad taste and brazen, even aggressive, vulgarity. Russia is of course my native country. But it is not a mother, rather more a wet nurse or nanny. Europe, on the other hand, is a mature love... Mother, father and wife...

***

In 1986 Natasha and I were visiting Pezin, the chairman of the USSR State Bank in London. He often invited selected compatriots to luxury lunches, paid for on expenses. That time, the banker's guests were academics. They were discussing, as almost all Soviet people were doing at the time, the strange new man in the Kremlin. They spoke very quietly for some reason, whispering... It even seemed to me that they were hissing... I did make out some of what they were saying.

"He's crazy! He can't do that! What does he want? To restore the New Economic Policy? What a nightmare! You can't imagine what he's doing... We will lose all our privileges! They'll kill him of course... And rightly so..."

I thought at the time, "What have they done to you, physicists-lyricists! Or is it you who have done it to yourselves? Can you really not see that somehow there is now a Man in charge! He wants radically to reform the system. We should be thinking about how to support him, and you have started hissing like snakes because you are so scared... You are ready to tear him limb from limb... Oh, Mikhail Sergeyevich, if even your academics have turned into such rats, who on earth have you got beside you? Nothing but cannibals? Hatchets? How are you going to carry your burden? Between the concrete heads of the Commies, and the terrified, drunken people, and the intellectual élite trembling for their sinecure?"

The scientists asked Pezin, "Is it true that Alkhimov's daughter ran off with Gavrilov?"

"Why don't you ask them yourselves?"

I shall never forget the expression of terror and feigned indignation on the faces of those Soviet scientists. They didn't ask me about anything, but quickly retreated in embarrassment. Only young Kapitsa stayed, gave my knee a squeeze and said, "Well, don't abandon us forever!"

I promised not to.

After lunch we went home. I had a heavy heart. I already understood that it was impossible to "restructure" Soviet Russia because it was impossible to change the people who lived there, even if you had half a century to do it.

I said to Natasha, "Do you know, I have a horrible premonition that there are going to be some terrible catastrophes really soon. I keep imagining something really awful... When Stalin was in power people built all those hydroelectric dams on Dniepre more or less in good faith. The enthusiasm of idiots, fear... But from Khrushchev onwards all these colossal Soviet projects have been fakes, tea-break work, imitations..."

It is dreadful when premonitions don't lie! Three months later Chernobyl happened. We watched in horror the satellite pictures on TV. We saw the lethal cloud that covered the territory round the broken reactor, and was gradually creeping to Belarus... We phoned Moscow, explained, begged our friends and family not to go outside and not to open the windows. Nobody believed us...

In August the same year the second omen happened – not far form Novorossisk the SS *Admiral Nakhimov* sank. More than 400 people were killed. In actual fact it was not the reactor that was exploding, and not the ship that sank – it was the whole USSR, rotten to the core, which was exploding and sinking...

At the end of 1986 I suddenly sensed that the Soviet mantrap had loosened its grip, and the following year I went back to

Moscow (as I had promised in my letter to Pete). Pete was the first of the bosses that Natasha and I went to see. He was very welcoming, did not whisper, spoke clearly, sensibly and in a friendly fashion. I had never seen him like that. He was fascinated to hear about our life abroad, asked a great many questions and even flirted with Natasha. He was like a luminous rose. When we got up from his huge, ministerial table and started to take our leave, he suddenly said to Natasha, "Well, please don't steal Andrei from us again!" and smiled sweetly. Natasha's jaw dropped in amazement, and she was unable to think of anything to say in response. That was the last time I met Nilych. Although only two years had passed since I left, I found myself in a different country.

The old USSR of Stalin or Brezhnev no longer existed. Lubyanka and Staraya Square and all the other institutions of the totalitarian state remained, however, and the bloody war in Afghanistan still continued. But academician Sakharov had already been allowed back from exile. Political prisoners were gradually being set free from incarceration. The refuseniks of many years were getting permission to leave the country.

Millions of Sovs developed the first justified hope they had in many decades that things might change for the better. It seemed to me that Gorbachev was trying to cut through the thousands of heads of the communist dragon to reach the tens of millions of Soviet citizens who had caught a whiff of fresh air. The country was in turmoil. Queues 100 metres long would form at newspaper kiosks to buy *Izvestiya* and *Ogonyok* that had suddenly become interesting to read. Even longer queues formed at the wine counters of Moscow shops. They published *Doctor Zhivago*. Soap disappeared from the shelves. Perestroika was taking place in the country.

My only input to perestroika was in facilitating the return of Vladimir Ashkenazy to his home country. TV presenters Molchanov and Listyev organized a number of programmes in which I participated. One of the things that was discussed in the programmes was the return of Ashkenazy. In modern society, television plays a truly fateful role, and back then, for the majority of the population in the USSR, television was something aligned with the divine voice and signs from God. What was shown and said on the telly was a command, the law... What was shown seemed to come true of its own accord, became not virtual, but true reality...

A miracle really did happen – just eighteen months after the first mention of the "return of Ashkenazy" in Molchanov's programme *Before and After Midnight*, Vladimir was already performing in the Moscow Conservatoire.

Years went by. After 2001 I started regularly visiting the new Russia with concerts. In 2003, my good friend, the journalist Larissa Alexeyenko managed to take a small interview with Gorbachev during the interval of my Bach concert at the House of Music.

Larissa asked Mikhail Gorbachev to talk about what happened in late 1986 when I had suddenly felt the disfavour lifted, and I was crossed off the list of enemies of the USSR, or even from the list of condemned men...

Gorbachev gave this answer: "I can't remember exactly, there was so much going on at the time. They gave me a list... There was Sakharov at number one, and in second place was Gavrilov. I knew who Sakharov was. But I had no idea who Gavrilov was. I asked who he was. I was told that he was a pianist. I wondered whatever he was on the list for. I signed it without a second thought..."

In 2004 Gorbachev came to see me in Nikitsky Boulevard. He was fresh, cheerful and wearing an elegant cap and leather jacket – good old Gorby! He asked his bodyguards to wait in the stairwell, so as not to make me feel uncomfortable. Emotions made it difficult for us to talk. I said, "Shall we go to the piano?"

"Let's," replied Gorby, "Music needs no words..."

I played him Suggestion diabolique by Sergei Prokofiev. Gorbachev listened attentively, literally breathing in the music, full of sarcasm, diabolic irony at the struggle between good and evil, and then he told me that he interpreted the piece as the anthem, the rhythm and the essence of perestroika... A diabolical suggestion or delusion? That is food for thought.

The father of perestroika is soon to celebrate his 80th birthday. I am not a politician, and not an analyst. I do not have the right to judge or glorify Gorbachev the politician. I do, however, want to pay tribute to his wonderful human qualities that have manifested themselves in his advanced age, after great personal losses. His wisdom, sense of humour, strength of will and heartfelt integrity. This man exudes warmth, light, tolerance, kindness and faith. He is full of energy, life and inner radiance. What a contrast to the unkind, dark, old Richter; hollow, lacking in faith and abhorrent to himself...

With Mikhail Gorbachev (2006)

Mafia

The musical world today is in a state of confusion. Many composers search, but cannot find. Accessible electronic playback technology has crushed creativity. I hope this is temporary. We are all living through an astonishing computer revolution which of course will give rise to a new aesthetic sooner or later, and with new instruments, a new style or symphony of styles...I do not know if a genius composer or top class performing musician will be required in the future. I do not know if a new Bach will occur, capable of squaring the circle and combining in his art all the musical currents and trends that have scattered in all directions like frightened mice... I know only one thing – humanity will be unable to live without high art. In almost all books about musicology, the authors obsequiously quote Nietzsche's famous phrase, "Without music, civilisation would be a mistake." Tens of millions of music lovers repeat this quotation. What a load of pompous twaddle! Without music, quite simply, civilisation would be impossible.

***

At the All-Union Competition in Minsk in 1971 I first encountered evil in the music world. Before this competition I was genuinely convinced that all musicians were one big happy family. The harassment started after I, an unknown ninth-grader from the Central Music School, played in the first round. They wouldn't let me sleep. The phone rang all night through until I finally thought to pull the plug out. It was not "wrong numbers" who called me; it was a planned and cynical attack on a novice. Various people kept knocking on my hotel room door, having "got the wrong door". Three grown men discussed openly amongst themselves (so that I could hear every word), exactly how they were going to break my arms and fingers on the staircase. I managed to play the second round successfully as well. At this point one of the competition directors distinguished himself. He announced outright, talking to the crowd of fans by the competition jury's meeting room, "Your

Gavrilov is never, not under any circumstances, getting through to the third round." It ended in farce, with the public bursting into the jury's room to control the voting process. A few fans called out, "If Gavrilov doesn't get through to the third round, nobody is leaving this room." Support like this was a great surprise to everyone, and it disrupted the pre-arranged plans for who would win and who would fail.

At the Tchaikovsky Competition in Moscow in 1974, it all happened again, but on a much larger scale and more dramatically. Interference by the public would have been insufficient there, but the foreign members of the jury stood up in my defence, all unanimously voting for me to win. In so doing they shuffled the deck for the Soviet jury members. Back then the wonderful elders of musical Europe were still alive, the last representatives of a generation of honour and merit.

Today, I am ashamed to be the winner of the Tchaikovsky Competition. When I understood that influential and super-rich Asians were buying the prizes of this formerly great musical competition for their offspring, I gave my gold medal away to be made into chains and rings for my beautiful ladyfriends…

Let us forget the USSR from those distant times. Let us talk about the here and now. Who wins musical competitions nowadays? Those who have been appointed to win by the members of the jury who are half-teacher, half-wheeler dealer, thrown out of art in their time and therefore loathing all living creativity! Over the last half century three generations of "musiciens" have arisen, along with consumers of their tacky art. It's a matter of supply and demand. The public feels perfectly happy with such idiot-proof performers. The opinions of the few, sensitive people who are devoted to true art are of no interest to anyone.

About 10 years ago, in a conversation with a leading major music promoter, I was bemoaning the state of affairs. He looked at me with pity and said, "There's high demand for the piano!"

He couldn't care less who is at the piano. As long as "it" has been "hyped". Preferably not by him. The bosses of the international music business are incredibly cynical. They spent the post-war years aggressively and inexorably striving for absolute power in the arts. And they got there. They changed from being service personnel for the musicians and audience, to being the sole masters of performance art. Until by now, money and fat cats determine the composition of the international music scene. There is no way of changing the situation.

The roots of decay should be sought in the activities of Karajan and similar talents, who learned how to squeeze colossal money out of classical music. They achieved this by gradually lowering the level of classical art until it was easily understood by the wider public. The main thing was for music to be easily swallowed by the public, and therefore to sell well. Today we are reaping the fruits of these efforts. It is no longer possible to squeeze the genie back into the bottle.

By the end of the 1970s, the western half of the international music scene had almost completely decayed. And Russia? The new, post-communist Russia quickly outstripped the West in anything to do with moral decay and bourgeois dissipation. But fell even further behind in all things good, I'm afraid. Russia seems to have returned to the times of Gogol and Dostoevsky, writers who showed in particularly sharp relief the corrupting power of money. The stokers of the Russian musical furnace pour across the world with the wild joyful whoops of Neanderthals released from communism. The eternal barbarity of Russia has burst out, blowing away and burying the few remaining fragments of "great Russian culture" that were still cherished in the USSR, for better or for worse.

What can be done? What can be done with a musical world that has had its heart deadened by horrifying trolls, like in the tale of the Snow Queen, and whose eyes have been pierced by shards of the diabolical mirror that distorts the world? Everyone who views him or herself as an honest musician should seek a personal path through the clouded, dangerous ocean of the financial and anti-cultural outrage that has taken the place of the cultural world. It is essential to foster within oneself strength of mind, demonstrate inventiveness and seek out unconventional approaches. We need to fight, otherwise we will perish, and be slowly and painfully tortured to death. In the modern world a great many new opportunities have opened up – for example the cheap production of discs. Even though I am opposed in principle to recordings, in view of the new conditions that are in place in the competitive struggle between good and evil, I plan to make recordings as often as possible.

If necessary I shall pay for them myself, jointly with sponsors, or however, but the main thing is to put pressure on the commercial mass of clones bearing the labels of the "leading world brands". The Internet is a superb platform for popularizing one's ideas in the most varied formats! Concerts from small to large auditoria, at total cost recovery. One needs to set an example to teach the public. When the public has the opportunity of comparing, they still chose beauty, for the time being.

The people who work in the music business are incompetent – from the presidents to the programme managers. In comparison with them, any bureaucrat from the Ministry of Culture of the USSR would look like Plato or a quick-witted Newton. From the mid-70s through to the early 90s, I worked in major Western recording companies. Even then the upper echelons of the business were riddled through with ignorance and corruption of all sorts. The main pursuit of these people was taking part in countless conferences, which were always held in the most beautiful spots on the planet. First-class tickets were always purchased to get to these usually pointless meetings. The most prestigious hotels were hunted out. Expensive wine was gulped down in vast quantities. Diverse sexual activities were also practised, and all on company expenses, of course.

Record companies treat musicians in the same way that slave-owners treat their slaves. They dictate what, when and with whom to record. Musicians have no say. Half-hearted resistance is suppressed severely. It is difficult to leave, as without these companies it is impossible to break through into the group of leaders. The companies juggle with people, exclude the talented and recalcitrant from the stage, and promote to prominence the mediocre and compliant. The major agencies determine who will give concerts where and when, and who will go on the big concert tours - solo and orchestral. In this work, the agencies are governed purely by the laws of the free market, not by considerations of cultural suitability, let alone supporting and developing the talent of a particular artist. Unfortunately, this "market" is only called "free", while in actual fact it is a totally corrupt structure organized by the mafia.

It is no small money that circulates in the music business. The leaders of the "music mafia" protect their interests using their favoured methods. I believe that nobody has been physically destroyed yet, but there is no need to. Performers are killed quietly, without loss of blood, by denying them the opportunity to perform. No concerts means no musician.

I know dozens of great musicians who have been exterminated by the "music mafia", no longer accepted as professionals for having made independent moves on the music scene. Mikhail Faerman was in my class at school, the winner of the Queen Elisabeth Music Competition in Brussels. He did not take up Israeli citizenship, did not go to live in Israel or America, and insisted on his own conditions when negotiating contracts.

For this he was excluded from concert life. That was how he was "killed". Even though this brilliant pianist had already attained the level of Gilels at a young age, but with even greater technical potential than Emil. The world lost in Faerman a concert pianist on a par with Horowitz! The Brussels Conservatoire acquired a superb professor…

The music mafia has no difficulty in shattering any musical star. Rumours start to circulate about an insubordinate musician regarding his unpleasant personal qualities, his unprofessionalism, his sexuality, unreliability, alcoholism, or his having AIDS. If that is not enough, the world music mafia announces a real boycott against a musician – nobody notices the musician's work, no reviews, no invitations, and anyone who dares to go against this in turn becomes a victim. There is no point expecting the music critics to help, because they feed off the crumbs that fall from the tables of the international agencies.

My whole life I have observed how performers of my generation have suffered once they are entangled in the net of the musical monster. For example, brilliant talents such as Zimerman and Pogorelić were terrified of interrupting "business" and constantly forced themselves too far, not giving their talents the chance to develop and establish themselves. Those who "kept business going" at whatever price, gradually slid down to the level of careless kitsch.

Instead of real musicians there are now musical robots from Asia who are pretty "key-tappers" and "bow-holders", and who play hilariously badly, with no understanding of the musical material they are dealing with. Recordings of these "extra-terrestrials" are sold in vast quantities. The world stage now features the children of the Samsungs, Toyotas, Yamahas, Sonys and Daewoos, along with many other Asian billionaires. It would appear that the producers of televisions, cameras and cars have taken a shine to this new sport. It imparts to them the cultural gloss that they lacked. The Asian performers are superb athletes and have turned European art into a "Chinese circus". The children of Christian civilization are brought up on the Asian circus traditions, and already totally reject true art, as it has nothing in common with "Nintendo music!"

A whole pleiad of clones, fools and sex kittens has appeared. Anne-Sophie Mutter made her contribution to all of this. In the 80s I was still working with EMI, and witnessed how the design department would spend hours in a meeting heatedly debating the plunge of the neckline on her dress. The picture was to be used on the cover of a record that was being prepared for release. As a result, Mutter was photographed from above, to show off her charms to the best advantage. The process did not stop at the décolletage of sexy female musicians. Backs, arms and legs were bared. The essential condition for entering the "élite" was the demonstration by a violinist of her semi-naked voluptuous form.

Female pianists were also active participants in the striptease competition, with the pioneers here being the Labèque sisters. The moment they were put on a piano, they were undressed to be put on the album covers!

Then onto the world stage came the musical fool, Nigel Kennedy, a violinist who seems unable to play a single clean note on his instrument. But Nigel does not let that get him down; he appears in public in striped shorts, sneakers, a green and red punk combat wig, then festoons himself in a kilogramme of hard rock knick knacks. He scrapes away at an insane tempo (to conceal the fact that he is out of tune, and hide how uneven and weak his little fingers are) to play Vivaldi's *Four Seasons,* unbearably hackneyed from frequent performance. Nigel is already in the charts for pop and classical music. Another two dozen different freak images, and Nigel is recognized as a Maestro of the violin!

Then there was the rather immodest daughter of the Singapore Godfather, Vanessa Mae, bursting onstage with out-of-tune screeches on her electric monster-violin, remembering periodically to hoik her skirt up. The audience are in raptures – the electricity will hide her inaccuracies and weaknesses, and the drummers will stuff the ears with a cotton wool of sound. This semi-nude Asian girl, carefully packaged by the British commercial machine, has already become the dream and role model for girls all over the world.

"The New Oistrakh" – Vengerov, the public favourite and internationally undisputed leading violinist – breaks into a nifty jig on stage at one of the most celebrated Philharmonic halls, and in well-simulated ecstasy breaks into a Cossack dance, clutching his Stradivarius and bashing out Sarasate all the while. Even the brilliant musician Gidon Kremer scrapes out a world tour and plays Argentian tango to the strains of the accordion. The public are entranced. Oh, Piazzolla, oh my goodness, I love it! This marvellous classical violinist as endearing restaurant fiddler. Taking the bread from the mouths of the virtuosos of the vodka, champagne and nibbles variety.

I have undergone a difficult, painful and lonely journey to strengthen my spirit and develop my individuality. I have managed to return to the principal podiums around the world since returning to the international scene in 2001, despite fierce opposition from the music mafia.

The difficulties recede with each passing year, and I can feel tremendous support from the musical youth who want to attain total freedom in art, unfettered by the chains of the financial market!

***

I completed my first ever trip to India. The Indians are astute in their understanding of European and Russian music. I was particularly impressed by my talks with people who were deeply and sincerely religious. There is not enough faith in Russia. Faith in my country has mutated into superstition. Young people have sunk into insolent, illiterate nihilistic scepticism. Without true faith, art wilts. Without God, the world is just a cellar full of spiders.

Tour in Russia 2010

I flew to Moscow. Then by train to Samara. The price for two tickets in a sleeper carriage leaves us stunned. It is 800 dollars for an overnight trip. In Europe train journeys are half the price. I don't understand who can afford a luxury of this sort. The food in the restaurant car is bad, stale and ridiculously expensive. They're all trying to rip you off. They don't print out receipts, they write them out by hand so that they don't get caught with their hand in the till…

The Samara Philharmonic Hall. The people work well and make an effort. There is an exhibition in the foyer, "Lights of the Samara Philharmonia". The public are wonderful, kind and attentive listeners. The orchestral musicians complain to me that their life is difficult, and housing unaffordable. They have to hold down several jobs to provide for themselves and their families. The Samarans were excellent when they played with me with enthusiasm and understanding.

It seemed to me that the general atmosphere in the town had worsened. In 2004 the Samarans took me round their city and told me about their plans for a renaissance of the city. We dreamed about walking along beautiful Dvoryanskaya Street, once it was renovated. The street never was renovated. The unique 19th-century architectural ensemble still bears the uninspiring name of Kuibyshev. The fire has also died down in the people themselves. Nobody any longer expects anything from anyone. The years have passed with nothing to show for it. The people have kept going somehow. The feudal lords have grown incalculably richer.

Moscow. The main impression is that Russia has fallen into a malignant perpetuity. It seems that this is the "special path" the country is taking. Throughout its harsh history the same cycles repeat themselves stupidly and mechanically.

Short periods of reanimation and thaw are then replaced by gloomy periods of reaction when the principle component in public life is its oppression and suffocation. Nobody can or wishes to learn from past mistakes. Modern Russian society is treading water, rotting and bruised. But with leaden stubbornness it does not wish to look at itself, to pull itself together and rise even one step higher. Russia does not wish to return to objective reality; it prefers to befuddle itself with renewed, but painfully familiar myths that are rotten to the core.

It is impossible to watch Russian television because it is, without metaphor or hyperbole, a Witches' Sabbath. Absolutely ALL the characters on screen have visible horns, tails, snouts and hooves. Avaricious, obtuse physiognomies, red slug-like lips, grabbing hands and the eyes of witches and vampires. They are special, national bogey monsters, not something from Goya's engravings or the paintings of Bosch. They are post-Soviet glamour. The moral stench that is mentioned in Dostoevsky's short story, *Bobok*, has filled Moscow in its entirety. It emanates from Russian "politicians" and "comedians", and their banal public. People are not living; they are functioning in malignant perpetuity, like robots. There are robot pimps and robot whores. A bestial passion for profit hangs in the air like an axe.

There is no real meaning in contemporary Russia. No big idea. THE KINGDOM OF EMPTINESS. Thoughts and ideas have left, together with the people who had them, or they have been chewed up and spat out like chewing gum waste. There is nobody to talk to and nothing to talk about. The feelings and reactions of the overriding majority of Muscovites are on the most primitive level. People are engaged in satisfying their needs. They are superficial, vulgar and evil as hardened crims. The lives and pain of other people is of no concern to anyone. Love, care, attention, mutual respect and amicability have abandoned these people's reality. The cosmic coldness of modern Russians chills to the core. The jaw drops at their effrontery.

I was walking round the Boulevard ring road late one evening. I looked into the eyes of passersby. What did I see there? Loneliness, hopelessness, intoxication with the pointlessness of existence and a brainless readiness to risk their lives. As well as imminent death from drink or drugs…

Beautiful naked female forms in the windows of the night clubs and discos of the centre of Moscow. Hookers dance and draw the punters in. There are dead smiles on their doll-like, rubber faces. They stretch their lips wide in front of a client in order to gobble him down, swallow him and then spit him out of their bellies and raze him from their memories.

The image of the new Moscow that has been built up over the last ten years is extraordinarily similar to its contents. It is of course not New London, not Paris, New York or Madrid. It is still the same old Potemkin village, blue bloated face, a bit of lippy and a covering of cheap blusher. Clothed in hollering stations. Everywhere and everything is vulgar, vile and fake, from the main replica cathedral along the replica boulevards and up to the replica sky scrapers.

The last romantic corners of old Moscow, which served as my constant source of inspiration in my past life, have all been destroyed or desecrated.

The architectural effrontery and lack of talent made my physically unwell, I felt nauseous. New Moscow is the embodiment of lack of talent, boorishness and the mental retardation of the rampaging louts who have got their hands on power! The city of Moscow no longer exists. It is Disneyland. A fairground ride of lethal anarchy. Freedom as interpreted by idiot gangsters, like at Gulyai Polye. A den of thieves. The mundane passivity of the post-Soviet masses is depressing, along with their mob-boss elders. The most terrifying phenomenon in life in New Russia, however, is the artistic intelligentsia. They are obese and stupid and have sold out, hook, line and sinker. They have trampled all that was humane within them in exchange for awards and undeclared cash payments from the KGB and the crime lords.

I always used to be offended by Rachmaninoff. In an interview in the 1930s an American journalist asked him if he missed Russia. He replied, "Russia no longer exists." Until very recently I thought that Rachmaninoff was wrong. It is only these most recent concerts in Moscow in 2010 that have made me realise that he was right.

Despite all this, I did notice several lovely, familiar faces from old times among the concert-going public. How have they survived in this crazy cesspit, at this licentious carnival of modern Daddy Makhnos? I imagined that in the cavernous halls there were tiny streams of life trickling through, and that people came there to breathe, away from deafening reeking reality.

The main mass of Muscovites have adapted to the lack of atmosphere in the megapolis. They like the putrid ambiance of captivity. They are incapable of living at liberty, in the fresh air. Nine hundred years of self-enslavement, followed by another 100 years of communism have left their mark. Liberated bondmen yearn for the lash of a whip. Old cons want to get back behind bars. The intellectuals who stayed behind long for the stools in the kitchen, rubbed smooth by sitting backsides. To have a giggle, drink a bit, tell a few jokes...

I flew to Magadan! It was an Aeroflot plane, a Boeing I was pleased to see. My relief was premature, however. Inside the aeroplane it was as cramped as a bad dream. The passenger in front lay on my legs for the whole flight. The seat was as narrow as a monkey's bum.

It was impossible to squeeze into the toilet. The flight lasted eight hours. I reclined the seat. The passenger behind me yelled, "What do you think you're doing?"

I roared back in response, "Complaining about your Aeroflot!"

As we approached Magadan I could see cheerless hills covered in snow. How awful it was to die here! There was a poster: Welcome to Kolyma, the Golden Heart of Russia!

Well, into the Heart I go! I walked through the streets. The people here seemed particularly primitive to me. On the faces of almost everyone I passed there was some indication of hard drinking. Puffy, worn-out, grey faces. Blurry eyes. Everyone drinks in this cold, Golden Heart of Russia. Even the staff at the Philharmonia. It seems that any other way is impossible. Many people in the streets have thuggish faces. Even young girls.

But, what a miracle! Even here the concert-going public was pleasant and nice. My concert. Comprehension, passionate success and tears of happiness.

The director was Jewish, happy and drunk. Aha, I thought, someone I can talk to! I was wrong. All that was left of the Jew in him was the wisdom not to interfere in anything except his own business. We spoke about the memorial project (in memory of the victims of political repression). He squirmed and pulled a contemptuous expression.

"Whatever for? How much can they keep banging on about that? Anyone who comes to see us in Magadan immediately starts talking only about the dead. We've had enough requiems! Let's live and have fun!"

I see, I see, Mr Director, I thought. The unspoken order from above has reached even the Golden Heart of Russia. A new song to an old tune. The Soviet Union wasn't all that bad. The most successful manager in Russia has directed it all. The Spiritual Father of today's Great Pretender. Well, you can drink and have fun, dance on the bones of your ancestors. Just do it without me.

I came down with pneumonia in Magadan. Perhaps it was caused by indignation?

Before leaving I went up onto Krutaya Hill. Perched on top stands the Mask of Sorrow, a 15-metre concrete monument by Ernst Neizvestny. Instead of a face it has a cross, instead of eyes it has a hole, with a prison cell inside. Newly-weds come up to the Mask of Sorrow. They do not come to mourn, however, they come to drink. The dogs need an excuse to clink their glasses, and a post to lift a leg against.

Our guide explained, "These concrete blocks symbolise the camps."

She was interrupted by a cracked voice, "Why don't you tell foreigners that 67 per cent of the prisoners in Kolyma were criminals? Only 33 per cent were politicals. And this monument is a lie, nothing but a waste of money to bullshit the foreigners…"

The voice belonged to a young man with an ugly face and sallow complexion. He was wearing a long, smart overcoat, with a childish knitted balaclava on his head. He was tall. He counts people in percentages, the bastard… Is he a goon? A far-right extremist? No, he's an ordinary modern young Putinoid, brainwashed by the new propaganda. He's a worthy son of a moronic father informer, the grandson of a prisonguard and great grandson of a commissar in a dusty helmet. He spews out the sort of bubonic loathing of all humanity that was rife in Soviet times.

In Yaroslavl I was unwell when I played my concert, but I enjoyed it. I played Mozart and Prokofiev, for music lovers who have not been annihilated by the new era. It was a full house. Happy faces. Even a few Muscovites made the effort to come; I noticed a number of familiar faces. Good for them! I so wanted to embrace them all with my music. To take them away from there for ever. Tears again. Happiness.

After the concert there followed four miserable hours in the car. A fever. Finally I was back home on Nikitsky Boulevard. I couldn't breathe I was coughing so much. I barely manage to crawl to bed. East, west, home's best. Not a bit of it! There were cars roaring outside the windows. I couldn't open the little top window as the smell of exhaust was unbearable. From upstairs, as though from the sky, came the never-ending din of a pneumatic drill and the infernal wine of an electric drill; the sounds of refurbishment. Plaster fell from the ceiling. It seemed to me in my feverish delirium that the ceiling was falling down and the sky was crumpling. Judgment Day. My illness developed complications because of the racket. Moscow coughed and spluttered. It was the city's cough that was ripping my throat and bronchial tubes.

The nouveaux riches have sucked up enough money and are renovating their glamorous homes. The New Moscow scum hopes to shut itself off from the world behind marble walls. From the world, from reality, the past and the present. You can't shut yourself off from destiny. Something tells me that payback time is not far off.

There was no reality, only noise. Rumblings, filth, people with frenzied faces. It was stifling. It never used to be so stifling at Nikitsky Boulevard. This had nothing to do with being ill. My body and soul were stifling, and my mind. Being at home had not helped. The hell of Moscow's oblivion reached me even here, although I lived here for so many years. I had prayed with thousands of hours of practising, sanctified the rooms and the walls with the music of geniuses.

I turned on the television. On the Nostalgia channel they were showing famous performers from the Soviet stage, from Bernes (*Where does Homeland Begin*) to Sofia Rotaru (*Be Happy, My Earth*). Then they started playing Soviet newsreels from the 60s and 70s... Party conferences, people's deputies, medals, eminent miners and milkmaids, presidiums...

A cosmonaut mumbled something patriotic from orbit, front-rank workers reported to the people and the Party about the progress of socialist emulation...

The announcers broadcast like psychiatrists putting their patients into a deep, hypnotic sleep.

Headstrong tractors crawled across the screen, stern victorious soldiers marched, sweaty steel workers produced record cast iron smelting, the engines on snow-white IL-62 airliners rumbled richly, and capable stewardesses smiled shyly...

A gleam of gold and the wonderful Friendship of the Peoples fountain sent its crystal jets into the heavens...

The criminal experiment to produce a "new humankind" succeeded. Many Russians never came out of their Soviet coma. Hundreds of millions of human experimental subjects were turned into primitive, biological dolls, and produced multiple offspring...

It is no surprise that more than 50 per cent of the population of Russia wants to return to the USSR, while over 70 per cent believe Stalin was a "great leader" and dream of a "firm hand". Having undergone multiple selection in the Michurin technique, and three generations of lobotomy, people are unable to live beyond the walls of the clinic.

Rozanov was right, "Lenin and his henchmen are so brave because they know that nobody will judge them, as the judges will have been eaten."

I looked on the Internet where the best Russian commentators publish their analytical articles. Many of them write about the "points of no return". Somebody thinks that the turning point in the history of Russia was the disbanding of the NTV channel, someone else believes it was the sinking of the Kursk, others that it was Beslan, or Nord-Ost... They all round off their critiques along the lines of, "One more step, and we will be on the brink of catastrophe!"

I have long been sick of this "brink". What are you talking about? What points of no return? What edge of the abyss? How much longer can you keep reassuring yourselves? How much longer can you keep lying to yourselves?

Russia has been buried under a layer of blood-soaked lava for the past hundred years. The lava is now filling up the last burrows, holes and caves where the contemporary Russian Nestors and Avvakums sit. The Russian apocalypse has exploded Russia, and it will be more than a century's wait for any green shoots of Russian culture.

Up until New Year 2011, everyone was eagerly discussing the TRIAL of two men. These two men retained their pride and dignity, which is why they were in court. Like two Gulliver's, they looked in amusement from their glass cages at the Lilliputians scurrying around them.

The "best brains" little realise that this is no trial, but the latest in a string of criminal gang rapes on all of us who grieve over what is left of our homeland...

One great "brain" insists that the crooked leaders should be banished from the country on a "ship of thieves" in order to cleanse the country of filth. The brilliant commentator forgot that it is not a ship that is required; rather a gigantic ark into which the vast majority of the mutilated population of the Soviet Union need to be stuffed...

I was quietly exultant on my way to the airport. I was not upset when the girl at the check-in desk had a little fit of hysterics over the additional kilogrammes in my luggage. I ran the 30 metres with my shoes off to the metal detector, out of breath, in a bit of a lather. I almost fainted, barely able to wait for take off.

"Gutte morga, Grützi" sang our beautiful, polite SWISS air cabin staff with their welcoming smiles. They were congenial from the heart, not as part of their job. There was a white cross on the red tail of the plane, with no masks of the killed and tortured.

All around me were people. I heaved a huge sigh and fell asleep. We landed in Zurich, the sun was shining. It was warm. Smiles. For some reason I didn't want to see it all, and knew that my soul was back there. What was here was nothing but the husk. Till the bitter end I will keep going back to my homeland. I shall die with the thought of its renaissance in my mind.

Piano Concerto No. 1

For quite a long time after winning the Tchaikovsky Competition and the triumph in Salzburg I did nothing but execute the music using the technical skills of a good school.

For five or six years I occupied the niche of "Russian marvel"... Eventually I got sick of that. I can remember that the management of EMI tried to limit my repertoire. Some very imposing chaps came to see me and told me, "You will play Rachmaninoff, Tchaikovsky, Prokofiev and a little Stravinsky." I put forward my condition, which was that I would fulfil their commission, and then record what I wanted to myself. I started to prepare Bach, Mozart, Schubert and Schumann. They vigorously opposed this. Why? Because Schubert and Chopin were played by Zimerman. Schubert and late Beethoven as well as Brahms were played by Brendel. It was all divided up, like the mafia carving up the streets of New York. The director of the marketing department came to see me and said, "People are confused, they don't know which composer to buy in your interpretation!"

To which I replied, "They can damn well buy me!"

***

The Tchaikovsky Concerto No. 1 is a huge hit nowadays.

No other classical piece is played so often, including performances at countless competitions. This constant repetition has discredited and exhausted the wonderful, delicate work. Abuse of Concerto No. 1 in the USSR and in Russia at all sorts of celebrations, in the past they were communist, and now they are patriotic, has led to the concerto setting the teeth on edge for many Russians, while in other countries it is often taken to be a musical apotheosis of Russian nationalist chauvinism.

This musical work, however, is woven from melodical modulations of the human soul, this singing, symphonic philosophy of life, this sweet Russian symphonic existentialism belongs possibly to the top ten greatest creations of human genius.

In order to perform Tchaikovsky's Concerto No. 1, a pianist must not only be technically perfect, but also have the appropriate life experience, be in tune with the wonderful Russian culture of the 19th century, and have a profound understanding of Russian religious philosophy or, as it is sometimes known, the organic wisdom of life.

I have been playing Tchaikovsky's First Piano Concerto all my life. This piece is connected in my soul with the image of my father, Vladimir Gavrilov, an artist who received recognition during the Khrushchev thaw. I remember his painting that hangs in the Tretyakov Gallery, entitled A Fresh Day. It depicts a girl in a white skirt, headscarf and short yellow cardigan. The girl is standing in a boat. A fresh wind is blowing from the lake, into her back. The girl is laughing and happy. When I play Concerto No. 1, I also want to be happy. To take delight in the marvellous music and mourn my prematurely departed father. Before my father left for his friend's exhibition in Tver, in 1970 (where my dad died suddenly at the age of 47), I had promised him that I would learn this concerto in a week. He had laughed and said, "I don't think that's very realistic."

The fresh, sweet, melodious wind of life that blows through my heart – that is the music of Tchaikovsky's Piano Concerto No. 1. I have been playing the concerto in this way for 35 years – carefree, happy and delighted. Revelling in the beauty of the harmonies, surrendering myself to them. At the same time I also felt that something in the fabric of the music was not entirely the sweetness and light of Russian Shrovetide celebrations, and that Tchaikovsky's music takes us back to something colossal, pre-Biblical. Against the background of the hymns of joy and plenitude of being there are horrors and disruptions slipping through in the music. One can hear fears, and guess at an agonising inner struggle. It is not only the azure vistas that open up, but also the chasms of darkness.

I thought a great deal about the Piano Concerto No. 1, and it often sounded in my mind; it came to me and suffused me. It would linger with me for a long while. One day this marvellous music detonated my consciousness. It was as though the "codes" of this wonderful piece were revealed to me in the sort of enlightenment that occurs in Zen Buddhism. Ever since then I have played the concerto differently. Unfortunately, not everything can be put into words. It is well known that music starts where words lose their power.

The Piano Concerto No. 1 is Tchaikovsky's cosmos, his Book of Genesis. In the introduction, Tchaikovsky presents the creation of the world. The mighty blows of the French horn are the days, the acts of creation. These are the words of the Creator, His voice. His pulse. The trumps of the archangels. The call of the ancestors. The forceful cry of the prophets.

The act of creation is continued by the blacksmith demiurge, the pianist. He forges the universe out of chaos with his hammer of harmony. Around him revolve the clouds of the melodic Glory of God.

The composer shows us the creation of the world from the viewpoint of the Creator. Tchaikovsky is not watching this scene, he does not hear it; he is himself creating. Not as the successor to creation, but as God.

The extraordinary popularity of the introduction is because the composer wrote music of such power and beauty that people submit to the author's will, without even understanding what the music is "about" and "what" it is. They heed the creation and admire it.

The beginning of Concerto No. 1 is the most famous music on the planet. In all my life I have never met a single person who did not know this tune, from peasants to kings.

The task of the performer is to play the introduction in such a way that the public feels with every fibre in their bodies, the creation of the world as a great exultation and sacrament. However many times a musician performs this piece, he has to become a demiurge, the creator of the universe during the introduction, every time. Then the introduction will not sound vulgar or pompous or frivolous, like a waltz. It will not sound falsely patriotic, revoltingly majestic or trivially nationalistic. God and Pyotr Tchaikovsky did not create Russia for the Russians, they created the WORLD! Day and night. Water and land. Air and fire. Plants, animals, fish, humankind. The peoples of the world. That is the scope of the start of this concerto. A universal, cosmic scope.

At the same time, starting with the main theme of the first movement, the music of Concerto No. 1 is the personal experiences of the composer. Tchaikovsky the musical genius was an exceptionally sensitive and vulnerable man. His homosexuality, against which he struggled for many years as a dishonourable sin, was difficult to integrate into the morals and concepts of society at that time and the milieu in which he had to live. In the mid 1870s Tchaikovsky felt like a man looking into a deep abyss. Life "outside the abyss", however, oppressed him. He was frightened of giving into his sensual nature, of hurling himself into the abyss. He was scared of smashing against the bottom of the chasm. His own Golgotha among his friends, the "court of honour" awaited him. This court in judgment upon himself took place in the composer's soul throughout his thinking life. Tchaikovsky wrote about his sufferings many times in his diaries and letters to his brothers.

The composer's sufferings were reflected in the first movement of the Concerto, filled with a love of life on the one hand, and on the other saturated with horror at the reality of life and his own fate. That was Tchaikovsky, constantly caught between horror and rapture. Simultaneously between ecstasy and the nightmare of reality.

Tchaikovsky wrote the Piano Concerto No. 1 while he was still subjecting himself to monstrous constraint to avoid gaining a reputation for buggery (active sodomy) and at least somewhat to conform to the image of a "normal man" in the society of the times. In 1876 he even got married. By the end of the 1870s he was already "living in the abyss". He was living as nature had genetically determined he should. But in the early 1890s Tchaikovsky did "smash" after all. Whether deliberately or with the aid of cholera is uncertain.

It is no accident that the main theme of the concerto is taken from an old sorrowful song by blind beggar musicians, and seems to carry within it Tchaikovsky's fatal fragility. His rejection, his otherworldliness. His sorrow. The second theme presents the other aspect of his personality – the tender, loving attachment to mortal life.

Having shown in the primary and secondary themes the two driving forces in his soul, Pyotr Ilyich provides a musical prophecy of what awaits him. He reconstructs the fatal train of events that will lead to his death in the future. Starting with Concerto No. 1, the theme of implacable fate exists in almost all of Tchaikovsky's symphonic works. In the first movement of the concerto, Fatum is manifested by the relentless trombones and sombre bassoons. At the end of the development section, Tchaikovsky reproduces a dialogue between his lyrical hero (the piano) and the powers of fate (the orchestra). The hero begs for salvation. This prayer and trepidation of a man faced with Fatum is represented also in the solo cadenza.

Starting with the "Allegro con spirito", performers usually play the first movement of the concerto at the wrong tempos. This more often than not leads to a disruption of the whole musical architecture of the piece. How can the right tempo allegro be found?

In the secondary theme it indicates – "Tempo primo". It is obvious, however, that the secondary theme must be performed in an unhurried manner, with love. "Tempo primo" of course refers to the main theme, not to the theme of the introduction. The "Tempo primo" of the secondary theme must be at the same tempo as the main theme "Allegro con spirito". Then it all makes sense.

Usually "Allegro con spirito" is performed one and a half, or two times faster than it should be. The F minor octaves in the culmination likewise seem absurdly fast, and they should be performed at tempo, with no slowing down of the speed. If the tempo is wrong from the start, then the whole piece naturally takes on a caricature form, loses its logic and falls apart. The secondary theme "poco meno mosso" is usually played too slowly. Only after a revision of the tempos such as this does it become clear exactly how profound and magical is the music written by Tchaikovsky. Only if the tempos are correct does it become possible to intonate every note with care and gentleness worthy of the composer.

In the second movement, sketched outlines for Eugene Onegin can be perceived. Peaceable pictures of Russian nature, the countryside, the manor estate. The "shot" in the reprise leads one to think of the duel between Lensky and Onegin. The short recitative by the piano reminds one of Onegin's muttered, "He is killed, killed…" There are also musical images that remind one of future themes in The Queen of Spades.

The old French folk song reminds us of the agonised delirium of an old woman remembering dances with French aristocrats in the 18th century. The finale of the concerto is optimistic. The composer moves away from the Bible and from his own problems and gives himself entirely over to an ecstatic Ukrainian feast day. In the concerto finale, magical Christmas landscapes stretch out, with heroes from early Gogol dancing, and the whole world rejoicing.

The first theme signifies the "male" element, the well-known Ukrainian song Viydi, viydi Ivanku, (Come, come Ivanku). The secondary theme manifests the female element, the physicality and contentment of Ukrainian beauties and handsome young men.

At the end, before the coda, Vakula the Smith soars across the musical heaven, riding the Devil to St Petersburg to the tsaritsa's court to ask for her boots for his beautiful Oxana. This ecstatic flight ends with the crash of a fall. Vakula lands in the palace, with the elegantly dressed courtiers dancing the polonaise all around him. The apotheosis of the scene is the majestic appearance of Catherine the Great.

Conclusion

In conclusion I should like to write a few words about my family and loved ones. I shall write in detail about my family and my childhood in a second volume to this book.

On my mother's side my ancestors were Armenians from Constantinople. According to family legend they also had Greek, Turkish and French blood in the mix. My great-great grandparents traded the famous Samsun tobacco in Istanbul, and then left for the east of the Ottoman Empire, going to Trebizond and Erzurum. In the terrible times of the Armenian genocide they came to the Caucasus. Some of them traded, some built, some were soldiers and some of them speculated on the stock exchange. Later, in the 20th century, the Egisseryan clan also married into German blood. I had an Auntie Emilia, born in Swabia, the wife of the brother of Granddad Melik. She never did learn to talk Russian. She had two sons, Alfred and Klim, who were miners in Donetsk. They were both awarded the title of Heroes of Socialist Labour. I loved my cousin Alfred. He would often come to visit us in the Caucasus. It was said in the family that he was desperately in love with my mother. All the German Egisseryans were enormously tall, lovely men.

Many of my Armenian ancestors from my grandmother on my mother's side threw themselves into politics, and became fanatical socialists of all hues. Some of them were put on trial for their beliefs and even refused the royal pardon issued to them on account of their large families. They died in penal hard labour, but never gave in. There were others who suffered at the hands of both the tsar and the Bolsheviks. Their noble stubbornness passed on to me.

My grandfather on my mother's side, Melik Egisseryan, married for the second time to Margarita Akopova, a young girl nineteen years his junior. They were faithful and loved each other till the grave. I loved my Granddad Melik very much, and Grandma Margarita.

They were like the granny and granddad from a fairy tale, only in real life – loving, tender and caring. They had no idea what Soviet power was, they only knew that they needed to defend themselves against it and defend their loved ones.

Granddad Melik, like many other people of his generation, did not sleep at night through the Stalin years. He would listen to the street and the courtyard to check if there was the sound of an engine. Was that a Black Maria stopping by the door to the house…? Granddad told me that weeping mothers, sisters and wives would run behind the cars that left after an arrest, along the streets of Sukhumi, Novy Afon and Gudauta. They would fall, exhausted in the middle of the road.

Melik and Margarita lived in Novy Afon. Granddad was the steward at the famous monastery. An enormous garden with fountains and exotic trees adjoined their large house. While they lived in this house, they had a son and a daughter – my mother. The boy was my uncle, who died of Hodgkin's disease at the age of 15. Melik and Margarita mourned him all their lives. When they spoke of him they were unable to say his name out loud, and just called him "manchuk" (the Armenian for boy). In our family it was taboo to talk about the dead, so I never did find out my uncle's name.

My grandparents called my mother by an ancient royal Armenian name – Assanetta. My mother was very beautiful, and combined in her features the Akopova fanaticism of Grandma's ancestors, which manifested itself in her selfless service to art, and the Egisseryan wisdom of my granddad. My mum graduated from the Moscow Conservatoire and became a pianist. She studied with some legendary teachers, including Heinrich Neuhaus.

When I asked Granddad Melik about anything to do with Soviet Russia, my granddad would shrug, smile helplessly and pull a silly face of incomprehension. He would take a flute from his old trunk and play me French songs. The trunk was enormous, mysterious and enticing. It was entirely covered in metal studs and secret locks. It could only be opened with one huge key with intricate grooves and teeth. First, one had to press the correct stud, and only then the brass plate that covered the main lock would slide away. Granddad would ceremonially place the key in the lock, turn it to left and right a certain number of times, and the heavy lid of the trunk would be opened... As a boy, the inside of Granddad's trunk seemed like the cave from *Ali Baba and the Forty Thieves*... Granddad kept in his trunk a few things that had survived from the old days – ivory dominoes, a few sumptuous old books, an exquisite golden pipe encrusted with amber, his flute and various other wondrous items... The locals stole everything when my father died and we were unable to go to the house in Gudauta for two years. My grandparents often had visitors.

They would sit around the table and play oriental card games. They would all talk in a strange mixture of Armenian, Russian, Turkish and French. In the 1960s, they were still discussing news from the stock exchange and prices for tobacco that were fifty years out of date. They argued about politics like field marshals, as though the USSR did not even exist. These old men and women lived out their lives as recluses in their own houses with their large gardens. They drank their own wine and rarely went outside...

I loved these fine old people, their quaint Caucasian accents. I felt that they were genuine people with roots, despite their advanced age... I would wait impatiently for them to come to visit. Before the Soviets came to power they had been prosperous people; one of them had been in charge of the Caucasus branch of the Singer sewing machine company, another had been a tycoon on the Tiflis stock exchange. The wise old Caucasians believed that Soviet power, although terrible, criminal and painful, would not last long. Nobody believed them, but they were right!

On my father's side my ancestors were Russian, Ukrainian and Polish. Hereditary Russian intellectuals. Engineers on the railways.

My dad's father, Granddad Nikolai, died from Typhus when he was evacuated to Ufa. He was 42. My grandmother, Ksenia Bondarenko, came from a merchant family. She was renowned for her feisty spirit. Grandma outlived her son, my father, Vladimir Gavrilov, by 17 years.

My father was an exceptionally talented man. He was also a wonderful artist and colourist who understood music brilliantly, sang in a beautiful baritone, improvised on the piano in neo-Scriabin style, and knew Wagner's *Ring Cycle* off by heart.

One of the best memories of my childhood was my parents making music at home in the evening. My father used to sing romances and songs from the song cycles by Schubert, Schumann, Tchaikovsky and Rachmaninoff while my mother accompanied him.

Papa lamented becoming a painter instead of a pianist. He missed having sounds to express his inner world. That is possibly why it seems to me, whenever I look at his paintings, that his paints and compositions give out sounds, that they ring with cheerful piano chords...

Until the late 1960s, near Sokol metro station, in Pokrovsky-Streshnevo, stood the old Gavrilov family house. It was a real Russian estate, like something out of *Eugene Onegin*. My father's family lived there. On Victory Day, 9 May, all the Gavrilovs would gather there. My father's cousin, Evgeny Gavrilov, was a war hero. In the garden was a spectacular lilac, just like in Vrubel's painting.

I used to admire the beauty of the spring blossom, breathe in their sweet, exciting aroma and the music of Rachmaninoff or Chopin would start up of its own accord in my mind.

The men would sit at a huge table and silently remember those who had died in the war. There were no pompous speeches, no showy reminiscences at the table. Real war veterans detested war. When I grew up, Uncle Evgeny told me not only about what the Fascists did, but also the atrocities of the Soviet soldiers in the lands they occupied.

My cousin Natasha was a typical girl from a story by Turgenev or Bunin. She was a timid, pretty, clever Russian girl who could in no way fit in with the squalid, aggressive, Soviet world. I think she never did get married. She could never find a worthy life companion.

The old folk, my dad's aunts and uncles, kept the spirit of the Russian estate as best they could. In their house I drank in the golden air of dignified olden times. It seemed to me that the house and its inhabitants retained a marvellous poetical substance, familiar to us from Pushkin's verse...

In the Gavrilov house they made jam, prepared liqueurs, baked pies and pastries, engaged in handicrafts and made lace. I was lucky enough as a child to run around the countless verandas, terraces and attics to my heart's content, as well as rummaging around in the many lofts and walking in the garden... The pictures, scents and sounds of this culture still live in me. They miraculously survived in Soviet Moscow which had been defiled by the tower blocks built by Stalin and Khrushchev. I have noticed that, without meaning to, I am trying to recreate the atmosphere of the old Gavrilov house at my own estate in Switzerland...

In the early 70s the Gavrilov house was demolished. The old folks were rehoused in modern flats.

Uncle Evgeny was killed by doctors during an appendectomy. Natasha had a nervous breakdown. My father died in unexplained circumstances in 1970. Suddenly the time-honoured Russian family of the Gavrilovs ceased to be.

My mother was left with two sons on her hands. The Sovs paid her 40 rubles a month "for loss of the breadwinner."

My brother Igor, an artist, died in Moscow from a heart attack in 2005, aged 52. He was deeply affected by the sudden, early death of our father, who was his God. As so often happens in families with two children, Igor was like our father, and I was like our mother. He was the first to hear the terrible news, at the Surikov Institute. He was handed a telegramme and told, "Bear up, lad, your father's died!" I believe that his heart was damaged by grief somehow right then... Later this inner trauma made itself felt...

My mother died four years ago, at my house in Switzerland after a long illness. She died one month before her 81st birthday.

Her illness did not stop her being happier at my house "than she ever had been in her life." My mum loved my wife, Yuka, her last pupil. They got on like a house on fire.

Mum managed to set our little son Arseny on the right track. He was named after my older friend, Arseny Tarkovsky, and without the help of his grandmother he would never have learned Russian. The Swiss doctors did everything possible to keep my mother from physical suffering. The last six years of her life she was unable to walk.

Two days before she died she was present at my solo recital for the Festival at the Piano in Lucerne. She was welcomed by the enormous, packed house. On that same day Yuka and I flew to Warsaw at the invitation of Penderetsky. I was playing an evening of Chopin. Playing Chopin in Warsaw is quite a challenge, especially for a Russian musician. The house gave me a standing ovation. I immediately told my mum.

"I'm happy, son. I'm going to bed," she said tenderly, and asked me to phone her again later to tell her the details.

We flew to Poznań for a concert. We received a phone call there and were told that my mother had died in her sleep.

I did not cancel the concert.

Index

Alexeyev, Dmitry, 38-41
Alliluev (Allilueva), Svetlana, 235
Alkhimov, Vladimir, 257 -2 60, 262 - 264, 278, 284, 289, 290, 305, 336
Alkhimova, Natasha, 6, 257 - 260, 262, 264, 275, 278, 279, 280, 281, 283, 284 - 287, 289, 292 - 295, 298 - 300, 303 - 305, 315, 335 - 337, 366, 367, 369
Ambartsumian, Levon, 13, 19, 41, 43
Anastasiev, Mikhail, 13, 21, 22
Andropov, Yuri, 201, 202, 258
Anechka, 75, 76, 106
Ashkenazy, Vladimir, 197, 214, 337, 338
Babadjanian, Arno, 275
Bach, Johann Sebastian, 7, 86, 159, 160, 162, 180, 191, 201, 204, 225, 246, 248, 250, 254, 255, 277, 278, 279, 299, 311, 338, 341, 357
Barabash, Yuri, 181
Bashkirov, Dimitry, 36
Bashmet, Yuri, 107, 244, 289
Beethoven, Ludwig van, 89, 162, 175, 195, 196, 224, 240, 244, 285, 357
Bobkov, Philipp, 262, 263, 281
Brezhnev, Leonid, 2, 54, 59, 61, 86, 93, 95, 96, 99, 100, 138, 141, 142, 159, 202, 208, 224, 250, 272, 337
Bruni, Alexei (Lyosha), 19
Buratinka (see also Rostropovich), 17, 101, 257, 327 - 334
Ceausescu, Nicolae, 86
Chizhik (Natasha Slobodyanik), 107, 108, 167, 192
Chopin, Frédéric, 5, 9 - 11, 14, 15, 18, 19, 27, 30, 52, 53, 66, 79, 85, 95, 100, 104, 109, 111, 125, 130, 131, 133, 139, 158, 188, 195 - 198, 216, 222, 239, 240, 248, 253, 285, 287, 288, 300, 311, 312, 317, 318, 321, 357, 366, 368
Cliburn, Harvey Lavan (Van), 166, 174 - 176
Demichev, Pyotr (see also Nilych and Pete), 94, 126, 137, 181, 292
Dmitriev, Sasha, 159, 246
Dorensky, 30
Dorliak, Nina, 122, 141, 171, 173, 202, 232, 277, 289
Dorokhov, Pavel, 131
Dostoevsky, Fyodor, 92, 119, 217, 258, 343, 350
Dzhigarkhanyan, Armen, 248
Egorov, Yura (Yuri), 23, 24, 26, 27, 37, 39, 40, 42, 290

Engerer, Brigitte, 149, 369
Faerman, Mikhail, 32, 345
Fellini, Federico, 45, 94
Fira (see also Richter and Slava), 2, 3, 33, 174, 228, 229, 310, 328, 329, 330
Flier, Yakov, 18, 24, 30, 31, 36, 38, 48
Friedman, Volodya, 169, 170
Furman, Nonna, 85
Furtseva, Ekaterina, 17, 22, 35
Gavrilov, Igor, 125, 136, 137, 281, 367
Gavrilova, Aida, 245, 247, 249, 250, 257, 264, 280, 281
Gilels, Emil, 32, 66, 67, 122, 174 - 176, 345
Ginzburg, Evgeny, 76, 107
Gold, Shelly, 277, 278, 299
Goldenweiser, Alexander, 30
Gonzaga, Pietro, 179, 180, 182
Gorbachev, Mikhail (see also Gorby), 73, 285, 305, 337, 338
Gorby (see also Gorbachev), 93, 335, 338
Gornostayeva, Vera, 192
Grieg, Edvard, 108, 195, 222
Grindenko, Tatyana, 308
Handel, George Frederick, 111, 114, 123, 125, 126, 130, 131, 151, 160, 179, 182, 185, 201, 203, 204, 210, 238, 244, 277
Heikinheimo, Seppo, 71, 141
Heinonen, Eero, 81
Hideko (see also Kobayashi), 151, 157 - 160, 244, 245, 249
Hurok, Sol, 299
Igolinsky, Stanislav, 39, 40
Ivanov, Pasha, 181, 218
Jagger, Mick, 5
Jankovic, Xenia, 13
Jordania, Vakhtang, 261
Kabakov, Ilya, 79
Kalganovich, Shabtai, 315 - 318, 370
Kaluzhsky, Lev, 21
Karajan, Herbert von, 71, 111, 127, 133, 135, 137, 138, 148, 175, 291, 343
Karlsson, Seppo, 63 - 67
Kennedy, Nigel, 346
Khachaturian, Aram, 57
Khazanov, Gennady, 56, 94, 96 - 98, 169
Khrennikov, Tikhon, 259, 260, 262, 309

Khormut, Lyuba, 77
Kimanen, Seppo, 75, 76
Kimanen, Yoshiko, 75, 76
Kimov, Valery, 126, 127, 138, 141 - 147, 153
Kinski, Klaus, 113
Kireyev, Anton, 89
Klimov, Elem, 309
Kobayashi (see also Hideko), 151
Kondrashin, Kirill, 65, 326
Kondratiev (von Benckendorff), Sergei, 237
Koprowski, Hilary, 319
Kozodov, Victor, 14
Kremer, Gidon, 72, 107, 108, 125, 280, 307, 312, 313, 347
Krylov, Andrei, 22
Kukharsky, Vasily, 56, 57, 130, 131, 181, 289
Lenin, Vladimir, 55, 58, 100, 104, 126, 286, 312, 326, 355
Liszt, Franz Joseph (Ferencz), 51, 121, 195 - 198, 288
Lively, David, 40
Mae, Vanessa, 347
Magidenko, Elena, 37
Maisenberg, Oleg, 280
Malinin, Evgeny, 36
Malkovich, Mark, 81 - 83
Mann, Freddy, 317
Maximova, Katya (Ekaterina), 56, 107
McCartney, Paul, 265
Mercury, Freddy, 5
Michelangeli, Arturo, 29
Mikhoels, Solomon, 286
Milstein, Yakov, 30, 196 - 199
Minzhilkiev, Bulat, 56
Mironov, Andrei, 169
Moiseyev, Igor, 58
Monsaingeon, Bruno, 118, 235, 238
Mordler, John, 264
Moroz, Vladimir, 228
Mozart, Wolfgang Amadeus, 49, 86, 91, 92, 188, 191, 195, 196, 222,
    225, 248, 267, 285, 291, 311, 353, 357
Mullova, Vika (Viktoria), 261
Muti, Riccardo, 111, 125, 129, 131, 133, 321
Mutter, Anne-Sophie, 346
Myung-whun Chung, 40

Naumov, Lev (Lyova), 23, 24, 30 - 34, 38 - 40, 43, 60, 126, 154, 244, 268
Neuhaus, Stanislav (Stasik), 18, 33, 40, 79, 149
Neuhaus, Heinrich, 31, 38, 364
Neuhaus, Silvia, 107
Nikolaeva, Tatiana, 30, 31
Nikulin, Yuri, 107
Nilovna (Elena Obraztsova), 55, 57, 94, 96, 97, 173
Nilych (see also Demichev and Pete), 94, 126, 129 – 131, 133, 134, 137, 181, 294, 297, 337
Novitskaya, Katya (Ekaterina), 32, 60
Nummi, Seppo, 63, 65, 75
Obolensky, Nikolai, 106 - 108
Oborin, Lev, 18
Oistrakh, David, 77, 129, 143, 175, 311, 347
Ozawa, Seiji, 321, 322
Paleyev, Nikolai, 243, 257
Parker, Chris, 264
Pete (see also Nilych and Demichev), 292, 297, 337
Peter, Andrew, 292
Petrosyan, Rona, 271, 273, 276
Petrosyan, Tigran, 270 - 276
Pirumov, Alexander, 36, 40
Pogorelić, Ivo, 13, 300, 345
Popiełuszko, Jerzy, 285, 286
Popov, Vladimir, 75, 76, 181
Prokofiev, Sergei, 52, 54, 353
Pugacheva, Alla, 56, 169, 309
Pushkin, Alexander, 92, 107, 142, 153, 214, 249, 273, 300, 366
Rachmaninoff, Sergey, 30, 40, 41, 60, 65, 111, 127, 135, 148, 165, 177, 216, 262, 264, 277, 283, 290, 298, 299, 323, 328, 351, 357, 366
Raikin, Arkady, 75
Ravel, Joseph Maurice, 51, 65, 192, 216, 240, 267, 268
Richter, Sviatoslav (see also Fira and Slava), 2, 33, 47, 49, 54, 65, 73, 90, 99 - 104, 107, 111, 112, 115, 118 - 123, 125 - 127, 129 - 131, 133, 135, 141, 147, 149 - 151, 160, 162, 165, 166, 171 - 173, 175, 176, 179, 180, 182, 183, 185 - 190, 192, 193, 196, 198, 199, 201 - 204, 207 - 211, 214, 216, 221 - 229, 231 - 240, 244, 253, 263, 264, 277, 278, 289, 311, 321, 328, 329, 332, 334, 339
Riefenstahl, Leni, 60
Rostropovich, Mstislav (see also Buratinka), 175, 272
Rozanov, Anatoly, 319, 355

Rubinstein, Anton, 322
Sakharov, Vadim, 24, 246
Sakharov, Andrei, 337, 338
Sato, Yoko, 260
Schaaf, Johannes, 231
Schiff, András, 40
Schlosser, Dorothea, 136
Schnittke, Alfred, 308, 309
Schubert, Franz, 108, 158, 191, 199, 207, 235, 238, 239, 312, 357, 366
Schwarzkopf, Elisabeth, 125, 371
Scriabin, Alexander, 30, 95, 121, 122, 165, 166, 214 - 216, 262, 264, 277, 283, 299, 366
Serkin, Rudolf, 299
Shalamov, Varlam, 76
Shauro, Vasily, 98
Shostakovich, Dmitri, 21, 39, 73, 118, 237, 260 - 262
Slava (see also Fira and Richter), 54, 73, 90, 99 - 108, 111 - 120, 122, 127, 131, 135, 136, 147 - 150, 153, 154, 165, 166, 171 - 176, 179, 180, 182, 185 - 194, 196, 199, 201 - 205, 207 - 211, 213 - 215, 221, 223, 224, 227 - 229, 232, 234 - 239, 243, 244, 277, 289, 321, 329, 330
Slobodyanik, Alik (Alexander), 85, 107, 108, 130, 167, 170, 172, 192, 253
Solzhenitsyn, Aleksandr, 262, 333
Speranskaya, Masha (Maria), 77
Stalin, Joseph, 14, 31, 53, 54, 65, 130, 190, 201, 216, 227, 233, 234, 235, 240, 286, 297, 309, 336, 337, 355, 364, 367
Suslov, Mikhail, 95, 202, 203
Svetlanov, Zhenya (Evgeny), 103, 159, 321, 323, 324, 325
Taneyev, Sergei, 171, 174, 175
Tarkovsky, Andrei, 215, 367
Tchaikovsky, Pyotr, 2, 17, 25, 26, 30, 35 - 37, 41 - 43, 45, 59, 60, 65, 66, 90, 100, 107, 111, 126, 160, 162, 166, 175, 214, 222, 231, 244, 260, 261, 263, 285, 308, 309, 321 - 324, 342, 357 - 361, 366
Temirkanov, Yuri, 159, 244
Timofeyeva, Lyubov, 20, 32
Toradze, Lexo, 244, 248, 261
Tsereteli, Zurab, 190
Travkin, 79, 80
Turgenev, Ivan, 217, 300, 366
Vasiliev, Volodya (Vladimir), 56, 57, 107
Vengerov, Maxim, 347

Vigers, Mark, 265
Vishnya (see Vishnevskaya), 17, 327 – 334
Vivaldi, Antonio, 160, 347
Voronets, Olga, 58
Vysotsky, Vladimir, 107, 185, 218, 286
Wagner, Richard, 20, 122, 233, 285, 366
Willan, John, 7, 264, 265, 291, 295
Wittgenstein, Paul, 268
Zak, Yakov, 18, 24, 30, 36, 174
Zemlyansky, Boris, 19, 33
Zetel, Isaac, 160, 185, 186
Zhuraitis, Algis, 310
Zimerman, Krystian, 300, 345, 357
Zykina, Lyudmila, 58

www.ingramcontent.com/pod-product-compliance
Lightning Source LLC
Chambersburg PA
CBHW060450170426
43199CB00011B/1148